SMALL ARMS

IDENTIFICATION SERIES

Wm. J. Ross - 1995

.303 RIFLE, No. 4

Marks I, & I*,
Marks 1/2, 1/3 & 2

Parts Identification & Lists, No. 4 Series Notes,

Exploded Parts Drawings, Descriptions,

Accessories & Fittings.

S.A.I.S.
No. 2

Ian Skennerton

REFERENCES:

"Identification List" *Australian Military Forces* 1945, M.G.O.
"Identification List" *War Office* 1946 & 1952, Army Council Command
"List of Changes in British War Material — 1940-1954" H.M.S.O.
"Local E.N.E. Instructions" *Canadian Armed Forces* 1946
"The Lee-Enfield Story" *Ian Skennerton* 1993, SKENNERTON

ACKNOWLEDGMENTS:

Peter Laidler, Marcham, Oxfordshire, England
James Alley Jr., Piqua, Ohio, U.S.A.
Robert Faris, Yuma, Arizona, U.S.A.
Brian Labudda, Kingaroy Firearms & Supplies
Robert Courtney, Curator of Weapons, Australian War Memorial

© *Ian Skennerton, 1994*
All rights reserved. No portion of this publication may be reproduced, stored in a retrieval system, or transmitted in any form or by any means, electronic, mechanical, photocopying, recording, or otherwise, without the prior permission in writing of the author and the publisher.

National Library of Australia
Cataloguing-in-Publication data:
Skennerton, Ian D.
ISBN 0 949749 20 6

Typesetting, layout and design by Ian D. Skennerton.
Published by Ian D. Skennerton, P.O. Box 433, Ashmore City 4214, Australia.
Printed and bound by Thai Watana Panich Press Co. Ltd., Rama 1 Rd., Bangkok, Thailand.

Distributors:

North America—	**Great Britain—**	**Australia—**	**New Zealand—**
I.D.S.A. Books	Jeremy Tenniswood	Ian D. Skennerton	Bruce Gorton
P.O. Box 1457	28 Gordon Rd.	P.O. Box 433	P.O. Box 917
Piqua	Aldershot	Ashmore City	Invercargill
Ohio 45356	GU11 1ND	Qld. 4214	South Island
U.S.A.	England	Australia	New Zealand

CONTENTS

No. 4 Rifle Genealogy	5
Model Identification Tables	9
Differences in Component Parts	11
Interchangeable Parts, Rifles No. 1 & No. 4 ...	17
Rifle Specifications	18
User Guide	19
Key Plate	20
Backsights and Bands	22
Barrel Assembly	26
Body and Breech Bolt Assemblies	28
Locking Bolt, Magazine, Butt Plate, &c.	30
Butt and Fore-end	34
Bayonets No. 4 & No. 9	36
Accessories	40
Stripping and Assembly	42
The Canadian Distinction	43
Parts Manufacture Identification	46

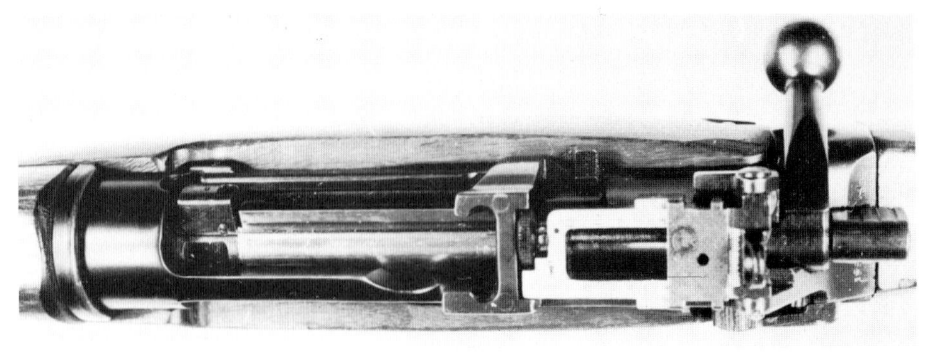

Top view of wartime Fazakerley No. 4 Mk I fitted with Mk I Singer backsight. *B. Labudda*

1933-dated Trials Rifle No. 4 Mk I. Note the Enfield mark and year of production, left side of butt socket. Early style cocking piece with button rim. *M.O.D. Pattern Room*

Stevens-Savage No. 4 Mk I* with Mk 2 backsight. Most of these are marked **U.S. PROPERTY**. Scooped safety catch was a manufacturing concession, not fitted to all rifles. *Brian Labudda*

No. 4 Mk I/3 conversion. Note the converted fore-end with wood inserts to replace original fore-end tie bracket. Most of these inletted were semi-circular rather than with squared corners as illustrated. *B. Labudda*

.303 RIFLE, No. 4

No. 4 RIFLE GENEALOGY

In 1926, the .303 Marks III and III* S.M.L.E. were redesignated Rifle No. 1 Mark III and Mark III*. The .22RF trainers became the Rifle No. 2 and the .303 Pattern 1914 became Rifle No. 3. Then in 1929 and 1930, a new model, the **No. 1 Mk VI** was produced at R.S.A.F. Enfield for extended troop trials. The Mark VI features aperture sights, a stronger action body, heavier profile barrel and a lightened nosecap. In 1931, after more improvements, this new model was re-designated the Rifle No. 4. It also fixed a short, spike bayonet which became known as the Bayonet, No. 4.

The **No. 4 Mark I Trials** rifle has its designation markings and factory of manufacture stamped on the left side of the butt socket, these are dated between 1930 and 1933. This trials model also had a higher, flat-sided wall for the left side of the receiver body, a feature of the No. 4 rifle series. Illustrated descriptions and comprehensive details of the No. 1 Mk VI and No. 4 trials rifles, comparisons and their development will be found on pages 173-175 and 191-195 of the *Lee-Enfield Story*.

The production **No. 4 Mark I** was a wartime requirement, hastily approved in November of 1939. Development of a self-loading rifle at the time was shelved, with war looming in the late 1930's. After the outbreak of war, newly-constructed Royal Ordnance Factories at Fazakerley and Maltby were supplemented by a new B.S.A. plant at Shirley, on the outskirts of Birmingham. The first wartime No. 4 rifles did not become available until mid-1941. The R.S.A.F. Enfield factory only manufactured No. 4 trials rifles during the early 1930's; machine gun production became the top priority during World War 2.

The .303 No. 4 rifle was also made in North America, where production actually exceeded that of the British factories. Parts for the No. 4 were also supplied by commercial contractors, R.O.F. Maltby acted more as an assembly plant. R.O.F. Fazakerley made most of the rifle components as did B.S.A. Shirley. Variations found in the No. 4 furniture and fittings do not necessarily indicate early or late production; parts were ordered from many and various contractors and the manufacture of early style sights, handguards, fore-ends bands and swivels was concurrent with that of the later marks, and certain production expediencies.

Canada's Long Branch and the U.S. Stevens-Savage plants commenced production late in 1941. Certain manufacturing shortcuts were applied as time progressed and so some variations may be noted in the shapes of component parts and their mode of fabrication. Such parts are the outer bands, sight protectors, backsights, magazines, safety catches, cocking pieces and trigger guards. The Canadians also produced some variations of the No. 4 (T) sniper rifle, using different telescopes and mounts.

The **No. 4 Mark I*** was produced from 1942 until 1944 at Stevens-Savage and into the 1950's at Long Branch. This particular model was only made in North America and it features streamlined receiver body production and a simplified bolthead release system. These rifles are usually found fitted with a 2-groove barrel instead of the more common 5-groove model. Most Stevens rifles are marked "U.S. PROPERTY", supplied to Britain under the Lend-Lease agreement. Many of the Long Branch rifles were purchased by Britain during the war and imported; these saw British service and are often found fitted with British parts as a result of repairs and upgrade programs. The .303 No. 4 rifle was only manufactured in Britain and North America; Australian and Indian factories continued with the No. 1 S.M.L.E. production during World War 2.

Some No. 4 sniping rifles were set up by Holland & Holland, these were designated the **No. 4 Mk I (T)**. Fitted with telescopic sights and detachable bracket, these units were so reliable and accurate that they survived the changeover from .303-in. to 7.62mm N.A.T.O. ammunition. Long Branch produced similar rifles on the Mk I* action, referred to as the **No. 4 Mk I* (T)**. The Canadian sights have different catalogue and Vocab. numbers because of variations from their British equivalents. The *".303 No. 4 (T) Sniper Rifle — An Armourer's Perspective"* by Laidler and Skennerton describes the No. 4 sniper rifles series to its grand finale, the L42A1.

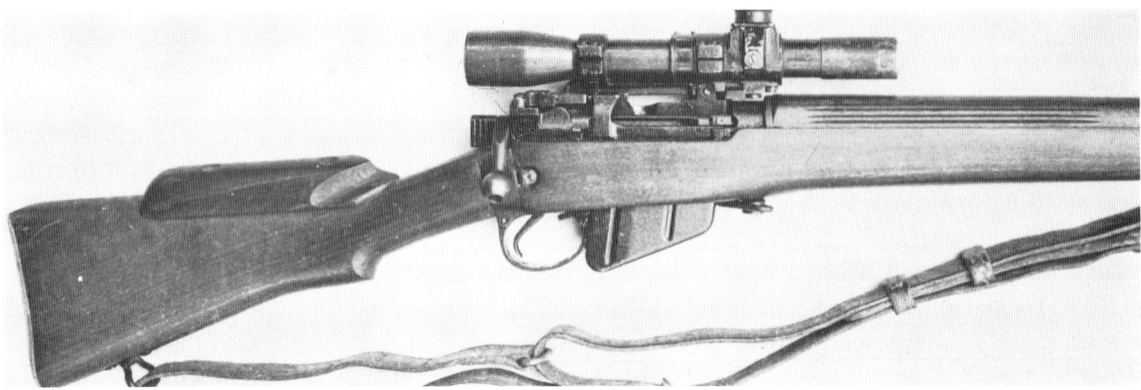

British No. 4 Mk I (T) sniper model, converted by Holland & Holland. *I. Skennerton*

As the 1939-45 war extended into the South-East Asian theatre, requests were made for a shorter, lightened model and the **No. 5 Mk I** was developed. This is commonly referred to as the "Jungle Carbine" and it was introduced in 1944. While its utility was unquestionable, the accuracy of this new model proved to be inconsistent and this "wandering zero" problem was never remedied. As a result, service of the No. 5 was relatively short-lived although its was very popular for its convenient weight and general handiness. At one point in time, it was about to replace the No. 4 rifle as the general British service arm.

Development of a new rimless cartridge and automatic rifle trials after the war were sidelined and a "hung trigger" modification was proposed for the No. 4 rifle. The trigger is mounted onto a bracket at the front of the butt socket. This **No. 4 Mk 2** model was approved in December 1947, but the final design and mode of conversion not finalised until 1949. About 70% of these rifles were new body forgings, with 30% being conversions of the earlier patterns. This model of No. 4 rifle was only produced at Fazakerley because the Maltby factory closed in about 1947. The Marks I and I* rifles were upgraded, to **No. 4 Marks 1/2** and **I/3** respectively. Engraved on the left side of the action body, these conversions retain the earlier markings and so they can be readily identified. The main difference between the Mk I/2 and Mk I/3 is in the position and form of the bolthead release slot.

The 7.62 x 51mm N.A.T.O. round was adopted in December 1953, along with the L1A1 self-loading rifle. No. 4 rifles were later converted for the new cartridge and the "L" series of nomenclature applied. This saw the end of the "Mark" designations in British service,

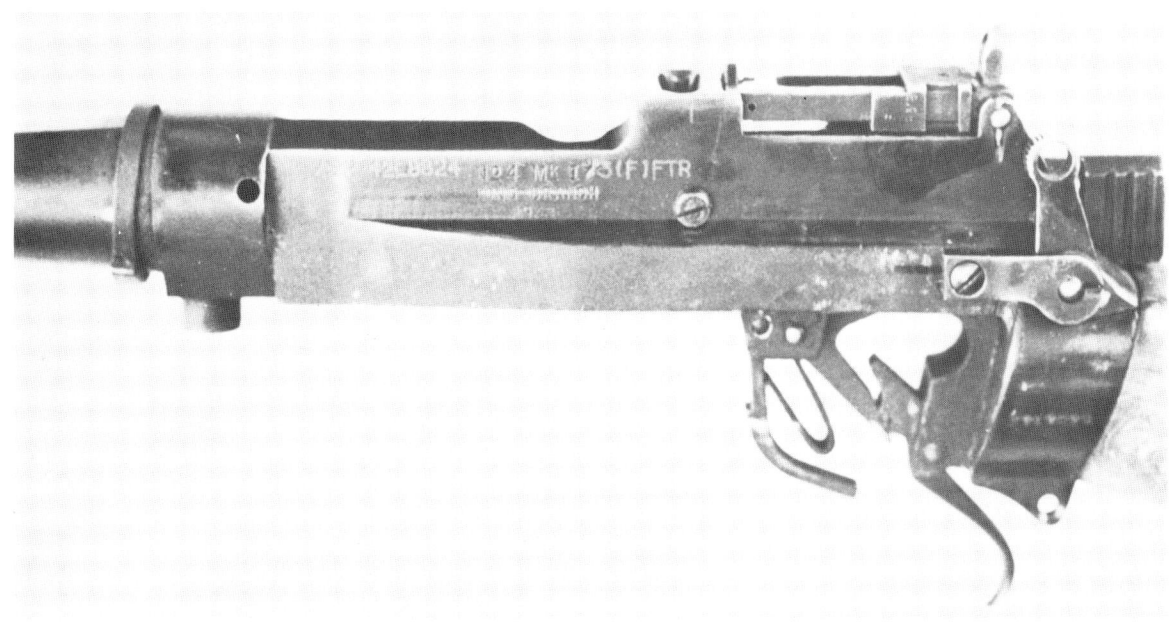

Above: Trigger mounted onto the action body, as for the No. 4 Marks 2, 1/2 and 1/3 rifles.
Below left: L8 and L42A1 7.62mm magazine compared with the .303 No. 4 magazine (at right).
Below right: Mk 2 series rifle fore-ends, wood removed at back for the trigger. One has the transverse screw fitted.

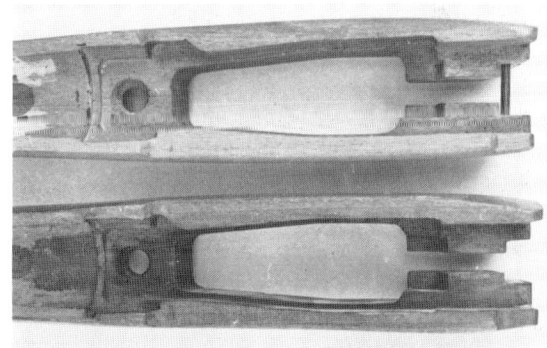

after nearly one hundred years. The various No. 4 rifles were converted as follows:
 .303 No. 4 Mk 2 ... 7.62mm **L8A1**   .303 No. 4 Mk I ... 7.62mm **L8A4**
 .303 No. 4 Mk 1/2 ... 7.62mm **L8A2**   .303 No. 4 Mk I* ... 7.62mm **L8A5**.
 .303 No. 4 Mk 1/3 ... 7.62mm **L8A3**

Merely patterns for proposed conversions, some L8 models were not produced in quantity. These were intended for police and such security forces rather than general military issue.

Sterling Armament also developed a system to enable commercial conversion of the .303 No. 4 rifles for the new 7.62mm round. Their ejector was repositioned in the No. 4 action body whereas the Enfield system utilised a lip on the magazine. It will also be noted that the .303 magazine is differently shaped to the 7.62mm version and the Sterling model too has a different silhouette to the service Enfield pattern. The 7.62mm extractor is differently shaped to the .303 version.

The **L39A1** was a special target model, the modified .303 No. 4 (T) sniper rifle became the **L42A1**. The L39A1 and L42A1 are half-stocked and utilise heavy barrels. The **L59A1** is a training model with skeleton cuts and milling to render it unfireable, stamped "DP" and painted as such on the left side of the butt and under the fore-end.

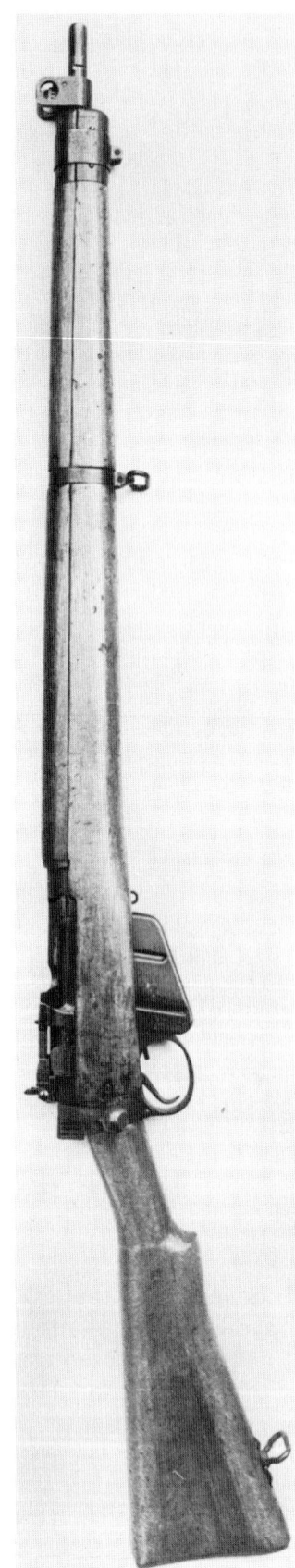

No. 4 Mk I, British manufacture. Note Mk I backsight and Mk II butt swivel. *B. Labudda*

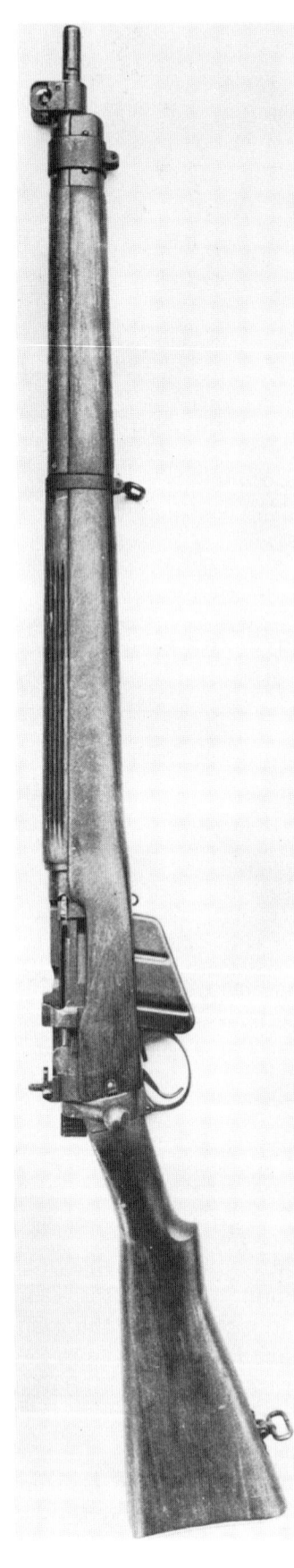

No. 4 Mk I*, by Stevens-Savage. Note Mk II backsight and grooved handguard. *I. Skennerton*

No. 4 Mk 2, Fazakerley. Note beech timber and screw at rear of fore-end. *J. Page*

MODEL IDENTIFICATION TABLES

Identification of the No. 4 Short Magazine Lee-Enfield rifle series is usually relatively easy as the particular Mark designation is engraved on the left side of the action body, on the flat external wall of the bolt-way. Converted models also recorded the factory upgrading and the new designation alongside or over the original markings. Only the original 1930's vintage trials No. 4 rifles were marked on the butt socket, on the left side; virtually all of these trials rifles were converted to No. 4 (T) sniper models or upgraded at the beginning of World War 2.

Rifle No. 4	Intro. year	Main changes	Other notes	LoC para	L.E.S. pages
Mk I Trials	1930	New model trials rifle; with slab-sided action, aperture backsight, heavy barrel, spike bayonet.	Rifle serial number, Enfield factory and the production year marked on left side of butt socket.	—	191-194, **426**
Mk I	1941	Mass production model, with bolthead release catch behind the charger bridge.	Marked as No. 4 Mk 1 on left side of action body. Made in England, U.S.A. and Canada.	B4737	195-205, **427**
Mk I*	1942	Similar to Mark 1 except for bolthead release slot at front of rib, near the chamber.	Not made in England, only at Long Branch in Canada and Stevens-Savage in the U.S.A.	C2791	214-217, **428** 286-291
Mk 1/2	1949	Conversion of Mark 1, the trigger bracket is on the action body rather than trigger guard.	Converted at Fazakerley; a few at B.S.A. Shirley. Transverse screw through rear of fore-end.	C3727	228-230, **429**
Mk 1/3	1949	Conversion of the Mark 1* model, otherwise similar to the Mark 1/2.	Conversions effected at R.O.F. Fazakerley. Transverse screw through rear of fore-end.	C3727	228-230, **430**
Mk 2	1949	New production model with the trigger hinged on the action body, rather than the trigger guard.	These Fazakerley-made rifles generally utilised newly manufactured component parts.	C3727	228-230, **429**

Intro. year denotes the year of introduction into British service, rather than the approval year. Production usually did not commence per the approval date.

LoC para records the paragraph number in "List of Changes in British War Material". Vols. I - IV only (1860-1918) published to date (edited Skennerton).

L.E.S. pages lists the general text pages in the "Lee-Enfield Story". The page reference in bold type denotes the illustrated description reference in the Rifle Descriptions, Chapter 12. Also check pages 481-482 for illustrated examples of the receiver body markings.

No. 4 ACTION BODY VARIATIONS

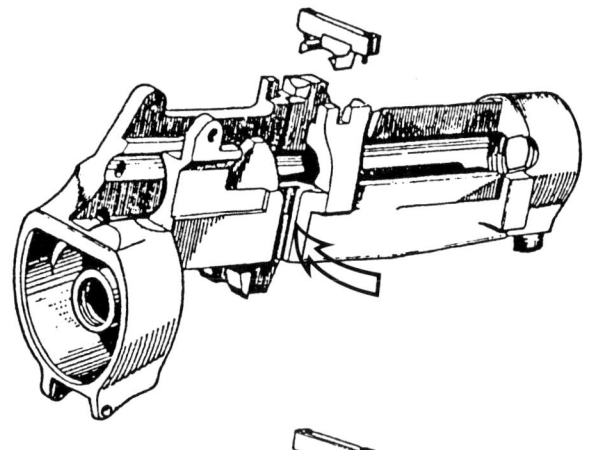

BODY Mk 1 with bolt release catch (indicated).
Rifle Type: No. 4 Mk I.
Makers: Enfield (early 1930's trials, with cut-off)
Fazakerley, Maltby, BSA Shirley,
early Stevens-Savage and Long Branch.

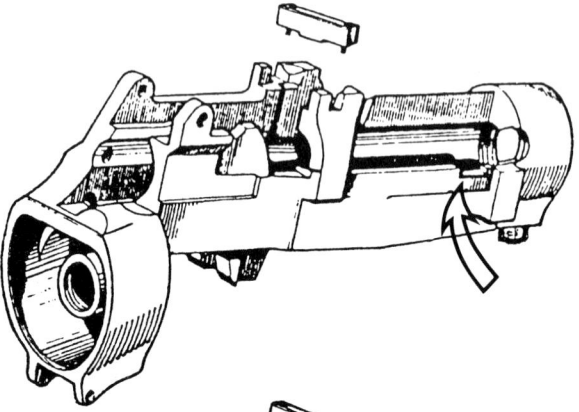

BODY Mk 2 with bolt release slot (indicated).
Rifle Type: No. 4 Mk I*.
Makers: Stevens-Savage, Long Branch.
Also note extra clearance under charger bridge piece.

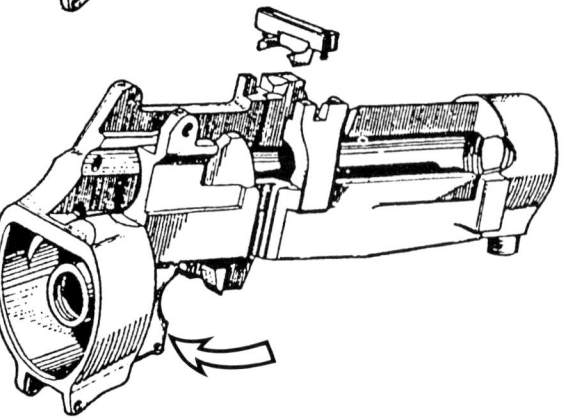

BODY Mk 3 with trigger mounted onto body (indicated).
Rifle Type: No. 4 Mk 2.
Maker: Fazakerley.

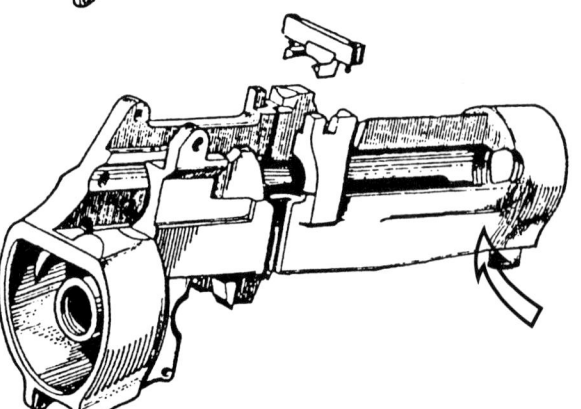

BODY Mk 4 with trigger mounted onto body,
no re-inforce (indicated).
Rifle Type: No. 4 Mk 2, late production (1955-56).
Maker: Fazakerley.

DIFFERENCES IN COMPONENT PARTS

This section illustrates and relates the differences found in those major component parts of the different models of No. 4 rifle. This is intended for use as a guide in examining, rebuilding or restoring any of the various No. 4 models. And for identifying various individual parts. During the war, virtually any model backsight, cocking piece, foresight or foresight assembly could be fitted to a No. 4 Mk I or Mk I* rifle in service. However, after 1945 and when many of these rifles underwent armourer repairs or F.T.R. programs, the better quality parts were reverted to on many of the rifles.

Regarding the particular action model, this will usually be found marked on the left side of the action body, with the rifle type number and mark *(e.g. No. 4 Mk I or No. 4 Mk 1/3)*. Unlike the S.M.L.E. and No. 1 Rifle series, virtually all the magazines, sights, cocking pieces and handguards are interchangeable between the various models. The main exception would be for the Mark 2 series (Mark 1/2, Mark 1/3 and Mark 2) which utilise a different fore-end and modified triggerguard.

Manufacturers of the British No. 4 rifles may not be as easy to ascertain from the action body markings as for the No. 1 and earlier Magazine Lee-Enfield series, and for a number of reasons. A code system was instituted during World War 2 for commercial contractors and manufacturers. These codes were stamped on most of the assorted parts, including the action body. Fazakerley rifles have the "F" mark, often in brackets thus "(F)". Most B.S.A. Shirley rifles have the wartime code "M4/C" marked on the left side at the butt socket, although this was not always clearly struck. Maltby rifles would be the hardest to identify, with variations of an "M" or "M" logo, or on earlier models, "R.O.F.M.". See pages 46-47 for lists of the various manufacturers' identification marks. The U.S. and Canadian receivers are easily identified as the Canadian models are marked "LONG BRANCH" and their U.S.-made counterparts have the squared "S" logo of Stevens-Savage.

On the No. 4 rifles, butts are not found stamped with the mark designation or such indicators, unlike many of the No. 1 rifles. The type of wood used on the No. 4 was generally softer than the walnut found on most No. 1 rifles.

No. 4 rifle serial numbers are usually found marked on the left side of the butt socket, rear flat of the bolt handle, and on the underside of the wooden fore-end at the front. An inspection of these numbers can help to ascertain if these parts have been exchanged in service or since disposal. The No. 4 does not have the serial number marked in as many places as its No. 1 predecessor, so it is not as easy to ascertain if parts such as the barrel, nosecap or sight have been replaced.

Line drawings have been used here rather than photographs because of the clarity in detail. Shadow, scale and projection angles can become a problem in some photographs and layouts when comparing parts, another reason for the use of the drawings.

No. 4 magazine cases, floorplates and auxiliary springs are interchangeable in this series, there was no advance in Mark, Number or Pattern during the life of the No. 4, until the introduction of the 7.62mm round. The No. 4 magazine is not interchangeable on the No. 1 rifle or Magazine Lee-Enfield, and while it may be forced into the magazine way, it is likely to cause damage.

Four vertical text columns have been used in the following four pages, each applying to a certain rifle type. Illustrations may disrupt these columns in some instances, but column headers at the top of each page apply to the specific text columns for that whole page. The part being described is named at the far left-hand side.

Rifle Model:	*No. 4 Mk I*	*No. 4 Mk I**	*No. 4 Mk 2*	*No. 4 Mk 1/2 & 1/3*
Body & Bolt	Bolthead release catch (a) behind the charger bridge. This push-down catch is depressed to withdraw the bolt-head fully to the rear. Turn bolt-head 90° upwards to clear the back of the action body. Then pull bolt assembly from the action.	No bolthead release catch. Instead there is a slot on the bolthead guide rib (b), just to rear of the chamber. To remove bolt, the bolthead is positioned over the slot cut-out, then bolt-head is raised 90° to enable the bolt assembly withdrawal.	Spring-loaded bolthead release catch is positioned behind the integral charger bridge (a), same design and operation as on the Mark I model. Parts usually marked with "F" and the production year.	Bolthead release catch is behind the charger bridge on the Mk 1/2, same as Mk I from which it was converted. The Mk 1/3 has its release slot towards the front of the bolthead guide rib (b), same as the Mk I* from which it was converted.
	Insufficient clearance under charger bridge for bolthead removal in the 90° raised position as with Mk I*. *[Marked (c), indicated behind charger bridge.]*	Extra clearance underneath charger bridge, enables withdrawal of the bolt with bolthead in raised position. *[Marked (c), indicated behind charger bridge.]*	No additional clearance under charger bridge same as Mk I model. *[Marked (c), indicated behind charger bridge.]*	Charger bridge clearance or lack thereof depends on whether conversion made from Mk I or I*. *[Marked (c), indicated behind charger bridge.]*
	Trigger hinged on trigger guard.	Trigger hinged on trigger guard.	Trigger mounted onto inside of body (d).	Trigger mounted onto inside of body (d).

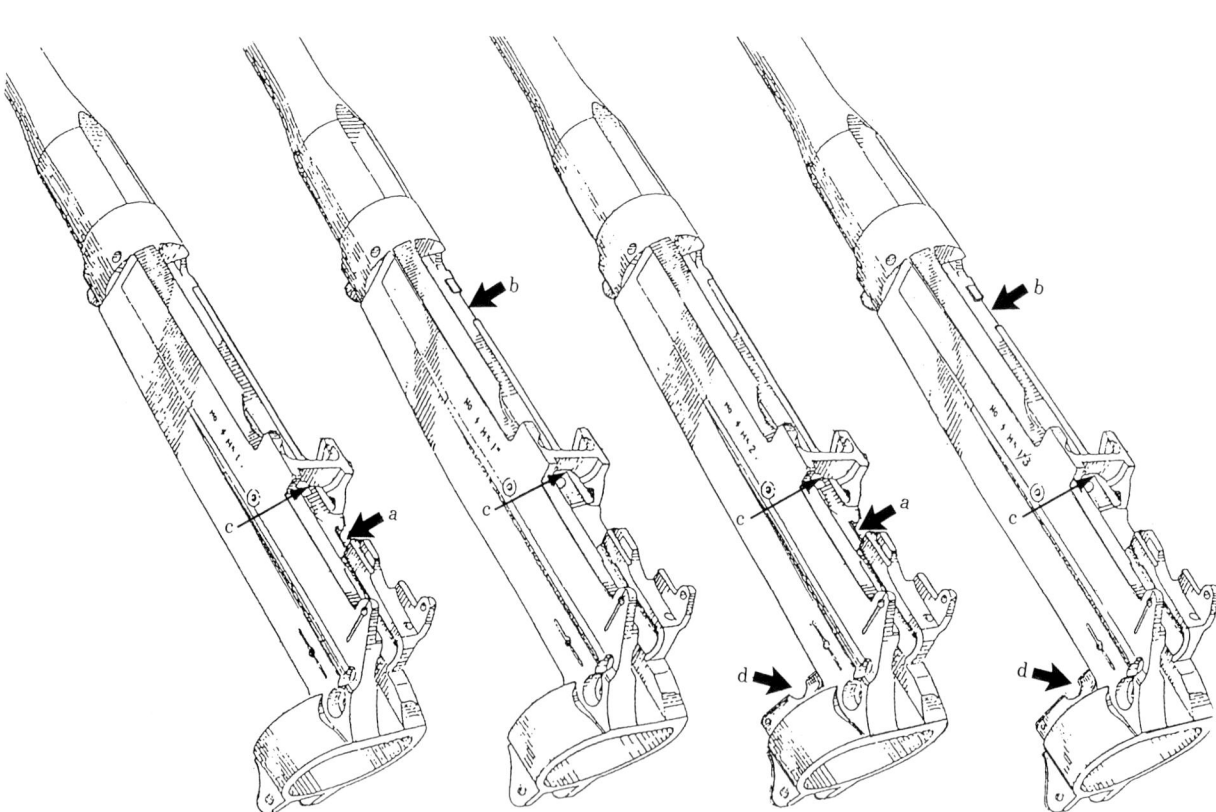

Left to Right:—
Rifle No. 4 Mk I ... Body Mk I
Rifle No. 4 Mk I* ... Body Mk 2
Rifle No. 4 Mk 2 ... Body Mk 3
Rifle No. 4 Mk 1/3 ... Body Mk 3

Also see illustrations of different bodies, page 28

Rifle Model:	No. 4 Mk I	No. 4 Mk I*	No. 4 Mk 2	No. 4 Mk I/2 & I/3
Cocking piece:	Mk 1 type had rimmed button end. Mk 2 is flat sided with three flutes each side. Some wartime Mk 2 had no flutes and/or half bent.	North American production from 1942, Mk 2, usually with "S" or "LB" logo marks. Mk 2 normally fitted.	These post-war rifles fitted with later Mk 2 type, marked "F" or "P" with manufacture year. Mk 2 cocking piece only.	As conversions which underwent FTR, usually refitted with late production Mk II type. Mk 2 should be fitted.

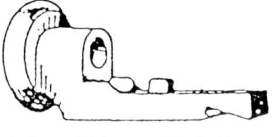

Left to Right:— Mark 1
Mark 2
Mark 2 later type

P50   F55

Locking bolt:	Two marks of locking bolt. Mk 2 is 3-piece, has no screw threaded spline; considered unsafe, especially with Mk II cocking piece without half-bent. Mk 1 is the usual type.	Mk 1 locking bolt only. The Mk 2 bolt without screw threaded spline was not made in the U.S. or Canada.	These post-war rifles fitted with Mk 1 locking bolt assemblies with the screw-threaded spline.	As rifles were repaired or converted, any still with Mk 2 locking bolts were refitted with the Mk 1 assembly.
	Three main styles of lever or "safety catch" as illustrated, third one is Canadian only.	Many of the later rifles were fitted with the distinct Long Branch "kicked leg" type.	Early style circular top with serrations for thumb grip reverted to; many were new-made.	Early style circular top with serrations for thumb grip was reverted to.

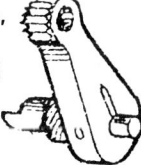
Original style, circular head with serrated thumb grip.

Production concession, "scoop" thumbgrip replaces serrations.

Long Branch "kicked leg" shape.

The locking bolt is also commonly referred to as the "safety catch".

Locking bolt spring:	Two types, early model (a) has machined screw block, later type (b) is a stamped pattern.	North American production generally fitted with machined pattern.	These post-war rifles fitted with the machined pattern.	As rifles were converted and repaired, machined pattern would have generally been refitted.

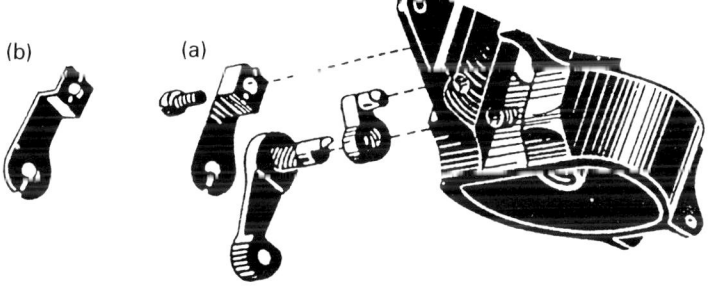

Rifle Model:	**No. 4 Mk I**	**No. 4 Mk I***	**No. 4 Mk 2**	**No. 4 Mk I/2 & I/3**
Fore-end:	Early fore-ends have more clearance below bolthead rib, and for bolthead release catch. From trials Mk I rifle with magazine cut-off. Rear of fore-end has a flat steel tieplate as a reinforce.	Basically the same as fore-end for Mk I rifle as made in North America. Similar to later British Mk I rifle production. Rear of fore-end has a flat steel tieplate as a reinforce.	Back end of fore-end is cut out for the trigger bracket. New-made fore-end has no reinforce for the transverse screw. A transverse screw is fitted across the rear of the fore-end.	Back end of fore-end is cut out for the trigger bracket. Converted fore-end has semi-circular wood reinforce in each side. A transverse screw is fitted across the rear of the fore-end.

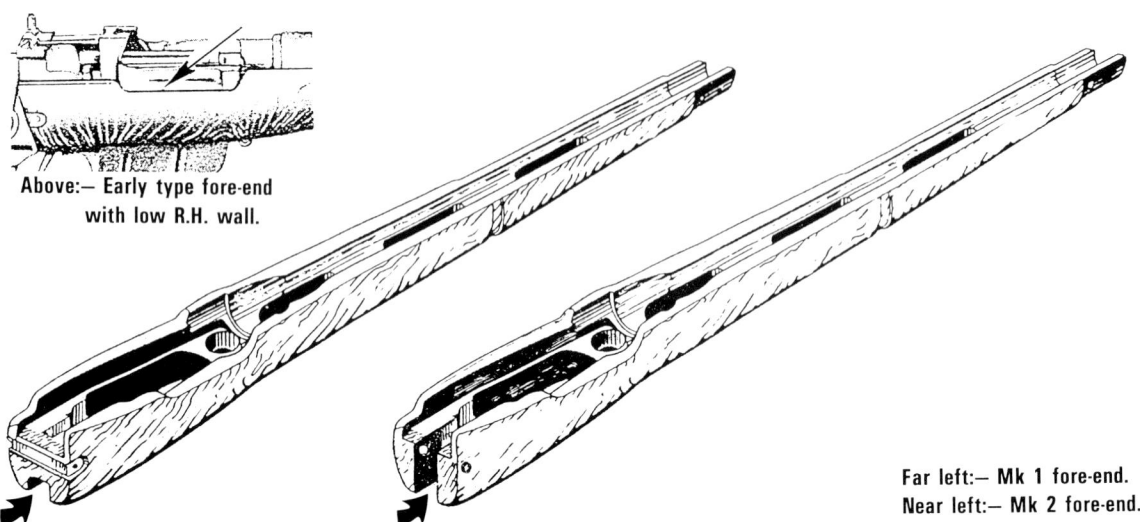

Above:— Early type fore-end with low R.H. wall.

Far left:— Mk 1 fore-end.
Near left:— Mk 2 fore-end.

Handguard— rear:	Some have longitudinal grooves for a better grip, not necessarily from early or later production.	Some have longitudinal grooves for a better grip, not necessarily from early or later production.	New handguards are usually light coloured beech timber. Maybe even grooved for a better hand grip.	New handguards were often fitted, although original ones were retained if they were in sound condition.

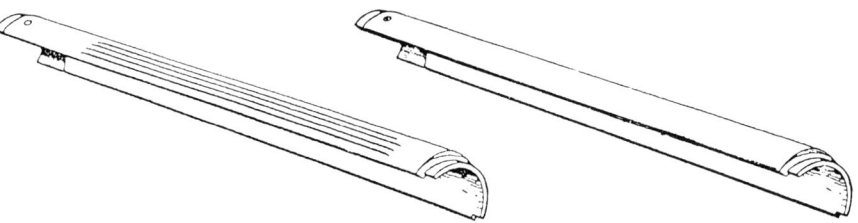

Trigger- guards:	Earlier production is milled from one piece. Wartime production or contractor's marks are usually evident.	Later fabricated type was made from square rod and inserts welded together. Different machining models.	No trigger axis pin, newly made from one piece casting. Has "P" or "F"" mark and year of manufacture.	Same as Mk 2, although could be converted by merely removing the original trigger and pin during the conversion.

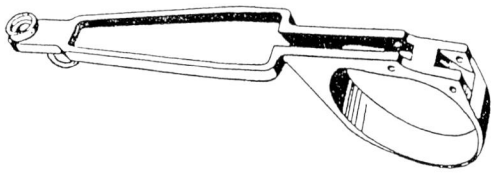
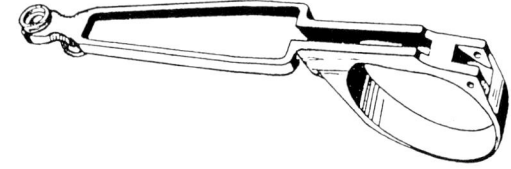

Rifle Model:	**No. 4 Mk I**	**No. 4 Mk I***	**No. 4 Mk 2**	**No. 4 Mk I/2 & I/3**
Backsight:	Four types were used in service. Early production usually had the Mk I pattern.	These rifles originally had Stevens-Savage and Long Branch manufactured sights fitted.	Mk 1 pattern sight was reverted to in this post-war production.	Generally, the Mk 1 pattern retrofitted in the post-war F.T.R. program.

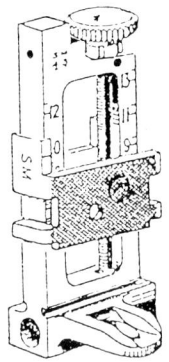
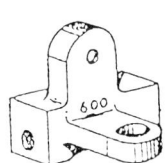
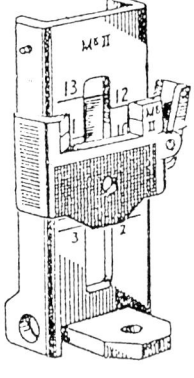
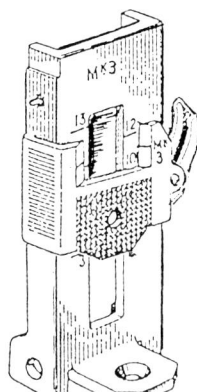

Left to Right:—
Mk 1 fine adjustment.
Mk 2, dual aperture only.
Mk 3, with Mk II leaf.
Mk 4, with Mk III leaf.

Note: Mks 2, 3 & 4 were wartime alternatives only.
Early Mk 1 sights have small diameter battle aperture.
Canadian Mk 3 sight with Mk 2 leaf is marked "C Mk II" or "C Mk 2".
Canadian Mk 4 sight with Mk 3 leaf is marked "C Mk 3".

Foresight Protector:	Early type 'waisted' as for No. 1 Mk VI and No. 4 trials models. Mk 1 altered pattern is solid construction but squared profile. Mk 2 fabricated patt. also used on North production. Some interchange during service. See *L.E.S.* pgs 201-2.	American Mk I* rifles originally fitted with Mk 2 fabricated type. Canadian production mostly Mk 1 altered pattern; some Mk 2. Many such parts were interchanged during service and F.T.R.'s. See *L.E.S.* pgs 201-2.	New Mk 2 production generally used solid Mk 1 altered pattern protectors rather than the manufacturing concession types. Many such parts were interchanged during service and F.T.R.'s. See *L.E.S.* pgs 201-2.	Most rifles were retrofitted with more solid type protectors rather than Mk 2 and manufacturing concession models. Can vary. Many such parts were interchanged during service and F.T.R.'s. See *L.E.S.* pgs 201-2.
Foresight:	Readily changed in service and F.T.R. programs.	Readily changed in service and F.T.R. programs.	Readily changed in service and F.T.R. programs.	Readily changed in service and F.T.R. programs.

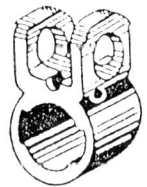
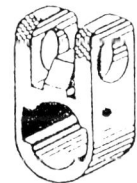

From left:— Foresight Protector Mk I (early type) & Foresight Bracket.
Foresight Bracket includes foresight ramp and mount.
Below, from left:— Foresight Protectors, Mk 1 (Altered Pattern) & Mk 2 Fabricated.
Block, band Mk 1 with Foresight Mk 1;
Block, band Mk 2 with Foresight Mk 1*.

Right above does not require the foresight block band. Others above and below fit around this block.

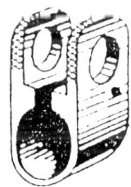

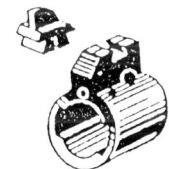

MAGAZINE ASSEMBLY:

Unlike the S.M.L.E. models, there were no successive Marks of the No. 4 magazine case, magazine platform or the auxiliary spring. This was mainly because there were no major changes introduced in the .303 round or its general projectile shape. This same magazine case and assembly was also used with the Rifle No. 5 or "Jungle Carbine".

Although the No. 4 magazine can sometimes be fitted into the No. 1 rifle and *vice versa*, force is often required to make the magazine latch on the receiver body engage over the magazine rib. Not recommended at all, as this causes undue wear on the engaging surfaces and the magazine is usually very hard to remove. To confirm that the correct magazine is fitted, the differences between the No. 1 and No. 4 magazines are shown in the illustration below. The No. 4 magazine has no extended or lower rib on the back of the case, or additional external spring. No. 4 magazine cases were generally serial numbered to the rifle, not so with the No. 1 rifle.

Certain manufacturing concessions were permitted during wartime production of the magazine, principally evident in some of the North American examples. Two separate sheets were bent up and then the halves welded together. Another form has the bottom of the case folded over on all four sides, and not welded. Therefore the sheet metal ends are quite evident on the bottom of the magazine. North American magazines are usually marked with the squared "S" logo for Stevens-Savage or "LB" for Long Branch.

Many of the No. 4 magazines were made by contractors, their code numbers, initials or trade marks will sometimes be noted on the magazine cases and cartridge platforms. Some of these codes will be found on page 47. A comprehensive listing of the contractors and parts will be found in the *Lee-Enfield Story*, pages 203 and 204. A full list of all the British wartime contractors, their addresses and codes is published in *British Small Arms of World War 2* (Skennerton).

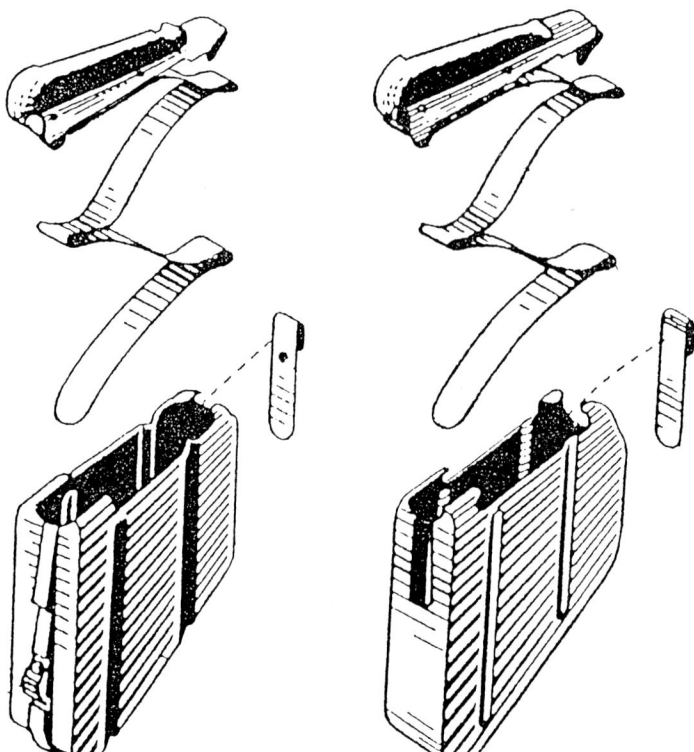

Far left:— Magazine for the No. 1 rifle, with exploded view of the magazine platform and spring, and the auxiliary spring.
Near left:— Magazine for the No. 4 rifle, similar projection of the exploded diagram.

Note the difference in form of the ribs at the back of the cases. The magazine platform is secured to the zig-zag spring by two rivets. Magazine platforms and the auxiliary springs are not interchangeable between the .303 No. 1 and No. 4 magazines. While the platform and zig-zag spring may well fit into the magazine case of its counterpart, this is likely to jam or misfeed cartridges.

COMPONENTS INTERCHANGEABLE

BETWEEN THE RIFLES, No. 1 & No. 4

Some component parts of the No. 4 rifle are interchangeable with those of the Rifle No. 1. However, few of the parts can be interchanged as most of the components are different. Threads of most screws were changed, making even these small parts non-interchangeable between the No. 4 series and earlier models.

Parts listed as interchangeable are:—

Body sear spring	This "V"-shaped spring also acts on the magazine catch, engaging into notches on each of these parts by means of nibs at each end of the spring.
Bolt mainspring	Often referred to as the firing pin spring.
Stockbolt washer	Steel.
Stockbolt wad	Leather, fitting on top of the stockbolt head.
Butt swivel assembly	Bracket, screw and swivel.
Sling swivel	No. 1 swivel is offset, longer side towards bolthandle.
Buttplate assembly	No. 1 buttplate was usually a brass composition.
Buttplate trap spring	Flat type spring.
Sling swivel screws	No. 4 screw has a flat head, No. 1 screws are rounded at top.
Butt stock	Later patterns of butt stock were nominated as interchangeable, with minor fitting required by an armourer, using a wood chisel.

OTHER NOTES:—

Serial numbers on the No. 4 rifles were marked on the body, bolt and fore-end, and later, on the magazine case as well. But not on the backsight or the nosecap as for No. 1 rifles; the No. 4 was of a different design and parts were more readily interchangeable. Their interchange did not affect the shooting of the rifle as much as with the earlier No. 1.

Screws for the bands, swivels and trigger guard (rear screw) are inserted from the left hand side, as on the Short Lee-Enfield and Lee-Enfield rifles and carbines. These swivel screws are some of the few interchangeable screws with those on the S.M.L.E. rifle.

The knobs on No. 4 bolt handles will be found to vary; some are rounded, others have a 5/16-in. diameter lightening hole and others, especially those of Stevens-Savage make, have a flat at the end. There was no specific "early type", "late type" or pattern change. Different contractors produced the parts to various specifications and in many instances, such production variations occurred concurrently.

Variations will be found in fore-ends and handguards. Some handguards are grooved, others are not; both types were produced at the same time. Early fore-ends have a recess on the right side of the action, provision for the cut-off on early trials rifles.

SPECIFICATIONS

RIFLE, No. 4 Marks I & I*

Lengths:
- Rifle, overall ... ... 3 ft. 8.5 in. [1130mm] *with normal butt*
- With bayonet fixed ... ... 4 ft. 4.8 in. [1341mm] *approximate*
- Barrel ... ... 25.2 in. [640mm]
- Bayonet, overall ... ... 10.0 in. [254mm] *No. 4, all Marks*
- Bayonet, blade ... ... 8.0 in. [203mm] *Cruciform & spike types*

Weights:
- Rifle, without bayonet ... ... 9 lb. 1 oz. [4.1 kg] *with empty magazine*
- Rifle, with bayonet ... ... 9 lb. 8 oz. [4.3 kg] *with empty magazine*
- Bayonet, Mk I ... ... 7 oz. [.2 kg] *without scabbard*
- Bayonet, Mks II & II* ... ... 8 oz. [.23 kg] *without scabbard*

Barrel:
- Rifling ... ... 5 groove, Enfield, Stevens & Long Branch
  2 groove, Stevens & Long Branch
- Rifling twist ... ... L.H., 1 turn in 10 ins. or 33 calibres
- Groove depth ... ... .005 in.
- Width of grooves ... ... .0936 in.

Sights: ... ... Mks I, 3 & 4; 200 – 1,300 yds.
Mk 2; 300 & 600 yds.
Blade foresight
Sighting radius, 2 ft. 4.6 in (28.6 in.)

Method of Operation ... ... Manually operated bolt, locking lugs at rear

Method of Loading ... ... 5-round charger clips

Cartridge ... ... .303-in. British

Muzzle Velocity, Mk VII ball ... 2,440 ft./sec. *approximate*

Production Costs: ... ... £8/5/0d (Mk I, 1941) *R.O.F., England*
£7/15/0d (Mk I, 1943) *R.O.F., England*

Service Accessories: ... ... No. 4 Bayonet & Scabbard
Webbing sling
Oil bottle
Pullthrough & Flannel

USER GUIDE

for PARTS and VOCAB. LISTS

IMPORTANT— Read this page first.

British, Canadian and Australian lists have been referred to; these have been edited, although the original vocabulary and format has been retained. The arrangement and format differ slightly from that in S.A.I.S. Vol. 1 on the S.M.L.E. rifle, mainly because the British, Canadian and Australian editions are not the same. British parts vocabulary has been used as the most widespread issues occurred there. Catalogue references from the early 1950's have been the principal sources.

REF. NO. is the number for parts shown and identified on the adjacent page. *PLATE* refers to the sheet illustration. *PART OR CAT. No.* is the service part catalogue or vocabulary number, usually marked on service packaging and labels. The letter prefix was also a service indicator. British lists have these part numbers prefixed by "B1/", dispensed with here in the parts vocabulary. Specific Canadian-made parts usually have an extra "C" in the prefix, *e.g.* "BAC", "BBC" or "BJC"; the "C" added to its British equivalent number. Canadian developed parts have a "CGR" prefix. A "GA" suffix indicates a General Arrangement, "A" is "Assembly" and "SA" for "Sub-Assembly".

The part no. prefixes commenced with "AA" during the earlier .303 S.M.L.E. era. "BA" and "BB" were applied to the No. 4 rifle for parts of wartime vintage. "BJ" was allocated to the Mk I* variant. "CR" part number prefixes for the No. 4 rifles are post-war and continued into the 7.62mm NATO era. An unusual prefix such as Z2/ZB 11412 (screw for the bayonet scabbard mouthpiece) indicates extra-service supply. An "SM" prefix denotes a different part series again.

DESIGNATION is the original service part name. Here, lines are indented where that particular line pertains to the previous one. For example, the Mk 3 Backsight slide catch pin, Mk I for the No. 4 Mk I Rifle, (page 13, illustrated as Part No. 23) is part of the Rifle Backsight assembly.

e.g.   RIFLE, No. 4 Mk I   *General Arrangement.*
      BACKSIGHT Mk 3   *Part group, applicable to Rifle No. 4 Mk 1.*
         SLIDE, Mk 2   *Part of the Mk 3 Backsight.*
           PIN, catch, Mk 1   *Component part of the Mk 2 Slide.*

Lower case text following the upper case part name serves as an additional description, *e.g.* "SPRING, plunger, adjusting screw" (item 15 on pages 22 & 23). An "#" indicator in the Designation column indicates that these parts were not provided for normal maintenance. Orders were to indicate that these parts were required to replace broken or worn items.

QTY is quantity required. *DRAWING NUMBER* is the manufacturer's part drawing. D.D.(E) is an Enfield drawing, those with S.A.I.D. and A.I.D. prefixes are also of British origin. C.S.A.I.D. is a Canadian variant. Roman numerals were previously used in service designations. By the time the No. 4 rifle series was in general service, this had largely been discarded for conventional numerals. So, "1" replaced "I" and the numeral "2" was used instead of "II". These changes are evident on body markings such as "No. 4 Mk 1/2" and "No. 1 Mk 2". Few O.M.L.E. rifle parts are interchangeable with those of the No. 4. Even for the metal screws, different thread pitches and types were used. These are noted in the *REMARKS* column where applicable.

A	Assembly.	hd	Head.
A/f	As for; same as	SA	Sub-Assembly.
B.A.	British Association.	SWG	Standard Wire Gauge.
Csk.	Countersunk. ‡		Item (usually assembly) not shown on plate.
GA	General Arrangement. #		Not supplied for normal maintenance.

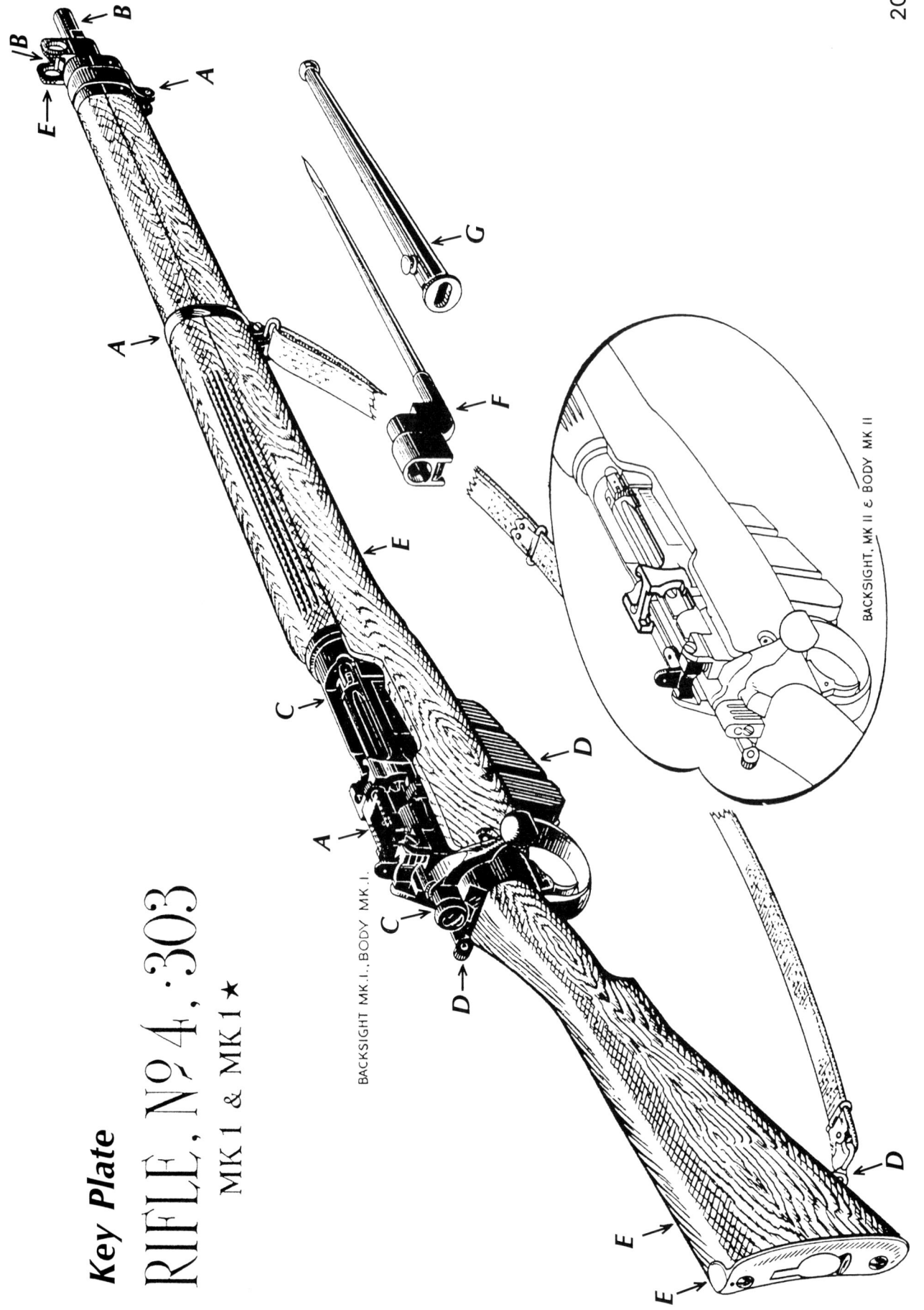

PLATES:—
- A1   Backsights   *pages 22 - 23*
- A2   Bands   *pages 24 - 25*
- B   Barrel and Foresight   *pages 26 - 27*
- C   Body and Breech Bolt   *pages 28 - 29*
- D   Locking Bolt, Butt Swivel, Magazine, &c.   *pages 30 - 31*
- E1   Butt Plate, Foresight Protector, &c.   *pages 32 - 33*
- E2   Butt and Fore-end   *pages 34 - 35*
- F   Bayonet   *pages 36 - 37*
- G   Bayonet Scabbard   *pages 38 - 39*
- H   Accessories   *pages 40 - 41*

				Old Series	REMARKS
RIFLE, No. 4 Mark I, .303-in.					
With **LONG BUTT**	—	Part or Cat. No.	B1/CR 27 GA	BA 8551	Long butt is ½-in. longer than normal.
With **NORMAL BUTT**	—	Part or Cat. No.	B1/CR 28 GA	BA 8022	Normal butt is not marked "L" or "S".
With **SHORT BUTT**	—	Part or Cat. No.	B1/CR 29 GA	BA 8552	Short butt is ½-in. shorter than normal.
RIFLE BODY	—	Part or Cat. No.	B1/CR 47 A	BA 10056	Mk I body has bolthead release catch.
BOLT, BREECH	—	Part or Cat. No.	B1/CR 66 A or BA 10095	BB 8566	
No. 4 Mk I Trials Rifle Magazine cut-off				*BB 8027*	
No. 4 Mk I Trials Rifle Magazine cut-off screw				*BB 8034*	
RIFLE, No. 4 Mk I*, .303-in.					
With **LONG BUTT**	—	Part or Cat. No.	B1/CR 30 GA	BJ 0001	Long butt is ½-in. longer than normal.
With **NORMAL BUTT**	—	Part or Cat. No.	B1/CR 31 GA	BJ 0002	Normal butt is not marked "L" or "S".
With **SHORT BUTT**	—	Part or Cat. No.	B1/CR 32 GA	BJ 0003	Short butt is ½-in. shorter than normal.
With **BANTAM BUTT**	—	Canadian only, Butt Part No. CGB 7404			
RIFLE BODY	—	Part or Cat. No.	B1/CR 48 A	BA 10045	Mk 2 body has bolthead release cut-out, near front of the body bolthead rib.
BOLT, BREECH	—	Part or Cat. No.	B1/CR 66 A or B1/BA 10095	BB 8566	
RIFLE, No. 4 E.Y., .303-in.					
Emergency	—	Part or Cat. No.	...	B1/BA 8665	Often used for grenade launching practice.
RIFLE, No. 4 Mk 2, .303-in.					
As above	—	Part or Cat. No.	B1/CR 17 & 19 GA	...	Mk 3 body has trigger mounted on the body.

21

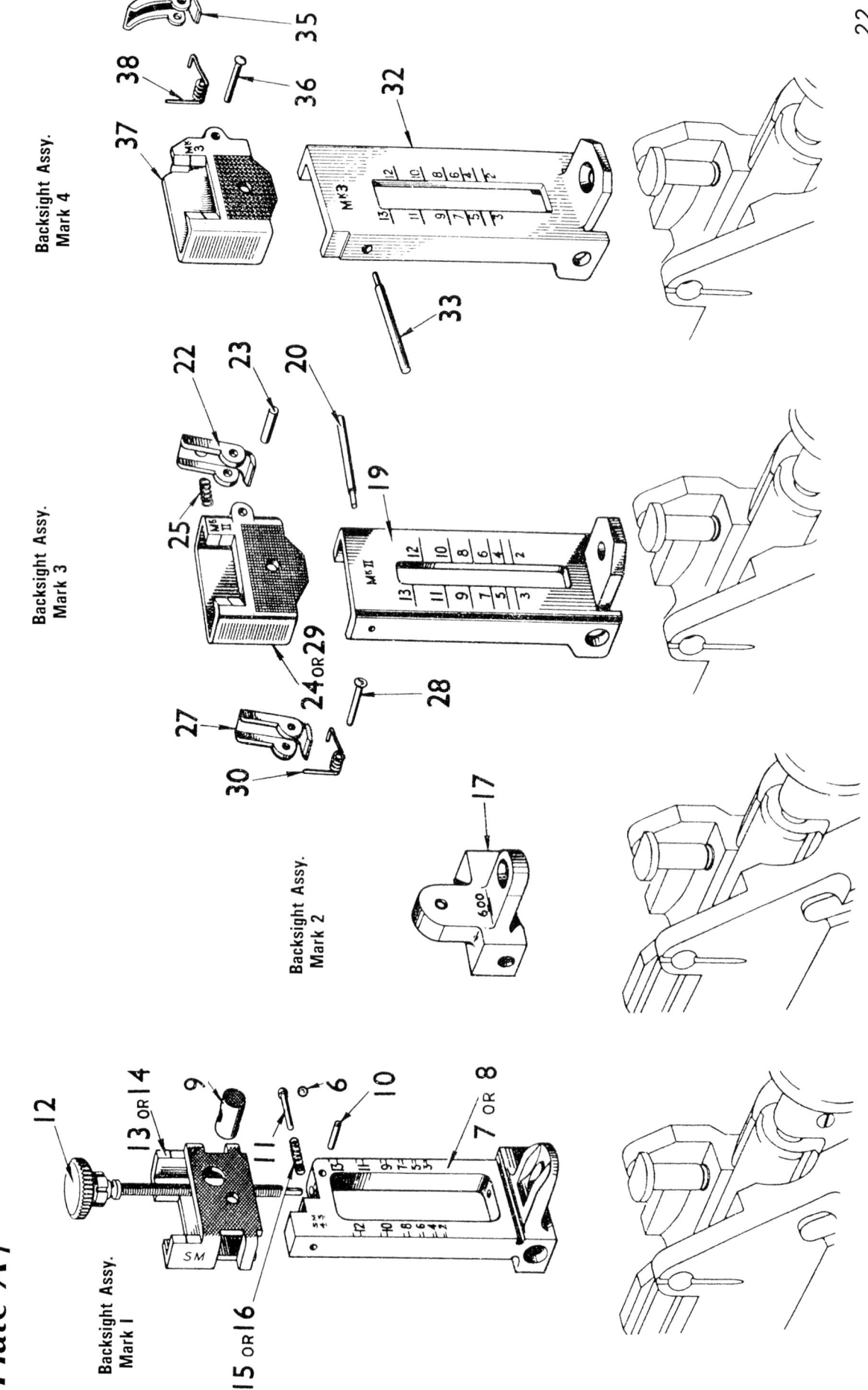

Plate A₁

Backsight Assy. Mark 4
Backsight Assy. Mark 3
Backsight Assy. Mark 2
Backsight Assy. Mark 1

REF. NO.	DESIGNATION	PART or CAT. NUMBER	PREVIOUS PART NO.	QTY.	DRAWING NUMBER	REMARKS
	Plate A1 RIFLE, No. 4 MK 1 & 1*					
5 ‡	BACKSIGHT (Mark I)	CR 39 A	BB 9023	1	DD(E) 450/A	Original Mk I Singer pattern.
6	BALL, steel, anti-friction, 3/32 dia. (b)	LV6/MT7/159		1		
7	LEAF	CR 403	BB 8589	1	DD(E) 450/28R	For Backsight Mk I.
8 or	LEAF	CR 669		1		Backsight Mk I only.
9	NUT, screw, adjusting	CR 314	BB 8590	1	DD(E) 450/30R	
10	PIN, retaining adjusting screw	CR 315	BB 8032	1	DD(E) 450/36	
11	PLUNGER, screw adjusting (c)	CR 316	BB 8599	1	DD(E) 450/47	
12	SCREW, adjusting	CR 317	BB 8604	1	DD(E) 450/55	
13	SLIDE	CR 318	BB 8620	1	DD(E) 450/67R	Slide Mk I.
14 or	SLIDE	CR 670		1		
15	SPRING, plunger, adjusting screw	CR 502	BB 8626	1	DD(E) 450/70	Coil type, stainless steel.
16	SPRING, plunger, adjusting screw (a) (d)	CR 319		1		Coil type, stainless steel.
17	BACKSIGHT, Mk 2 (a)	BB 8662		1	DD(E) 450/109	Dual 300 & 600 yds only.
18 ‡	BACKSIGHT, Mk 3 (a)	BB 8673		1	DD(E) 450/K	With C Mk2 leaf, BBC 8673.
19	LEAF, Mk 2	BB 8676		1	DD(E) 450/100	Canadian patt., BBC 8676.
20	PIN, stop	BB 8678		1	DD(E) 450/102	
21 ‡	SLIDE, MK 2	BB 8679		1	DD(E) 450/103	Canadian patt., BJC 8679.
22	CATCH, Mk 1	BB 8674		1	DD(E) 450/98	Uses coil type spring.
23	PIN, catch, Mk 1	BA 10053		1	DD(E) 450/101	
24	SLIDE, Mk 2	BA 10054		1	DD(E) 450/103	Coil type, stainless steel.
25	SPRING, Mk 1	BB 8680		1	DD(E) 450/104	Alternative.
26 ‡ or	SLIDE, MK 2	BB 8679		1		Uses mousetrap spring.
27	CATCH, Mk 2	BA 10052		1	DD(E) 450/121	
28	PIN, catch, Mk 2	BJ 0104		1	DD(E) 450/122	
29	SLIDE, Mk 2	BA 10054		1	DD(E) 450/103	
30	SPRING, Mk 2	BJ 0106		1	DD(E) 450/123	Mousetrap, stainless steel.
31	BACKSIGHT, MK 4 (a)	BJ 0101		1	DD(E) 450/L	With C Mk3 leaf, BJC 0101.
32	LEAF, Mk 3	BJ 0103		1	DD(E) 450/102	Canadian patt., BJC 0103.
33	PIN, stop	BB 8678		1		
34 ‡	SLIDE, Mk 2	BA 10082		1	DD(E) 450/124	Cdn. patt. Mk 2, BJC 0105.
35	CATCH, Mk 3	BJ 0102		1	DD(E) 450/126	
36	PIN, catch, Mk 2	BJ 0104		1	DD(E) 450/122	
37	SLIDE, Mk 3	BJ 0105		1	DD(E) 450/125	
38	SPRING, Mk 2	BJ 0106		1	DD(E) 450/123	Canadian patt., BJC 0106.

(a) Obsolescent.
(b) & (c) Alternative.
(d) For use with CR 3·6 only.

\# Part not provided for normal maintenance; the demand (order) should be endorsed "To replace broken part, or worn out part", etc.

‡ Item numbers do not appear on the plate illustration, they are assemblies.

23

Plate A₂

REF. NO.	DESIGNATION	PART or CAT. NUMBER	PREVIOUS PART NO.	QTY.	DRAWING NUMBER	REMARKS
Plate A2 **RIFLE, No. 4 MK 1 & 1*** (continued)						
39 ‡	BAND, LOWER	CR 56 SA	BA 10083	1	. . .	Tapped for No. 2 B.A.
40	BAND	CR 411	BB 8554	1	DD(E) 450/2	3 types; machined, lugs welded on, or stamped with blocks brazed to lugs. Production concession.
41	BAND, Canadian pattern . .	CR 321	BBC 8554 BB 8037	2 or 3	DD(E) 450/65	Same as on Rifle No. 1.
42	SWIVEL, sling . . .	CR 322	BB 8043	1	DD(E) 450/82A	Mark I.
	or					
43 ‡	BAND, LOWER	CR 57 SA	BA 10084	1	. . .	Production alternative,
44	BAND	CR 412	. . .	1	. . .	also see 40.
	or					
45	BAND	CR 518	. . .	1	DD(E) 450/65	Production alternative.
46	SCREW, swivel . . .	CR 321	BB 8037	2 or 3	DD(E) 450/65	Same as on Rifle No. 1.
47	SWIVEL, sling . . .	CR 322	. . .	1	. . .	
48 ‡	BAND, UPPER	CR 58 SA	. . .	1	. . .	
49	BAND	CR 413	BB 8555	1	DD(E) 450/91A	Hinged type, obsolete.
50	SCREW, swivel . . .	CR 321	BB 8037	1	DD(E) 450/65	No. 2 B.A. thread (SMLE).
	or					
51 ‡	BAND, UPPER	CR 59 SA	. . .	1	. . .	
52	BAND	CR 414	BE 8555	1	DD(E) 450/91A	Solid type, tap No. 2 B.A.
	BAND, Canadian pattern . .	. . .	BEC 8555		. . .	Production concession.
	or					
53	BAND	CR 519	. . .	1	. . .	Tapped for No. 2 B.A.
54	SCREW, swivel . . .	CR 321	BE 8037	1	DD(E) 450/65	No. 2 B.A. thread (SMLE).

\#   Part not provided for normal maintenance: the demand (order) should be endorsed "To replace broken part, or worn out part", etc.

‡   Item numbers do not appear on the plate illustration, they are assemblies.

N.B.:— Canadian-made components may be noted to differ slightly in machining and/or profiles.

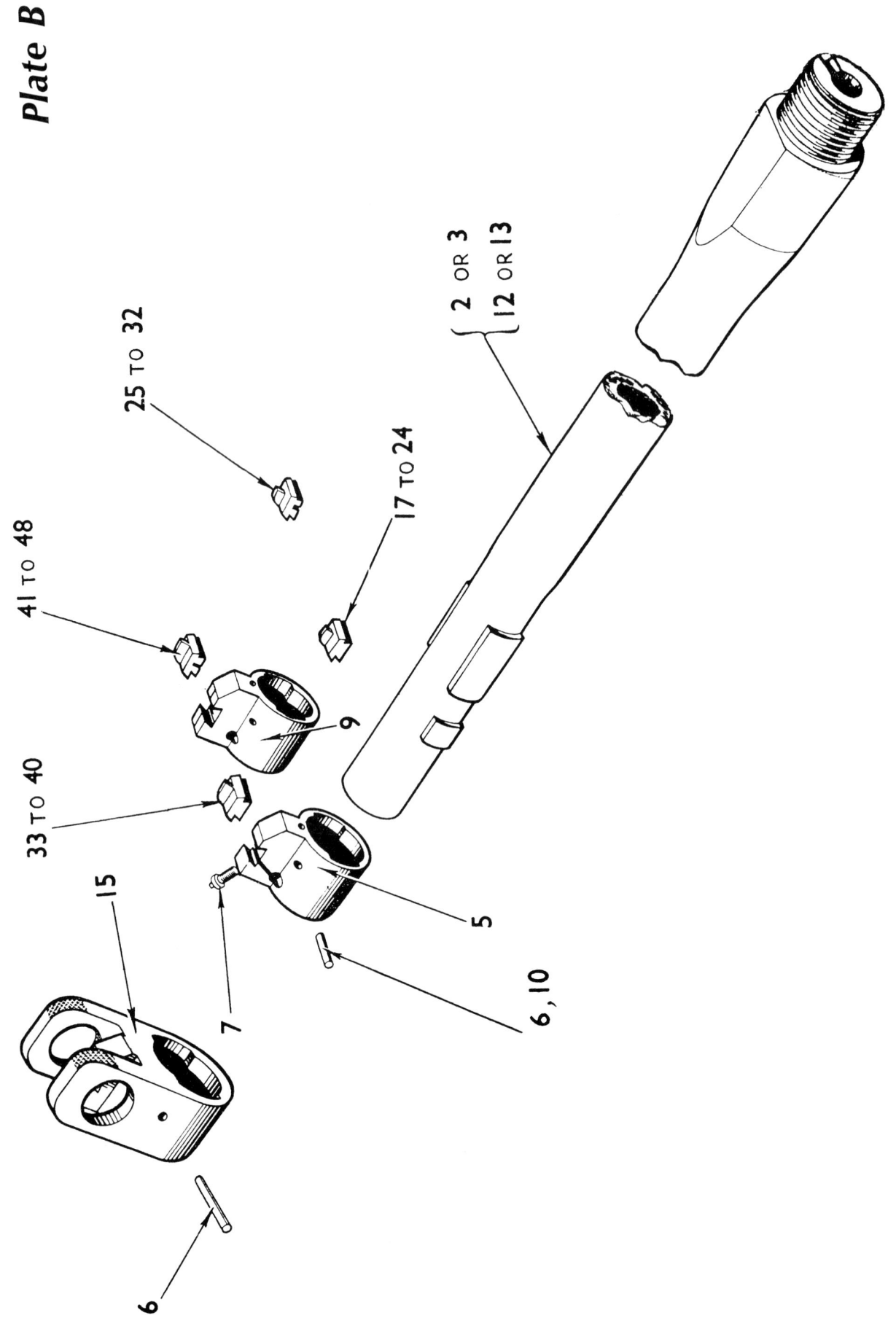

REF. NO.	DESIGNATION	PART or CAT. NUMBER	PREVIOUS PART NO.	QTY.	DRAWING NUMBER	REMARKS
Plate B	**RIFLE, No. 4 MK 1 & 1* (continued)**					
1 ‡	BAFREL	CR 41 A	BA 10089	1	DD(E) 450/A	(Mk 3, BB 8682 obsolete.)
2	BARREL, Mk 1	CR 415	BB 8557	1	DD(E) 450/3	5-groove rifling.
3	BARREL, Mk 2 (a)	CR 8683	BB 8681, 8683	1	DD(E) 450/110	2-groove rifling.
4 ‡	BLOCK, BAND, FORESIGHT, MK 1	CR 60 SA	BB 8568	1	. . .	Use solid blade foresight.
5	BLOCK, Mk 1	CR 416	. . .	1	DD(E) 450/5	
6	PIN	CR 312	. . .	1	DD(E) 450/35	
7	SCREW, blade, foresight	CR 418	BB 8033	1	DD(E) 450/56	Foresight block band Mk 1.
8 ‡ or	BLOCK, BAND, FORESIGHT, MK 2	CR 61 SA	. . .	1	DD(E) 450/96	Use solid blade foresight.
9	BLOCK, Mk 2	CR 419	. . .	1	. . .	
10	PN	CR 312	. . .	1	DD(E) 450/35	
11 ‡ or	BARREL	CR 42 A	BA 10092	1	DD(E) 450/A	Serial for Mk I* rifle.
12	BARREL, Mk 1	CR 415	BB 8556	1	DD(E) 450/3	5-groove rifling.
13	BARREL, Mk 2 (a)	CR 8683	BB 8681	1	DD(E) 450/110	2-groove rifling.
14 ‡	BRACKET, FORESIGHT	CR 62 SA	. . .	1	. . .	Uses split blade.
15	BRACKET	CR 420	. . .	1	. . .	
16	PIN	CR 421	. . .	1	DD(E) 450/120	Tapered pin.
17	BLADE, foresight, -.030-in., Mk 2	CR 422	*or* 33	BLADE, foresight, -.030-in., Mk 1	#	BB 8560
18	BLADE, foresight, -.015-in., Mk 2	CR 423	34	BLADE, foresight, -.015-in., Mk 1	#	BB 8561
19	BLADE, foresight "0", Mk 2	CR 424	35	BLADE, foresight, "0", Mk 1	#	BB 8562
20 #	BLADE, foresight .015-in., Mk 2 (b)	CR 425	36	BLADE, foresight, .015-in., Mk 1	#	BB 8563 (a)
21	BLADE, foresight .030-in., Mk 2	CR 426	37	BLADE, foresight, .030-in., Mk 1	#	BB 8564
22	BLADE, foresight .045-in., Mk 2 (d)	CR 427	38	BLADE, foresight, .045-in., Mk 1	#	BB 8565
23	BLADE, foresight .060-in., Mk 2	CR 428	39	BLADE, foresight, .060-in., Mk 1	#	BB 8666
24	BLADE, foresight .075-in., Mk 2	CR 429	40	BLADE, foresight, .075-in., Mk 1	#	BB 8667
or						
25	BLADE, foresight -.030-in., Mk 3	CR 353	41	BLADE, foresight, -.030-in., Mk 1*	#	BB 8685
26	BLADE, foresight -.015-in., Mk 3	CR 352	42	BLADE, foresight, -.015-in., Mk 1*	#	BB 8686
27	BLADE, foresight "0", Mk 3	CR 351	43	BLADE, foresight, "0", Mk 1*	#	BB 8687
28 #	BLADE, foresight .015-in., Mk 3 (b)	CR 350	44	BLADE, foresight, .015-in., Mk 1*	#	BB 8688 (a)
29	BLADE, foresight .030-in., Mk 3	CR 349	45	BLADE, foresight, .030-in., Mk 1*	#	BB 8689
30	BLADE, foresight .045-in., Mk 3 (c)	CR 348	46	BLADE, foresight, .045-in., Mk 1*	#	BB 8690
31	BLADE, foresight .060-in., Mk 3	CR 347	47	BLADE, foresight, .060-in., Mk 1*	#	BB 8691
32	BLADE, foresight .075-in., Mk 3	CR 346	48	BLADE, foresight, .075-in., Mk 1*	#	BB 8692

Canadian Patt. Mk 1 Foresight Blade — BBC 8560-8670. Drawing CSAID 1-1238.   Canadian Patt. Mk 1* Foresight Blade — BBC 8685-8692.   Also see pages 43-45.

(a) Obsolescent.
(b) Fitted as required.
(c) For use with CR 61 SA & CR 62 SA.
(d) For use with CR 60 SA.

\#   Part not provided for normal maintenance; the demand (order) should be endorsed "To replace broken part, or worn out part", etc.

‡   Item numbers do not appear on the plate illustration, they are assemblies.

27

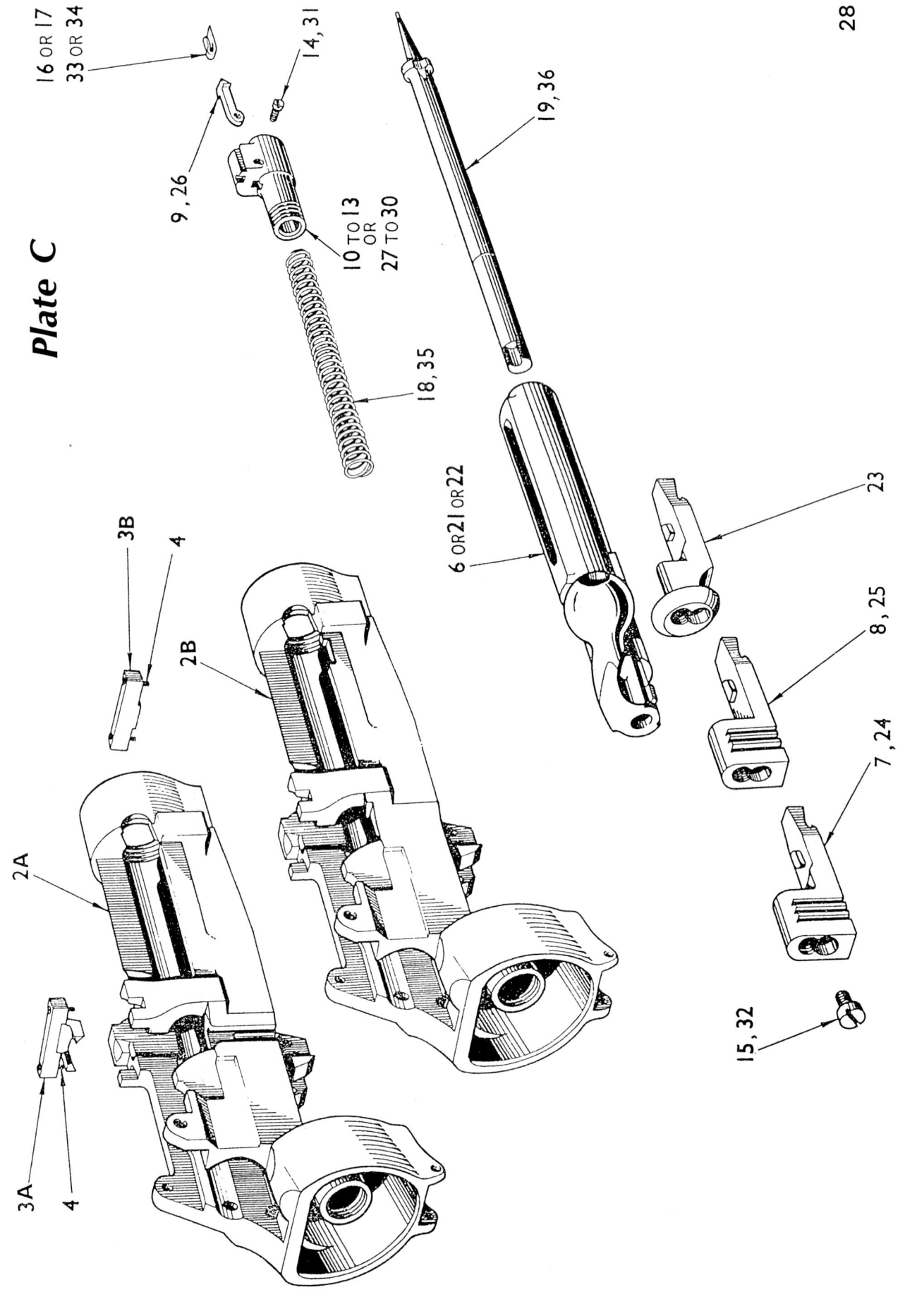

REF. NO.	DESIGNATION		PART or CAT. NUMBER	PREVIOUS PART NO.	QTY.	DRAWING NUMBER	REMARKS
Plate C RIFLE, No. 4 MK 1 & 1* (continued)							
1A ‡	BODY	#	CR 47 A	EA 10055	1	DD(E) 450/A	Not supplied as spare.
2A	BODY, Mk 1	#	CR 417	EA 10056	1	DD(E) 450/6R	
3A	BRIDGE, Mk 1 (a)	#	CR 494	EJ 0090	1	DD(E) 450/11	(b) not required when (a) is welded to body.
4	SCREW, bridge (b)	#	CR 495	BB 8652	2	DD(E) 450/57	
1B ‡	BODY, Mk 2	#	CR 48 A	BB 8658	1	DD(E) 2838/1	Not supplied as spare.
2B	BODY, Mk 2 (a)	#	CR 499	BA 10045	1	DD(E) 450/3	Mk 1* rifle has Mk 2 body.
3B	BRIDGE, Mk 2 (b)	#	CR 500	BA 10046	1		See above for (a) & (b).
5 ‡	BOLT, BREECH	#	CR 66 A		1	DD(E) 450/C	Some have drilled knob.
6	BOLT	.	CR 430	BB 8566	1	DD(E) 450/7	Unassembled.
7	COCKING-PIECE	.	CR 431	BB & BBC 8650	1	DD(E) 450/18A	Mark I, obsolescent.
8	*or* COCKING-PIECE	.	CR 432	BA 10060	1	DD(E) 450/18B	Mark II model.
9	EXTRACTOR	.	CR 433	BB 8028	1	DD(E) 450/22	
10	HEAD, breech-bolt, No. 0	.	CR 434	BB 8584	1	DD(E) 450/26	From sizes "0" to "3",
11	*or* HEAD, breech-bolt, No. 1	.	CR 435	BB 8585	1	DD(E) 450/26	increases in length
12	*or* HEAD, breech-bolt, No. 2	.	CR 436	BB 8586	1	DD(E) 450/26	are by increments of
13	*or* HEAD, breech-bolt, No. 3	.	CR 437	BB 8587	1	DD(E) 450/26	.003-in.
14	SCREW, extractor	.	CR 438	BB 8608	1	DD(E) 450/54	
15	SCREW, striker	.	CR 330	BB 8616	1	DD(E) 450/60B	
16	SPRING, extractor	.	CR 439	B3 & BBC 8041	1	DD(E) 450/72A	(Sheet 1)
17	*or* SPRING, extractor	.	CR 440	BA 10096	1	DD(E) 450/72A	(Sheet 2)
18	SPRING, main	.	CR 441	BB 0754	1	DD(E) 450/74	Same as for Rifle No. 1.
19	STRIKER	.	CR 442	BB 8634	1	DD(E) 450/79A	
20 ‡	BOLT, BREECH	(c) #	BA 10095		1	DD(E) 450/C	(c) means Obsolescent.
21	BOLT	(c) .	BB 8566		1	DD(E) 450/7	Unassembled. Some bolt-handles have drilled knob.
22	BOLT	(c) #	CR 430	BE 5859	1	DD(E) 3579/6	(c) means Obsolescent.
23	COCKING-PIECE, Mk 1	.	CR 431	BE 8650	1	DD(E) 450/18A	
24	COCKING-PIECE, Mk 2	.	CR 432	BA 10060	1	DD(E) 450/18B	
25	*or* COCKING-PIECE, Mk 2	.	CR 433	BB 8028	1	DD(E) 450/22	
26	EXTRACTOR	.	CR 434	BB 8584	1	DD(E) 450/26	
27	HEAD, breech-bolt, No. 0	.	CR 435	BB 8585	1	DD(E) 450/26	
28	*or* HEAD, breech-bolt, No. 1	.	CR 436	BB 8586	1	DD(E) 450/26	
29	*or* HEAD, breech-bolt, No. 2	.	CR 437	BB 8587	1	DD(E) 450/26	
30	*or* HEAD, breech-bolt, No. 3	.	CR 438	BB 8608	1	DD(E) 450/54	
31	SCREW, extractor	.	CR 330	BB 8616	1	DD(E) 450/60B	
32	SCREW, striker	.	CR 439	BB 8041	1	DD(E) 450/72A	Vary .620-in. to .628-in.
33	SPRING, extractor	.	CR 440	BA 10096	1	DD(E) 450/72A	Vary .625-in. to .630-in.
34	*or* SPRING, extractor	.	CR 441	BB 0754	1	DD(E) 450/74	Vary .630-in. to .635-in.
35	SPRING, main	.	CR 442	BB 8634	1	DD(E) 450/79A	Vary .635-in. to .640-in.
36	STRIKER	.					

Plate D

REF. NO.	DESIGNATION	PART or CAT. NUMBER	PREVIOUS PART NO.	QTY.	DRAWING NUMBER	REMARKS
Plate D	**RIFLE, No. 4 MK 1 & 1* (continued)**					
1 ‡	BOLT, LOCKING	CR 63 SA	BB 8714	1	DD(E) 450/8	Mark I assembly. Nos. 2, 5, 6 & 8 differ in shape or construction.
2	BOLT	CR 340	BB 8026	1	DD(E) 450/17	
3	CATCH, safety	CR 343	BB 8576	1		
4	BOLT, LOCKING Mk 1 (a)	BB 8714	...	1	DD(E) 450/8 S-1	Machined solid.
5	BOLT (a)	BB 8026	...	1	DD(E) 450/8 S-2	2-piece assembled w/ pin.
6	*or* BOLT (a)	BA 10097	...	1	DD(E) 450/17	3-piece, not threaded.
7	CATCH, safety	CR 343	BB 8576	1	DD(E) 450/8 S-3	
8	BOLT, LOCKING Mk 2 (a)	BB 8664	BB 8567	1	DD(E) 450/9	
9	BOLT, stock	CR 510	BA 10098	1		
10 ‡	BRACKET, Mk 1	CR 64 SA	BB 0664	1	DD(E) 450/10	For butt swivel, demand under Rifle No. 1. Used with Swivel, sling, Mk I. And Bracket, CGB 7399.
11	BRACKET	CR 443	BB 8605	1	DD(E) 450/48	
12	SCREW, swivel (axis screw)	CR 321	BB 8043	2 or 3	DD(E) 450/82A	
13	SWIVEL, sling (Mk I)	CR 322	BB 6188	1		For butt swivel, used with Swivel, sling Mk II. Not with Bracket Mk I. Not on Rifle Mk I*.
14 ‡	*or* BRACKET, Mk 2	CR 65 SA	BB 8672	1	DD(E) 450/93	
15	BRACKET	CR 444	BB 8671	1	DD(E) 450/94	
16	SWIVEL, sling (Mk 2)	CR 445	BB 8574	1	DD(E) 450/16	
17	CATCH, head, breech bolt	CR 342	BB 8575	1	DD(E) 450/15	
18	CATCH, magazine	CR 446	BB 8579	1	DD(E) 450/19	
19	COLLAR	CR 344		1	DD(E) 450/99	For trigger guard screw.
20	COLLAR, backsight (a)	BB 8675		1	DD(E) 450/D	For backsight axis pin.
21 ‡	GUARD, HAND, FRONT	CR 66 SA	BE 8580	1	DD(E) 450/12B	
22	CAP	CR 448	BE 8571	1	DD(E) 450/23B	
23	*or* CAP	CR 520	BA 10062	1	DD(E) 450/29	
24	GUARD	CR 449	BE 8588	2	DD(E) 450/44	
25	LINER	CR 450	BA 10061	4	DD(E) 450/33	
26	RIVET, cap	CR 451	BE 6273	2	DD(E) 450/E	
27	RIVET, liner	CR 452	BE 8581	1	DD(E) 450/24	
28 ‡	GUARD, HAND, REAR	CR 67 SA	BA 10099	2	DD(E) 450/29	
29	GUARD	CR 450	BB 8588	2	DD(E) 450/33	
30	LINER	CR 452	BB 6273	1		
31	RIVET, cap	CR 357	BB 8582	1	DD(E) 450/25	BBC 8582 welded assembly.
32	GUARD, trigger	BB 8582 and	BB 5863	1	& DD(E) 3579/9	Patterns obsolescent.
33	GUARD, trigger	CR 44 A	BB 8029	1	DD(E) 450/F	Production concessions result in different assembly types; with same part no.
34 ‡	MAGAZINE, case	CR 454	BB 8572	1	DD(E) 450/14A	
35	CASE	CR 60 SA	BB 8597	1		
36 ‡	PLATFORM, MAGAZINE	CR 455	BB 6275	1	DD(E) 450/43	
37	PLATFORM	CR 456	BB 8656	2	DD(E) 450/46	
38	RIVET, spring	CR 457	BB 8694	1	DD(E) 450/75	With spring assembled
39	SPRING	CR 458	BB 8622	1	DD(E) 450/68	
40	SPRING, auxiliary	CR 359	BB 8030	1	DD(E) 450/32A	
41	PIN, axis, backsight	CR 360	BB 8031	1	DD(E) 450/27	
42	PIN, retaining backsight axis pin	CR 459	BB 8591	1	DD(E) 450/38	
43	PIN, sear, Mk 1	CR 459	BB 8591	1	or DD(E) 2838/3	Pin, sear Mk 2, BB 8669.
44	PIN, trigger					Same as Pin, sear.

31

Plate E₁

REF. NO.	DESIGNATION	PART or CAT. NUMBER	PREVIOUS PART NO.	QTY.	DRAWING NUMBER	REMARKS
Plate E1 **RIFLE, No. 4 MK 1 & 1*** (continued)						
1 ‡	PLATE, BUTT	CR 45 SA	BE 8595	1	DD(E) 450/G	A/f Rifles Nos. 1 & 2.
2	PLATE	CR 460	BE & BC 8716	1	DD(E) 445/40A	Brass, Mazak alloy, steel.
3	SCREW, spring, trap	CR 366	BB 8614	1	DD(E) 450/64	Bolt locking spring screw.
4	SPRING, trap	CR 462	BB 0762	1	DD(E) 450/78	Same as for Rifle No. 1.
5 ‡	TRAP, BUTT PLATE	CR 69 SA	BB 8636	1	DD(E) 450/84	With pin, assembled.
6	PIN	CR 463	BB 8592	1	DD(E) 450/34	BBC 8592, Canadian patt.
7	TRAP	CR 464	BB 8717	1	DD(E) 450/84	
8	PLATE, catch, head, breech bolt	CR 465	BB 8596	1	DD(E) 450/41A	Only on Mk I action body.
9	PLUNGER, backsight	CR 362	BB 8598	1	DD(E) 450/50R	
10 ‡	PROTECTOR, FORESIGHT, MK 1	CR 70 SA	BA 10104	1	DD(E) 450/39 (Sheet 1)	
11	PROTECTOR	CR 466	BB 8600	1	DD(E) 450/39	Early, waisted type.
12	SCREW	CR 467	BB 8036	1	DD(E) 450/62A	
13 ‡ *or* PROTECTOR, FORESIGHT, MK 1		CR 71 SA	BA 10105	1	DD(E) 450/39 (Sheet 2)	
14	PROTECTOR	CR 468	BA 10106	1	DD(E) 450/39	Alternative pattern.
15	SCREW	CR 467	BB 8036	1	DD(E) 450/62A	
16 ‡ *or* PROTECTOR, FORESIGHT, MK 2		CR 72 SA	BA 10107	1	DD(E) 450/95 (Sheet 1)	
17	PROTECTOR	CR 469	BB & BBC 8693	1	DD(E) 450/95	
18	SCREW	CR 311	BB 8610	1	DD(E) 450/58	A/f Screw, guard.
19 ‡ *or* PROTECTOR, FORESIGHT, MK 2		CR 73 SA	BA 10108	1	DD(E) 450/95 (Sheet 2)	
20	PROTECTOR	CR 471	BA 10109	1	DD(E) 450/95	
21	SCREW	CR 311	BB 8610	1	DD(E) 450/58	
22	RING, retaining, rear hand guard	CR 288	BB 8602	1	DD(E) 450/45	
23	SCREW, bracket	CR 472	BB 8037	2	DD(E) 450/65	Also Canadian BBC 8037.
24	SCREW, catch, magazine	CR 473	BB 8606	1	DD(E) 450/49	
25	SCREW, ejector	CR 474	BB 8035	1	DD(E) 450/53	
26	SCREW, guard, trigger, back	CR 311	BB 8610	1	DD(E) 450/58	A/f F'sight protector Mk 2.
27	SCREW, guard, trigger, front	CR 475	BB 8611	1	DD(E) 450/59	
28	SCREW, plate, butt	CR 476	BB 8613	1	DD(E) 450/61	Wood screws.
29	SCREW, spring, locking bolt	CR 366	BB 8614	1	DD(E) 450/64	A/f Spring, trap, buttplate.
30	SEAR	CR 477	BB 5864	1	DD(E) 3579/16	
31	SEAR (a)	...	BB 8618	1	DD(E) 450/66	Also U.S. patt., "chunkier".
32	SPRING, bolt, locking	CR 363	BB 8040	1	DD(E) 450/77 (Sheet 1)	
33 *or* SPRING, bolt, locking		CR 478	...	1	DD(E) 450/77 (Sheet 2)	
34	SPRING, catch, head, breech bolt	CR 367	BE 8623	1	DD(E) 450/71	Only on Mk I action body.
35	SPRING, plunger, backsight	CR 368	BE 8625	1	DD(E) 69/R	
36	SPRING, sear	CR 479	BE 8627	1	DD(E) 450/76	Same as on Rifle No. 1.

33

Plate E₂

REF. NO.	DESIGNATION	PART or CAT. NUMBER	PREVIOUS PART NO.	QTY.	DRAWING NUMBER	REMARKS
Plate E2 **RIFLE, No. 4 MK 1 & 1*** (continued)						
37 ‡	RIFLE, LONG BUTT, No. 4 Mk 1	CR 74 SA	BB 8629		...	Canadian, BBC 8629.
38 ‡	STOCK, BUTT- LONG	CR 480	BA 10101	1	DD(E) 450/80	Stamped "L".
39	STOCK . #	CR 285	BB 0778	1	DD(E) 450/87	Same as for Rifle No. 1.
40	WASHER, bolt .	...	...		...	
41 ‡	RIFLE, NORMAL BUTT, No. 4 Mk 1	CR 75 SA	BB 3630		...	Canadian, BBC 8630.
42 ‡	STOCK, BUTT- NORMAL	CR 481	BA 10102	1	DD(E) 450/80	
43	STOCK . #	CR 285	BB 0778	1	DD(E) 450/87	Same as for Rifle No. 1.
44	WASHER, bolt .	...	...		...	
45 ‡	RIFLE, SHORT BUTT, No. 4 Mk 1	CR 76 SA	BB 3631		...	Stamped "S".
46 ‡	STOCK, BUTT- SHORT	CR 482	BA 10103	1	DD(E) 450/80	
47	STOCK . #	CR 285	BB 0778	1	DD(E) 450/87	Same as for Rifle No. 1.
48	WASHER, bolt .	...	...		...	
	also STOCK, BUTT, BANTAM	...	CGB 7404		...	Canada only, 12.3-in. long.
49 ‡	RIFLE, No. 4 Mk 1	CR 77 SA	BB 8632	1	DD(E) 450/H	Succeeded by CR 78 SA.
50 ‡	STOCK, FORE-END	CR 483	BB 8573	1	DD(E) 450/13C	
51	CAP .	CR 496	...	1	DD(E) 450/13C	Alternative.
52	*or* CAP	CR 484	BB 8594	2	DD(E) 450/31A	
53	PIN, CAP	CR 375	BB 8603	1	DD(E) 450/37A	
54	RIVET, tie-plate #	CR 388	BA 10064	1	DD(E) 450/81R	
55	STOCK . #	CR 374	BB 8635	1	DD(E) 450/42	
56	TIE-PLATE . #	CR 485	BB 8638	1	DD(E) 450/85	
57	TRIGGER .	CR 486	BB 0777	1	DD(E) 450/86	Same as for Rifle No. 1.
58	WAD, bolt, stock .	CR 517	...	1	DD(E) 450/86	Alternative.
59	*or* WAD, bolt, stock .	CR 387	BB 8640	1	DD(E) 450/89	Sheet steel.
60	WASHER, screw, front, trigger guard	CR 389	BB 8641	1	DD(E) 450/90	Steel, 2 complete turns.
61	WASHER, spring, stock bolt .					

(a) Obsolescent
A/f Also for

\# Part not provided for normal maintenance; the demand (order) should be endorsed "To replace broken part, or worn out part", etc.

‡ Item numbers do not appear on the plate illustration, they are assemblies.

35

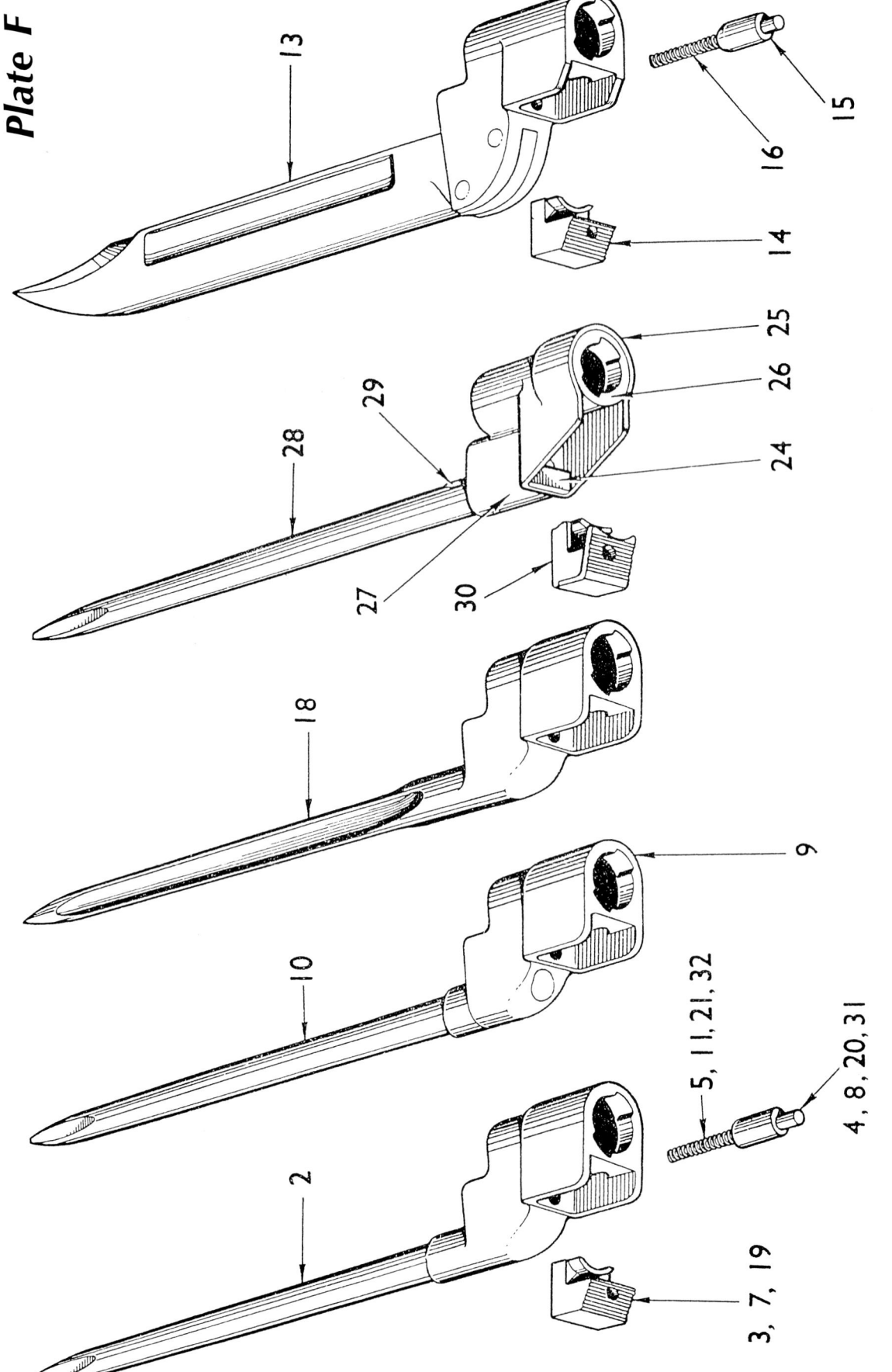

REF. NO.	DESIGNATION		PART or CAT. NUMBER	PREVIOUS PART NO.	QTY.	DRAWING NUMBER	REMARKS
Plate F	**BAYONET, NO. 4**						
1 ‡	BAYONET, NO. 4 MK 2	. .	CR 90 A	BA 6260	1	DD(E) 2605	Made by Singer in U.K., Long Branch and Stevens in North America.
2	BLADE	#	CR 732	BB 6265	1	DD(E) 2605/1	
3	CATCH	#	CR 488	BB 6252	1	DD(E) 340B/2	
4	PLUNGER, catch	. .	CR 733	BB 6253	1	DD(E) 340B/3	
5	SPRING, plunger, catch	. .	CR 489	BB 6254	1	DD(E) 340B/4	
	or						
6 ‡	BAYONET, NO. 4 MK 2*	. .	BA 6261	. . .	1	DD(E) 2679	Made in U.K. by Baird Eng., Prince Smith & Stells, Lewisham Eng., Baird Eng.
7	CATCH	#	CR 488	BB 6252	1	DD(E) 340B/2	
8	PLUNGER, catch	. .	CR 733	BB 6253	1	DD(E) 340B/3	
9	SOCKET	#	BA 10115	. . .	1	DD(E) 2679/2	
10	SPIKE	#	BA 10116	. . .	1	DD(E) 2679/1	
11	SPRING, plunger, catch	#	CR 489	BB 6254	1	DD(E) 340B/4	
	or						
12 ‡	BAYONET, NO. 9 MK 1	. .	CR 46 A	. . .	1	CR 46 A	Made by Enfield & Poole.
13	BLADE	. .	CR 487	. . .	1	CR 46 A	
14	CATCH	#	CR 488	. . .	1	DD(E) 340B/2	
15	PLUNGER, catch	. .	CR 128	. . .	1	DD(E) 340B/3	
16	SPRING, plunger, catch	. .	CR 489	. . .	1	DD(E) 340B/4	
17 ‡	BAYONET, NO. 4 MK 1 (a)	. .	BA 6138	. . .	1	DD(E) 340B	Cruciform blade. Made by Singer Mfg. Co., in U.K.
18	BLADE	#	BA 6251	. . .	1	DD(E) 340B/1	
19	CATCH	. .	CR 488	BE 6252	1	DD(E) 340B/2	
20	PLUNGER, catch	. .	CR 733	BE 6253	1	DD(E) 340B/3	
21	SPRING, plunger, catch	. .	CR 489	BE 6254	1	DD(E) 340B/4	
22 ‡	BAYONET, NO. 4 MK 3 (a)	. .	BA 6263	. . .	1	DD(E) 3453	Fabricated pattern. Made by J. Lucas in U.K. Separate parts are listed for the socket assembly.
23 ‡	BAYONET, HEAD	#	BA 10033	. . .	1	DD(E) 3453	
24	BRIDGE-PIECE	#	BA 10117	. . .	1	DD(E) 3453	
25	HEAD, casing	#	BA 10118	. . .	1	DD(E) 3453	
26	LOCATING-PIECE	#	BA 10119	. . .	1	DD(E) 3453	
27	SHIELD, reinforcing	#	BA 10120	. . .	1	DD(E) 3453	
28	SPIKE	#	BA 10121	. . .	1	DD(E) 3453/1-8	
29	TONGUE	#	BA 10122	. . .	1	. . .	
30	CATCH	. .	BA 10123	. . .	1	DD(E) 3453/3	
31	PLUNGER, catch	. .	CR 733	BB 6253	1	DD(E) 340B/3	
32	SPRING, plunger, catch	. .	CR 489	BB 6254	1	DD(E) 340B/4	
. .	BAYONET, NO. 7 MK I (a)	. .	. . .	CF 9A	1	CR 9A	Canadian issue, short time.

(a) Obsolescent.

37

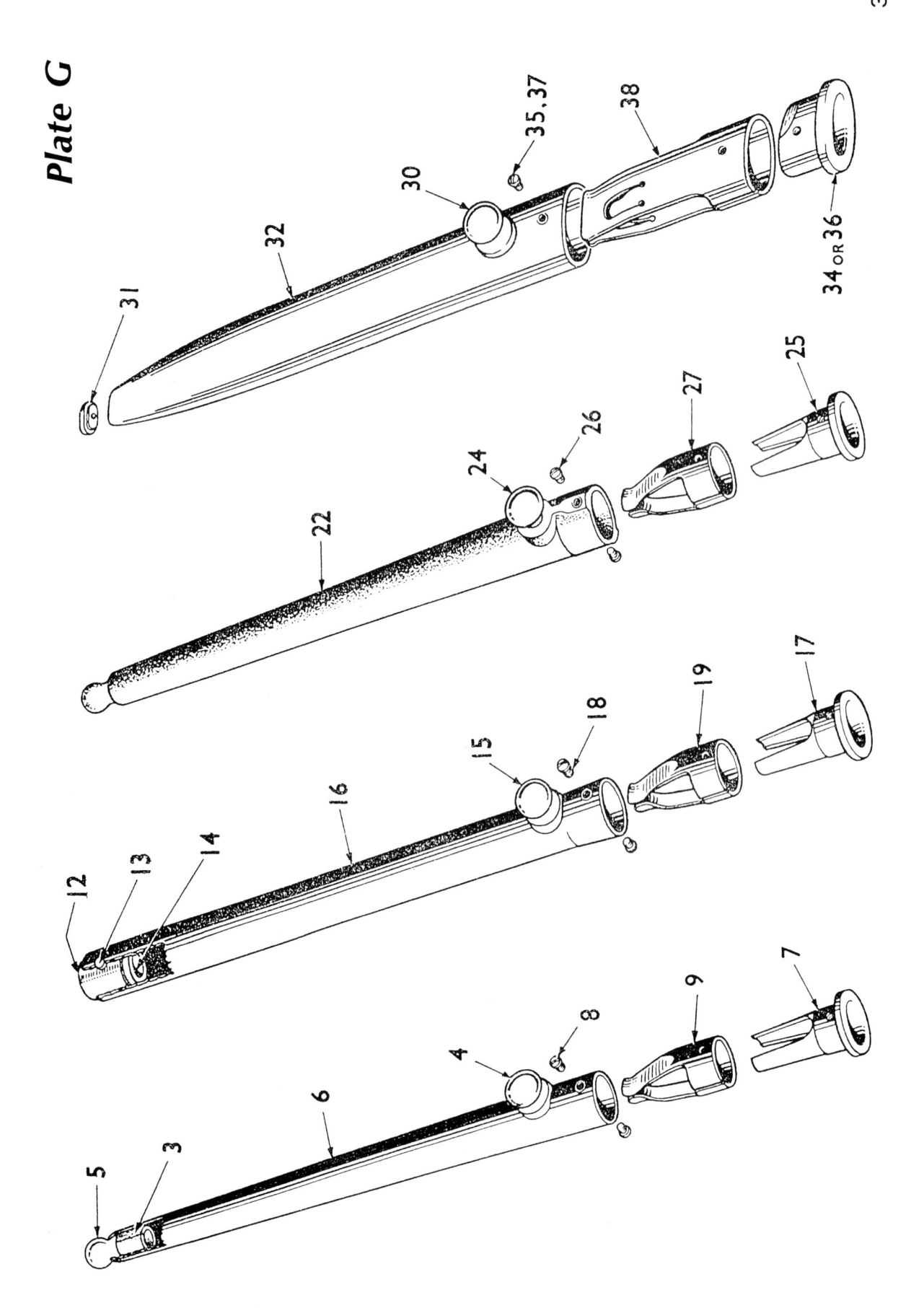

Plate G

REF. NO.	DESIGNATION	PART or CAT. NUMBER	PREVIOUS PART NO.	QTY.	DRAWING NUMBER	REMARKS
Plate G	**SCABBARD, BAYONET, NO. 4**					
1 ‡	SCABBARD, BAYONET, NO. 4 MK 1 (a)	BA 8354	...	1	DD(E) 463B	With tapered body.
2 ‡	BODY #	BB 8321	...	1	DD(E) 463/A	Tapered body.
3	LINER .	BA 10110	...	1	DD(E) 463/1	
4	STUD, body #	SM 515	BJ 0088	1	DD(E) 463/5	
5	TIP, body #	BA 10111	...	1	DD(E) 463/6	
6	TUBE, body #	BA 10112	...	1	DD(E) 463/7	
7	MOUTH-PIECE .	SM 517	BB 8322	1	DD(E) 463/2	
8	SCREW, mouth-piece .	SM 518	BB 8323	2	DD(E) 463/3	
9	SPRING mouth-piece	SM 519	BB 8324	1	DD(E) 463/4	
10 ‡ or	SCABBARD, BAYONET, NO. 4 MK 2 (a)	SM 53 A	BA 8523	1	DD(E) 463B/A	With parallel body.
11 ‡	BODY #	SM 18 SA	BB 8557	1	DD(E) 2664/A	
12	CUP .	SM 512	BJ 0085	1	DD(E) 2664/2	
13	PIN, plug	SM 513	BJ 0086	1	DD(E) 2664/4	
14	PLUG .	SM 514	BJ 0087	1	DD(E) 2664/3	
15	STUD, body #	SM 515	BJ 0088	1	DD(E) 463B/5	
16	TUBE, body #	SM 516	BJ 0089	1	DD(E) 2664/1	
17	MOUTH-PIECE .	SM 517	BB 8322	1	DD(E) 463B/2	
18	SCREW, mouth piece .	SM 518	BB 8323	2	DD(E) 463B/3	Also for Scabbard Mk I.
19	SPRING, mouth piece	SM 519	BB 8324	1	DD(E) 463B/4	
20 ‡ or	SCABBARD, BAYONET, NO. 4 MK 3 (a)	BA 6267	...	1	DD(E) 3572/A	With plastic body.
21 ‡	BODY #	BB 6264	...	1	DD(E) 3572	
22	BODY #	BA 10113	...	1	DD(E) 3572/1	
23	LINER .	BA 10110	...	1	DD(E) 463B/1	
24	STUD, body #	BA 10114	...	1	DD(E) 3572/3	
25	MOUTH-PIECE .	SM 517	BB 8322	1	DD(E) 463B/2	
26	SCREW, mouth-piece .	BB 6266	...	2	DD(E) 3572/2	
27	SPRING, mouth-piece	SM 519	BB 8324	1	DD(E) 463B/4	
28 ‡	SCABBARD, BAYONET, NO. 5 MK 1 (b)	SM 54 A	BA 5878	1	DD(E) 3681	Interchangeable, bayonets L1A1, No. 5 & No. 9.
29 ‡	BODY #	SM 19 SA	BB 5879	1	DD(E) 3681/A	
30	BUTTON #	SM 437	BJ 0096	1	DD(E) 3681/2	
31	TIP #	SM 520	BJ 0097	1	DD(E) 3681/5	
32	TUBE #	SM 521	BJ 0098	1	DD(E) 3681/1	
33 ‡ or	TUBE #	SM 436	...	1	...	
34	MOUTH-PIECE .	SM 522	BB 5880	1	DD(E) 3681/3	
35	SCREW, B.A., B.S., instrument hd, No.6 x 3/16" #	Z2/ZB 11412	...	1	...	Production alternative.
36 or	MOUTH-PIECE .	SM 523	...	1	...	
37	SCREW, B.A., B.S., instrument hd, No.6 x 3/16" #	Z2/ZB 11412	...	1	...	Production alternative.
38	SPRING .	SM 524	BB 5881	1	DD(E) 3681/4	

(a) For use with Bayonet No. 4   (b) For use with Bayonet No. 9 Mk 1

39

Plate H

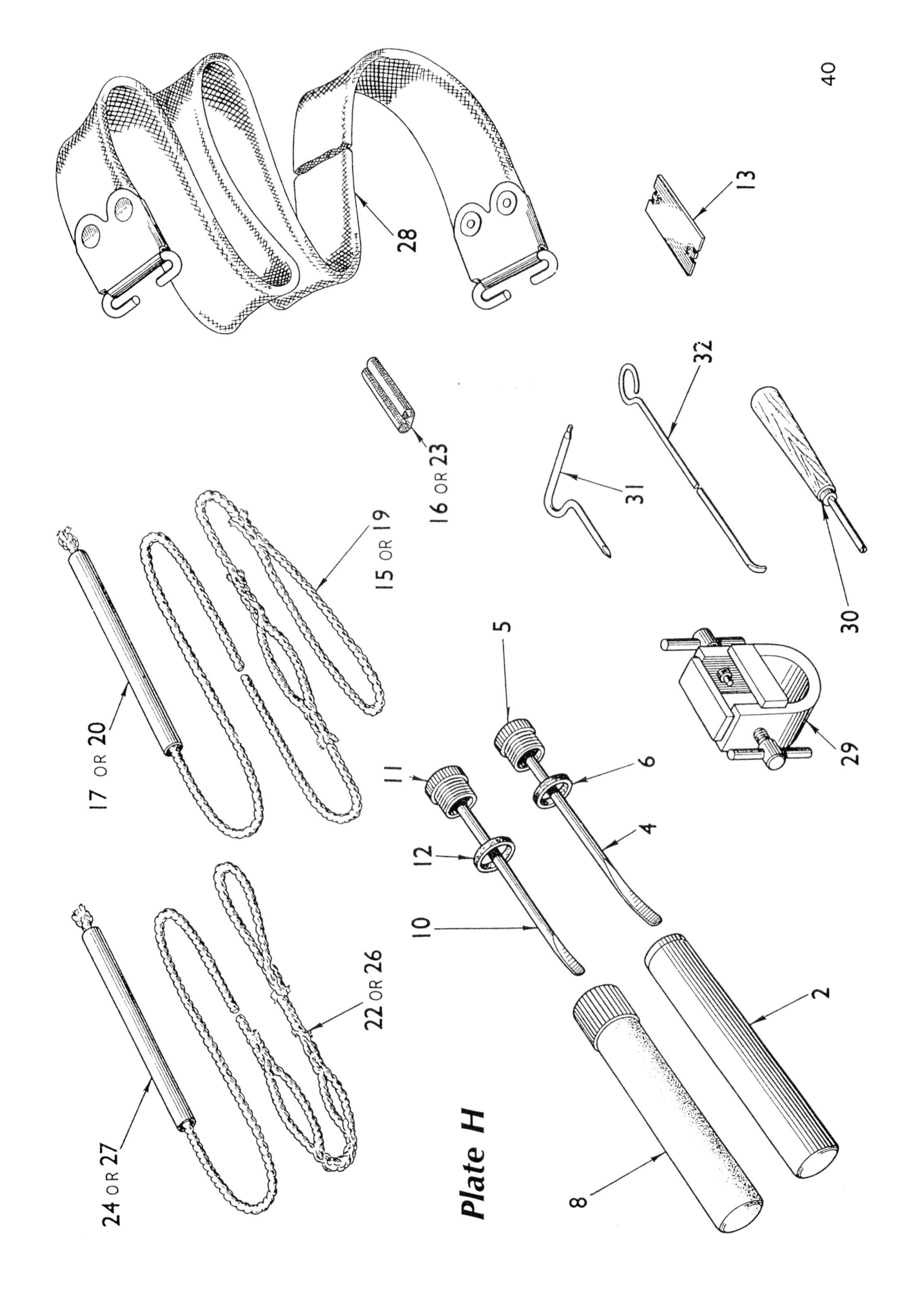

REF. NO.	DESIGNATION	PART or CAT. NUMBER	PREVIOUS PART NO.	QTY.	DRAWING NUMBER	REMARKS
Plate H **ACCESSORIES**						
1 ‡	BOTTLE, OIL, MK 4	BA 0053	...	1	SAID 939A	Brass w/ stopper & washer.
2	BODY #	BA 10048	...	1	SAID 939	
3 ‡	STOPPER #	BB 0055	...	1	SAID 939	
4	SPOON #	BB 0054	...	1	SAID 939	With spoon.
5	STOPPER #	BB 10049	...	1	SAID 939	
6	WASHER #	BB 0056	...	1	SAID 939	
or						
7 ‡	BOTTLE, OIL, MK 5	SM 52 A	BA 6320	1	DD(E) 2562	Plastic.
8	BODY #	SM 507	BJ 0084	1	DD(E) 2562/1	Canadian patt. BAC 6320. And BJC 0084, BBC 6321
9 ‡	STOPPER #	SM 17 A	BB 6321	1		BBC 6328 & BBC 6327.
10	SPOON #	SM 508	BB 6328	1	DD(E) 2562/2	
11	STOPPER #	SM 509	BB 6327	1	DD(E) 2562/4	
12	WASHER .	SM 510	BA 6326	1	DD(E) 2562/3	
13	GAUGE, ARMOURERS, STRIKER PROTRUSION, NO. 4 MK 1 #	SM 143	...	1	CIA (Gauges)	
14 ‡	PULLTHROUGH, DOUBLE, MK 1A	BA 0515	...	1	SAID 257	With wire gauze.
15	CORD #	BB 0519	...	1	SAID 257	Canadian patt. BAC 0515. And BBC 0519, BBC 0521,
16	GAUZE	3B 0521	...	1	SAID 257	& BBC 0522.
17	WEIGHT	BB 0522	...	1	SAID 257	
or						
18 ‡	PULLTHROUGH, DOUBLE, MK 1B	BA 0516	...	1	SAID 257	Without wire gauze.
19	CORD #	BB 0519	...	1	SAID 257	Canadian patt. BAC 0516.
20	WEIGHT	BB 0522	...	1	SAID 257	And BBC 0519 & BBC 0522.
or						
21 ‡	PULLTHROUGH, SINGLE, MK 4A #	BA 0517	...	1	SAID 257	With wire gauze.
22	CORD .	BB 0520	...	1	SAID 257	Cdn patt. BAC 0517, &c.
23	GAUZE .	BB 0521	...	1	SAID 257	Wire pieces 1.4 x 2.5-in.
24	WEIGHT	BB 0522	...	1	SAID 257	
or						
25 ‡	PULLTHROUGH, SINGLE, MK 4B #	BA 0518	...	1	SAID 257	Without wire gauze.
26	CORD .	BB 0520	...	1	SAID 257	Canadian patt. BAC 0518.
27	WEIGHT	BB 0522	...	1	SAID 257	And BBC 0529 & BBC 0522.
28	SLING, RIFLE, Web	AA 1657	...	1		Also for Rifle No. 1
29	TOOL, FORESIGHT CRAMP, NO. 3 MK 1 #	CR 29 A	BC 8881	1	DD(E) 2996	
30	TOOL, removing, foresight screw #	BC 8796	...	1	DD(E) 1294	
31	TOOL, spring, extractor, No. 2 .	BC 8797	...	1	DD(E) 2432	
32	TOOL, wad #	BC 4100	...	1	SAID 983	

\# Part not provided for normal maintenance; the demand (order) should be endorsed "To replace broken part, or worn out part", etc.

‡ Item numbers do not appear on the plate illustration, they are assemblies.

Projector, Grenade, No. 4 Rifle, Mk I . . . SM 3GA

41

STRIPPING & ASSEMBLY

A PRACTICAL GUIDE

Many weapons in private collections have been abused or damaged by improper stripping, faulty servicing or careless repairs. To learn the armourer's trade in a short space of time is not feasible, but some simple rules and a little thought can prevent most mishaps. Values of ex-military and collectors' arms are significantly reduced where the wooden furniture has been cracked, screws damaged or stripped, parts marked by improper use of a vice or stillson wrench, or components broken or lost.

Knowledge and the use of proper tools are the two prime elements. For the former, a gunsmith or armourer could be asked; or maybe a service manual or suitable reference checked. Regarding the latter, many armourers' tools and gunsmithing implements are available today on the open market. A good set of screwdrivers, a vice with wooden or soft metal jaw inserts, pin punches, and a soft-headed mallet are essential. Screwdrivers need good square edges, hollow ground tips are best. A few different sizes are needed to obtain a good fit in the screw head, for the full length and width of the slot. This is important for removing tight or seized screws; a penetrating lubricant is also useful.

Specialist armourers tools are usually required for tasks such as removing the firing pin, extractor spring, and the leather wad in the butt. Headspace gauges, striker protrusion gauges, spring weighing gauges and foresight cramps are not required by most collectors, unless the rifles are likely to be fired. The first Small Arms Information Series book, *".303 Rifle No. 1"*, contains a precis of the 1917 Ordnance College manual; some details apply to the No. 4 rifle as well. Centre-punching was sometimes used to secure screws such as the front trigger guard screw, although not to the same extent as the No. 1 rifle. These can usually be removed with the appropriate, tight-fitting screwdriver.

Stripping and assembly of the No. 4 rifle is not as specialised as for the No. 1. Its design was intended to simplify manufacture and maintenance and the net result makes it an easier firearm to strip, assemble and rebuild. To coax the best from these rifles for competitive shooting, however, is another matter, the armourer's realm. Headspacing the bolt or changing a barrel are well-enough understood by gunsmiths. Numbered boltheads range from size "0" to "4", varying by about .005-in. through each stage; from .620 - .625-in. + for the "0", .625 - .630 for "1", .630 - 635-in. for "2", .635 - 640-in. for "3" and .640 - 645-in. for "4". Headspacing is effected in the same way as for the No. 1 rifle; .067-in. is the "GO" gauge and .074-in. is the "NO-GO".

Collectors are often indifferent with firearms safety. When first handled, a firearm should have the action opened and chamber and magazine inspected for ammunition. "Unloaded" firearms are the most common cause of accidents and unauthorised discharges. Safety and courtesy also dictates that the muzzle not be pointed in the direction of any other person.

THE CANADIAN DISTINCTION

Stevens-Savage No. 4 production took only three years from mid 1941, so there was little ongoing development or manufacturing differences over this period. Long Branch continued until the 1950's and produced some special sniper rifles, rimfire trainers, target and lightweight variants. Due to the extended production time at Long Branch, and domestic considerations, some features of the Canadian parts differ from the British patterns. Stevens-Savage production was on British contract, so most of these rifles were shipped to Great Britain, the balance of 40,000 being sent to China. About one-third of Long Branch production (330,000) were British orders, shipped to England during the war.

Early North American production was the No. 4 Mk I; most of the U.S. and Canadian rifles were the Mk I* variant. And because of other variations and manufacturing concessions, many Canadian parts have different Vocabulary and parts numbers.

Parts numbers have indicators of Canadian variation in the Vocab. No. prefixes. For comparison with the British components, the next few pages list these Canadian parts. In most cases, a "C" (Canada) was added to the British "BA", "BB" or "BJ" prefix, special Canadian parts with no British equivalent have prefixes such as "CGB". Some British Vocab. Nos. are provided for comparison, refer to parts lists from page 23.

Component	Vocab. No.	Remarks
BAND, lower	BB 8554 BBC 8554	Three patterns. Machined; lugs welded on; or stamped with blocks brazed to lugs. All patterns tapped No. 2 B.A.
BAND, upper	BB 8555 BBC 8555	Hinged type; or solid type of two patterns machined or fabricated. All patterns tapped No. 2 B.A.
BARREL, Mk I	BB 8557	5-groove.
BARREL, Mk 2	BB 8683	2-groove. British part number, this was a British concession. 6-groove; some Canadian. Stevens also, 2 or 6 groove.
BLADE, foresight Mk I	BBC 8560 to 8570	Same blade heights as British equivalents. Drawing is CSAID 1-1238, higher base shoulder, wider base.
BLADE, foresight Mk I*	BBC 8685 to 8692	Same blade heights as British equivalents, but higher base shoulder, wider base.

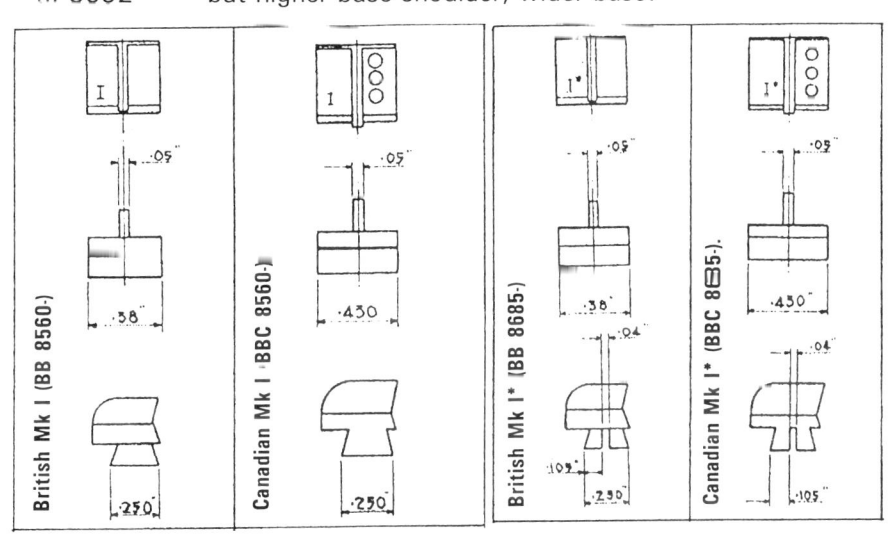

Note the higher base shoulder on the Canadian variant, and extra Canadian base width (.430-in. compared with .380-in.)

British Mk I (BB 8560-) | Canadian Mk I (BBC 8560-) | British Mk I* (BB 8685-) | Canadian Mk I* (BBC 8685-)

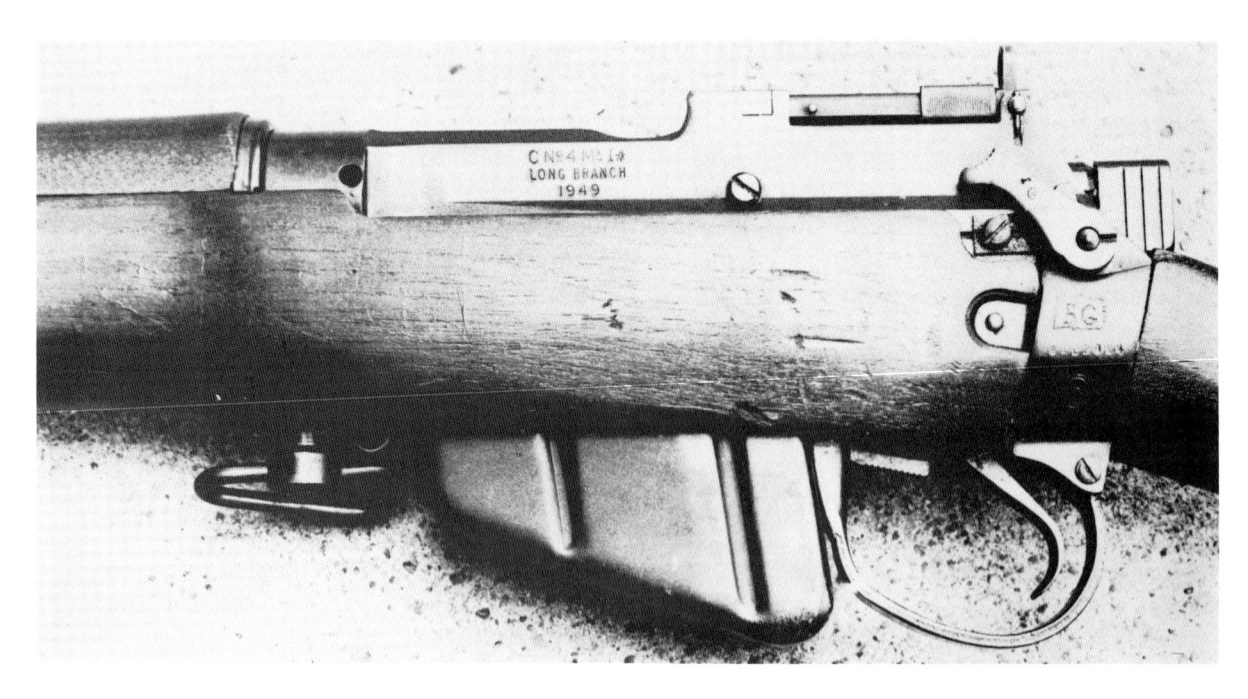

Canadian "C No. 4 Mk I*". Note distinct safety catch, pressed trigger guard and backsight, Mk 2 locking bolt spring and sling swivel. This particular example was a factory special competition model.

BOLT, locking, Mk I	BB 8026	Safety catch on some Long Branch rifles is differently shaped, with a distinctive "kicked leg" shape. Part numbers of locking bolts are the same as they are interchangeable.
CATCH, backsight Mk 2, Canadian pattern Drawing B1-764	BAC 10052	Straight type. Formed from No. 22 B.G. (.0313-in.) stock. Width .22-in. For use with Spring, catch, backsight Mk 2 or Mk 2 Canadian pattern.
CATCH, backsight Mk 3, Canadian pattern	BJC 0102	For Backsight Mk 4, Canadian pattern. Same form as Catch, backsight Mk 3.
COCKING-PIECE, Mk 2, Canadian pattern	BBC 8650	Same design as British Mk 2. Angle of bent of cocking-piece to vertical 4°.
GUARD, trigger, Canadian pattern	BBC 8582	Welded assembly with wire loop riveted in place.
LEAF, backsight Mk 2, Canadian pattern	BBC 8676	For Backsight Mk 3 Canadian pattern. Stamped. Leaf welded to machined base. Pin BB 8678 assemblies from right side. Not used on sniper rifle [Mk I (T) or Mk I* (T)].
LEAF, backsight Mk 3, Canadian pattern	BJC 0103	For Backsight Mk 4 Canadian pattern. Same as British Leaf Mk 3 but welded to a base which does not require Collar BB 8675. Aperture in battle sight drilled No. 38 (.101-in.). Aperture later changed to .02-in. Not used on sniper rifle [Mk I (T) or Mk I* (T)].
PIN, trap, butt plate Canadian pattern	BBC 8592 CGB 7411	Length .60-in., dia. .102-in. (British patt. .104-in. dia.). Steel S.A.E. 1020.
PLATE, butt, Canadian pattern	CGB 7403 BBC 8716	Pressed steel.

44

PROTECTOR, foresight, C Mk 2	BBC 8693	Steel with inserts welded in place. Same length and thread as BB 8600.
SCREW, bracket, Canadian pattern	BBC 8605 CGB 8605	No. 10 wood screw, 1.25-in. long. Screw head slot .05-in. wide. British pattern is 1.0-in. long. [For butt swivel.]
SCREW, spring, trap, butt-plate, Cdn. patt.	CGB 7403	Length .25-in., dia. .160-in., threaded for .21-in. No. 3 B.A. Dia. of screw head .245-in. British equivalent is .32-in. long, head dia. .248-in., will not fit on Cdn. patt. buttplate.
SCREW, swivel Canadian pattern	BBC 8037	Length .64-in., dia. .185-in., threaded No. 2 B.A. Dia. of head .280-in. End drilled No. 47 to depth of .06-in. British equivalent is end drilled to depth of .125-in.
SEAR	BB 8618	Same Vocab no. for British, Canadian and U.S. manufacture, though U.S. pattern is a little different, but interchangeable.
SLIDE, backsight, Mk 2 Canadian pattern	B3 1514 (drawing no.)	For Backsight, Mk 3 Cdn. patt. Assembly. Pointers to indicate range adjustment. Formed from No. 18 B.G.
SLIDE, backsight, Mk 3 Canadian pattern	BJC 0105	For Backsight, Mk 4 Cdn. patt. Assembly. Formed pointers to indicate range adjustment. No. 18 B.G. (.049-in.)
SPRING, catch, back-sight, Mk 2	BJC 0106 B1 805 (drawing no.)	A 5½ coil spring of .02-in. wire with arm at each end forming 130° including angle. Length of coil portion .14-in. Mean dia. of spring .035-in.
SPRING, extractor Canadian pattern	BBC 8041	Formed leaf spring, similar to British equivalent. Length .67-in., width .156-in., thickness .03-in. British pattern is .153-in. wide and the two British patterns also differ thickness and in contour of lower leaf.
STOCK, butt, bantam	CGB 7404	Overall length 12.3-in.
STOCK, butt, long Canadian pattern	BBC 8629	Overall length 13.8-in. (same as British equivalent)
STOCK, butt, normal Canadian pattern	BBC 8630	Overall length 13.3-in. (same as British equivalent)
STOCK, butt, short Canadian pattern	BBC 8631	Overall length 12.8-in. (same as British equivalent)
TRAP, butt plate Canadian pattern	BBC 8717 CGB 7410	Steel; external profile differs from British equivalent. Drawing B1-812.

ASSEMBLIES:—

BACKSIGHT, Mk I	BB 8023	When fitted to (T) Rifles, battle-sight portion removed.
BACKSIGHT, C Mk 3	BBC 8673	May be fitted to any Rifle.
BACKSIGHT, C Mk 4	BJC 0101	May be fitted to any Rifle.
PLATE, BUTT	BBC 8595	All components may be used with Plate BB 8716. Assemblies BB 8595 and BBC 8595 interchangeable.

PARTS MANUFACTURE IDENTIFICATION

An examination of the factory and contractor's markings on component parts will help to establish originality of the rifle because different logos and code indicators were applied. Inspection marks are not as abundant on the No. 4 rifles as on the S.M.L.E. Codes were applied during World War 2, the full listing of these British contractors will be found in *British Small Arms of World War 2 — the Codes and Contracts*. Page 493 of the *Lee-Enfield Story* lists those applied to No. 4 production. Most rifles in long-term service are likely to have had replacement parts fitted at some time.

Receiver Manufacturer Markings: The No. 4 rifles were marked on the left side of the receiver or butt socket with factory code or name and, in most cases, the production year. British rifles will usually be found to have "ROF(F)", "FY", "F" or "UF" for Fazakerley, "ROFM", "RM" or an "M" logo for MALTBY, and M47C for BSA Shirley. Conversion and FTR (Factory Thorough Repair) markings and the year were applied alongside or over the original designation during the Fazakerley overhauls. See the *Lee-Enfield Story* pages 485-486 for illustrated examples. Canadian rifles are marked "LONG BRANCH" while the Stevens-Savage models have a square "S" logo. Serial numbers on the Long Branch rifles contain an "L" while the U.S. models have a "C", *e.g.* 8L6092 and 24C3283. Chapter 8 of the *Lee-Enfield Story* (North American Production) details the Canadian and U.S. models and characteristics.

Parts Markings: Inspection marks were not as critical during wartime production. Original Fazakerley and BSA Shirley rifles would have had nearly all original factory parts. Maltby, however, mostly assembled component parts "farmed out" to sub-contractors. These are marked with contractors codes, initials or logos, see *Lee-Enfield Story* page 493. Some original early 1930's Enfield trials No. 4 rifle parts may be found on No. 4 rifles too as they were interchanged in service repairs and refits. These Enfield parts have the usual Enfield inspection mark of an "EFD" logo.

Stevens-Savage components usually have the squared "S" logo, while Long Branch parts have an integrated "LB" stamp. Some Canadian contractors also produced No. 4 rifle parts; Canadian Cycle and Motor, Border City Industries, Kelvinator and Regina Industries. Their initials or logos may be noticed on the Canadian rifle parts.

Enfield marks:	ENFIELD EFD Ð UE	**B.S.A. Shirley marks:**	B M47C 85B BS UB
Fazakerley marks:	ROF(F) FY F UF	**Long Branch marks:**	ᴸB ⊕
Maltby marks:	R.O.F.M. O.F.M. R.M. *or* RM M	**Stevens Savage marks:**	⌐S⌐ 5

Contractors' Parts Codes & Markings: Codes were only applied to the British parts. North American contractors generally used their initials, so these are not as difficult to determine, although some British makers did use their initials too *(e.g. Singers used S.M.C.).*

The lists in *Lee-Enfield Story* and *British Small Arms of World War 2* detail the components the various contractors supplied, and their addresses. The following tabulation is by codes.

Code	Manufacturer	Code	Manufacturer
M1	Accles & Pollock Ltd., Oldbury	S3	Adams Bros. & Burnley Ltd., Harrow
M3	Albion Pressed Steel Metal Co., Birmingham	S12	L. Benn & Sons, Leytonstone, London
M8	Anstey & Wilson Ltd., Birmingham	S21	British Salmson Aero Engines Ltd., London
M14	W. & T. Avery Ltd., Birmingham	S40	Graylon Engineering Co., London
M17	Baker & Finnimore Ltd., Birmingham	S51	Holland & Holland Ltd., London
M29	Birmingham Tempered Spring & Presswork Ld.	S56	Imperial Engineering Co., London
M33	Bloore & Pillar Ltd.	S68	Lines Bros. Ltd., Merton, London
M46	J. B. Bruce Ltd., Birmingham	S76	Metal Box Co. Ltd., London
M47C	B.S.A. Guns, Shirley, Birmingham	S77	Metal Box Co. Ltd. Acton, London
M56	W. C. Cheney & Son Ltd., Willenhall	S87	Nash Engineering (Staines) Ltd., Staines
M66	Crown Bedding Co. Ltd., Tyseley	S88	National Cash Register Co. Ltd., London
M94	W. W. Greener Ltd., Birmingham	S91	R. B. Page & Co., Kingston-on-Thames, Surrey
M99	Guest, Keen & Nettlefold Ltd., Birmingham	S95	G. D. Peters & Co., Windsor Works, Slough
M119	Hildick & Hildick Ltd., Walsall	S98	Pruners Ltd., Kilburn, London
M130	G. W. Hughes, Legge Lane, Birmingham	S99	J. Rawson & Sons Ltd., Tunbridge Wells
M151	B. Lilley, Birmingham	S104	Sidcup Tool & Gauge Co., Sidcup, Kent
M158	J. Lucas Ltd., Birmingham	S105	Silversmiths & Jewellers War Prod., London
M159	Ludlow Bros. (1913) Ltd., Birmingham	S106	J. W. Spear & Sons Ltd., Enfield
M175	M. Myers & Son Ltd., Oldbury	S113	Trafalgar Engineering Co., Deptford, London
M189	Peterborough Die Casting & Machine Co. Ltd.	S117	United Motors Ltd., Islington, London
M194	A. Poole & Son, Redditch	S122	Waddells Ltd., Brimsdown, Enfield
M215	George Salter & Co. Ltd., West Bromwich	S123	Howard Wall Ltd., London
M216	Sanbra Ltd., Birmingham	S124	Weir Larsen Tool Co., Potters Bar
M217	Savaker Ltd., Birmingham	S126	C. E. Welstead, Croydon
M232	Spring Washer Co. Ltd., Wolverhampton	S128	Wembley Tool Co., Bridge Works, Willesden
M241	Streetly Tools & Stampings, Birmingham	S131	Wright Bros., London
M249	W. Trueman & Sons, Birmingham	S132	L. S. Mayer Ltd., Tottenham, London
M250	Tube Fittings Manufacturing Co., Coseley	S134	Addressograph & Multigraph, Cricklewood
M254	Universal Stampings Ltd., Birmingham	S156	J. Boss & Co., London
M260	Walls Ltd., Birmingham	S166	Burdon & Miles Ltd., Barnett
M262	Ward & Sons, Birmingham	S167	British Oxygen Co. Ltd., Edmonton, London
M269	W. J. Wild Ltd., Birmingham	S171	Cogswell & Harrison, East Acton, London
M601	I. L. Berridge & Co. Ltd., Leicester	S174	Cope & Timmins Ltd., London
M603	British United Shoe Machinery Co., Leicester	S176	George Cotton & Son, London
M607	General Presswork & Stampings Ltd., Leicester	S189	Fisheries Foils Ltd., Wembley
M612	A. T. Ralphs (N.C.H.) Ltd., Leicester	S215	Holland & Caesar Ltd., London
M614	Messrs. Wildt, Leicester	S223	E.S.S. (Signs) Ltd., Bristol
M630	Woodhouse & Smith Co. Ltd., Nottingham	S232	G. S. Mascalls & Sons, Tottenham, London
M633	S. B. Grundy & Co., Derby	S238	C. F. Moore & Sons Ltd., London
M638	North Bridge Engineering Co., Leicester	S252	Philco Radio & Television Corp., Greenford
M639	Hardwick Engineering Co., Leicester	S259	Flexal Spring Co., Hanwell, London
		S261	Rex Meters Ltd., Kingsbury Rd., London
N22	John Curtis & Son Ltd., Leeds	S262	Roneo Ltd., Romford, Essex
N23	G. P. Dennis Ltd., Chester	S282	H. B. Thomas Co. Ltd., London
N37	Lang Pen Co., Liverpool	S300	Zip Fasteners Co., Edmonton, London
N45	Metal Box Co., Hull	S301	Bellgrett Industries, London
N46	Metal Box Co. Ltd., Newcastle-on-Tyne	S312	Aero Zipp Fasteners, London
N49	H. Morris & Co. Ltd., Glasgow	S314	Associated Brassfounders, Willesden
N56	Prince-Smith & Stells Ltd., Keighley	S316	R.B.H. Tool & Gauge Co., Teddington
N64	Sheffield Steel Products Ltd., Sheffield	S323	Chambon Ltd., London
N67	Singer Manufacturing Co. Ltd., Clydebank	S329	Greville Engineering Ltd., London
N74	William Sykes Ltd., Horbury	S332	Milliken Precision Tool & Turning Co., London
N76	Tempered Spring Co., Sheffield	S360	Southern Railways, Eastleigh
N77	Thomas Turner & Co. Ltd., Sheffield	S362	Metal Box Co., Barclay & Fry Branch, London
N79	Viners Ltd., Sheffield	S378	K. Garage & Service Station, Watford, London
N80	Walker & Hall Ltd., Sheffield	S381	A. C. R. Greene, Harrow
N85	Wilkinson's Ltd., Bradford	S385	Junction Engineering Co., Harlesden, London
N88	John Wilson Ltd., Sheffield	S390	Spikins Ltd., Twickenham
N89	John Wilson & Son Ltd.	S403	Colostat Combustion, London
N94	Metal Box Co., Carlisle	S415	Bifurcated & Tubular Rivet Co., Aylesbury
N95	Moore & Sons Ltd., Sheffield		
N132	Manchester Die Casting Co. Ltd., Manchester		

47

Other titles by this author:—

"The LEE-ENFIELD STORY" *Skennerton*
Hard cover, 11 x 8¾in., 503 pages, nearly 1,000 illustrations. Dust jacket.
Updated, much-improved and expanded "British Service Lee". New illustrations.

"The ENFIELD .380 No. 2 REVOLVER" *Skennerton & Stamps*
Hard & Soft covers, 9½ x 6in., 126 pages, 80 illustrations.
"Poor cousin" of the Webley, the first in-depth study of this model.

".303 No. 4 (T) SNIPER RIFLE" *Laidler & Skennerton*
An Armourer's Perspective; the Holland & Holland Connection.
Hard & Soft covers, 9½ x 6in., 126 pages, 75 illustrations.
A practical study of the No. 4 (T) and 7.62mm L42A1 series.

"AUSTRALIAN MILITARY RIFLES & BAYONETS" *Skennerton*
Hard & Soft covers, 9½ x 6in., 124 pages, 205 illustrations.
200 years of service longarms and bayonets, from Brown Bess to 5.56mm F88.

"AUSTRALIAN SERVICE MACHINEGUNS" *Skennerton*
Hard & Soft covers, 9½ x 6in., 122 pages, 150 illustrations.
100 years of machine & sub-machine guns, from .450 Gatling to 5.56mm Minimi.

"S.L.R. - AUSTRALIA'S F.N. F.A.L." *Skennerton & Balmer*
Hard & Soft covers, 9½ x 6in., 122 pages, 200 illustrations.
Study of Australia's L1A1 service rifle, variants, parts lists, &c.

"BRITISH SMALL ARMS OF WORLD WAR 2" *Skennerton*
Complete Guide to the Weapons, Maker's Codes & 1936-1946 Contracts.
Hard cover, 9½ x 6in., 110 pages, 36 illustrations.
Rifles, Pistols, Machine Carbines, Machine Guns, &c. List of Wartime Codes.

"BRITISH & COMMONWEALTH BAYONETS" *Skennerton & Richardson*
Hard cover, 11 x 8¾in., 404 pages, approx. 1,300 illustrations.
Standard reference on a popular subject, 1650 to current issues.

"The HANDBOOK of BRITISH BAYONETS" *Skennerton*
Soft cover, 5¾ x 4in., 64 pages. Pocket reference for "British & Commonwealth Bayonets".

"LIST OF CHANGES IN BRITISH WAR MATERIAL"
Hard covers, 8½ x 5½in., projected 5 volume series.
Official text, descriptions of Rifles, Pistols, Edged Weapons & Accoutrements.
VOL. 1 (1860-1866), 170 pages, 100 illustrations.
VOL. 2 (1886-1900), 201 pages, 75 illustrations.
VOL. 3 (1900-1910), 216 pages, 80 illustrations.
VOL. 4 (1910-1918), 192 pages, 35 illustrations.

"INTRODUCTION TO BRITISH GRENADES" *Skennerton*
Soft cover, 9½ x 6in., 56 pages, 130 different grenades illustrated.
Descriptions of the numbered series of grenades from 1908 until the 1960's.

"BRITISH SPIKE BAYONETS" *Skennerton*
S.A.S. No. 2. 9½ x 6in., 32 pages, 30 illust. The No. 4 and Sten bayonets.

"SMALL ARMS IDENTIFICATION SERIES, No. 1 — .303 RIFLE No. 1" *Skennerton*
Soft cover, 11 x 8¾in., 48 pages, 60 illustrations.

"SMALL ARMS IDENTIFICATION SERIES, No. 3 — 9mm AUSTEN & OWEN SMG's" *Skennerton*
Soft cover, 11 x 8¾in., 48 pages, 60 illustrations.

OUT OF PRINT -
"Australian Service Longarms"
"Australian Service Bayonets"
"A Treatise on the Snider"
"British Sniper"
"British Service Lee"
"De Lisle Commando Carbine"
"U.S. Enfield"

NO LONGER THE PROPERTY
OF THE
UNIVERSITY OF R.I. LIBRARY

TOPICS, TERMS, AND RESEARCH TECHNIQUES:

Self-Instruction in Using Library Catalogs

by

RICHARD R. STRAWN

The Scarecrow Press, Inc. Metuchen, N.J. & London

1980

Examples used in Exercise Frame E 1 are reprinted by permission of the American Library Association from Guide to Reference Books, 9th edition, Eugene P. Sheehy, copyright © 1976 by the American Library Association.

Library of Congress Cataloging in Publication Data

Strawn, Richard R   1923-
  Topics, terms, and research techniques.

  1. Library catalogs and readers--Handbooks, manuals, etc. 2. Library catalogs and readers--Programmed instruction. 3. Research--Methodology--Handbooks, manuals, etc. I. Title.
Z710.S87   025.3'1'0202   80-12569
ISBN 0-8108-1308-4

Copyright © 1980 by Richard R. Strawn

Manufactured in the United States of America

This program was prepared with the aid of a grant from the Council on Library Resources and matching funds from Wabash College.

CONTENTS

Preface vii

A. How to Read a Library of Congress Catalog Card 1
    Pre-Test 1
    Exercise Frames 2
    Summary 13

B. Words as Possible "Subject Headings" 14
    Pre-Test 14
    Exercise Frames 15
    Summary 22

C. How to Use Subject Headings 24
    Pre-Test 24
    Exercise Frames 26
    Summary 40

D. Specificity 42
    Pre-Test 42
    Exercise Frames 42
    Summary 45

E. Subdivisions 47
    Pre-Test 47
    Exercise Frames 48
    Summary 54

F. Filing 56
    Pre-Test 56
    Exercise Frames 57
    Summary 64

Answers to Exercises 65

PREFACE

The six sections of this handbook will help you first in deciding exactly what you are looking for when you begin compiling information on a research topic. Then it will aid you as you move through a library's card catalog or its indexes and bibliographies, preventing you from getting stopped in dead ends. The manual takes you step-by-step through the following sections:

- A. How to read a Library of Congress catalog card--or any other card of that sort--and distinguish among author cards, title cards and subject cards.

- B. Words to use as possible "subject headings."

- C. How to use subject headings, starting from a term in your topic.

- D. Specificity. What to do when you come to a dead end with a term that is too specific for your library's card catalog.

- E. Subdivisions. What ones to expect.

- F. Filing. What "alphabetical" means to you in the card catalog.

You can use the book on your own, testing yourself as you go. There are several ways to make the book do its job for you. One is to take the pre-test at the start of a section, to see what you need to know; then go to the summary at the end of the section in order to be told it. Another way is to follow the highroad through each section, doing only the main illustrations and none of the extra exercises. Yet another way is to do all of the exercises included here--which you will want to do only if you feel shaky about certain points.

The book is based on the Library of Congress classification system and Library of Congress subject headings. It uses LC cards as illustrations and obliges you to handle the mechanisms of <u>Library of Congress Subject Headings</u>, 8th edition. It uses as examples actual topics that Wabash College students have had to treat in the last several years. Sections A, C, and E require you to use an actual card catalog in a library.

Each batch of instruction, called an exercise frame, guides your observation and then puts a problem to you. The solution appears in the back of the manual, so that you can check yourself as you move step-by-step. You should feel free to move about in the book as you please, but you will usually find that to do a later frame you need to know what earlier frames teach.

The instruction in the book relies heavily on using your wits and also on your willingness sometimes to take a stab in the dark, sometimes to put up with trial and error. You will often be expected to guess or to "try tentatively"--just to see. At those points, the problem put to you will be marked by the sign: ?(.

Don't hesitate to try; at worst you can only be temporarily wrong, and often that kind of

"worst" is "good." You can get along efficiently by ruling out some wrongs rather than waiting until you are sure you can choose the right answer.

The book is aimed at high school and college students, as well as library aides and technicians. If you take none of the short-cuts, it should take you about seven hours to do the entire book, Section C being the longest. If you take the short-cuts, you will be done in about four hours--half a day.

Richard R. Strawn

SECTION A

HOW TO READ A LIBRARY OF CONGRESS CATALOG CARD

INTRODUCTION

In this section you will learn how to distinguish author cards, title cards and subject cards. To find out whether you already know how, take the short test below. If you do this section, you will need to go to an actual card catalog in a library.

Answers to tests and exercises in Section A begin on page 65.

PRE-TEST

The cards in the list on the right are arranged alphabetically by

   a) author
   b) title
   c) subject
   d) place of publication
   e) classification

In the card for the book by John McCorkle, the added entry "1. Quantrill, William Clarke, 1837-1865" indicates

   f) an author
   g) a title
   h) a subject

For the book by John McCormick, the <u>title</u> card will begin with

   i) McCormick, John
   j) The complete aficionado [lower case]
   k) THE COMPLETE AFICIONADO [upper case]
   l) BULL-FIGHTERS

For the book by Jack C. McCormac, the <u>subject</u> card will begin with

   m) McCormac, Jack C.
   n) Structural analysis [lower case]
   o) STRUCTURAL ANALYSIS [upper case]
   p) Structures, Theory of
   q) STRUCTURES, THEORY OF

1. McCorkle, John, 1838–
    Three years with Quantrell; a true story, told by his scout John McCorkle. Written by O. S Barton. New York, Buffalo-Head Press; distributed by J. F. Carr, 1966.
    157 p. ports. 24 cm.
    Reprint of the 1914 ed.
    1. Quantrill, William Clarke, 1837-1865. 2. Guerrillas. 3. U. S.—Hist.—Civil War—Personal narratives—Confederate side. 4. Missouri—Hist.—Civil War. I. Barton, O. S., d. 1925. II. Title.
    E470.45.M14 1966   973.78'2   67-6851

2. McCormac, Jack C.
    Structural analysis, by Jack C. McCormac. 2d ed. Scranton, International Textbook Co. [1967]
    xvi, 494 p. illus. 24 cm. (International textbooks in civil engineering)
    Bibliographical footnotes.
    1. Structures, Theory of. I. Title.
    TA645.M3 1967   624'.171   67-16236

3. McCormack, Mark.
    Golf '67: world professional golf; the facts and figures. London, Cassell, 1967.
    xiv, 310 p. plates, tables. 22 cm. 25/-
    1. Golf—Yearbooks. I. Title.   (B 67-14785)
    GV961.M3   796.352'64'05   67-95300

4. McCormick, John.
    The complete aficionado [by] John McCormick and Mario Sevilla Mascareñas; illustrated by Roberto Berdecio. London, Weidenfeld & Nicolson [1967].
    xi, 276 p. illus. (incl. ports.), diagrs. 24½ cm. 63/-
    Bibliographical footnotes.   (B 67-11638)
    1. Bull-fighters. I. Sevilla Mascareñas, Mario, joint author. II. Title.
    GV1108.A1M35 1967a   791.8'2   67-93030

When arranged alphabetically by <u>title</u>, the order of the title cards for the four books in the list above will be _____.

If you choose not to do the following exercises, you will find a summary of the contents of Section A on page 13.

1

Reading a Catalog Card

EXERCISE FRAME A 1

Go to some drawer in the card catalog and leaf through until you come to a <u>main-entry author card</u> that begins with an author's name, like this one (avoid works in foreign languages for the time being):

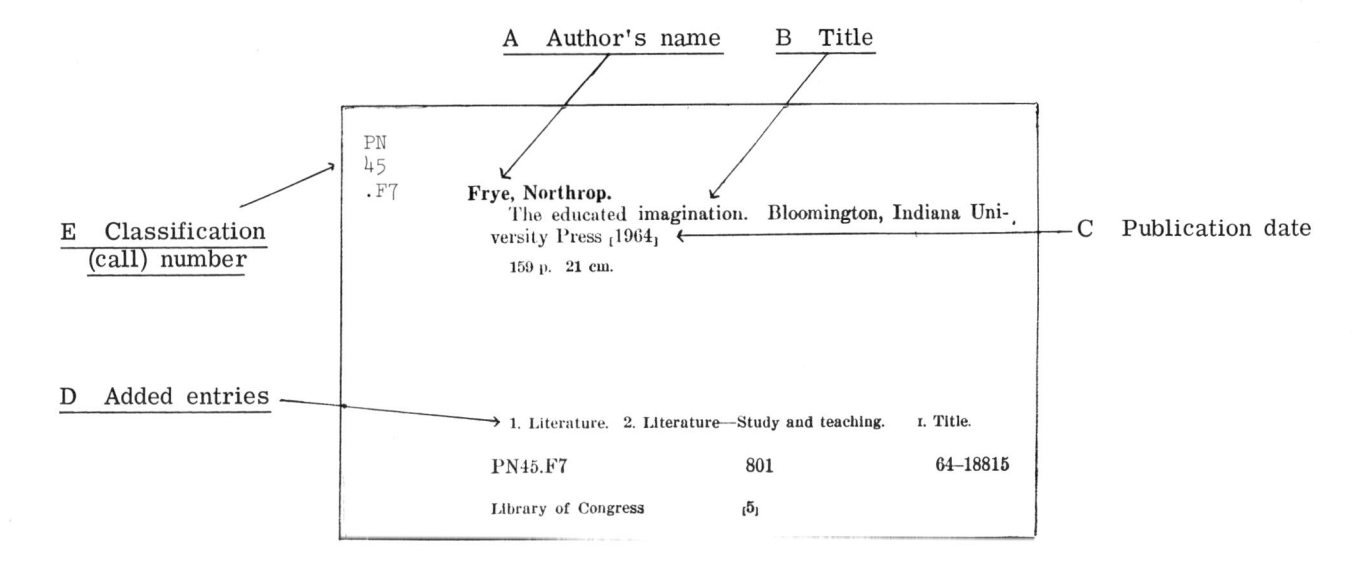

```
                              A  Author's name      B  Title

    PN
    45
    .F7
                      Frye, Northrop.
E  Classification          The educated imagination.  Bloomington, Indiana Uni-
   (call) number          versity Press [1964]                                    C  Publication date
                          159 p.  21 cm.



D  Added entries
                         1. Literature.  2. Literature—Study and teaching.   I. Title.

                       PN45.F7                801                    64-18815

                       Library of Congress         [5]
```

You can tell that your card begins "like this one" because your card

    a) has a call number in the PN's.
    b) is for a book published in 1964.
    c) begins with an author's name typewritten above another author's name.
    d) begins with an author's name printed bold face or typewritten just above the title.
    e) has a title typed at the top.
    f) "I <u>can't</u> tell and that's the trouble."

NOTE: Some libraries now use cards produced by a computer. They use only one typeface. Here is the <u>main-entry author card</u> to correspond to the example above:

```
              LITERATURE.
    PN
    45         Frye, Northrop.
    .F7           The educated imagination. Indiana
               University Press [1964]
                  159 p.




                  1. Literature.  2. Literature--Study
               and teaching.  I. Title

    InCW    15 JAN 79    325732   IWCMdc     64-18815
```

EXERCISE FRAME A 2

Now that you've turned up a main-entry author card, go to the drawer that will include the

title card to match your author card, and turn to the title card. Here, for instance, is the title card to match the author card in frame A 1:

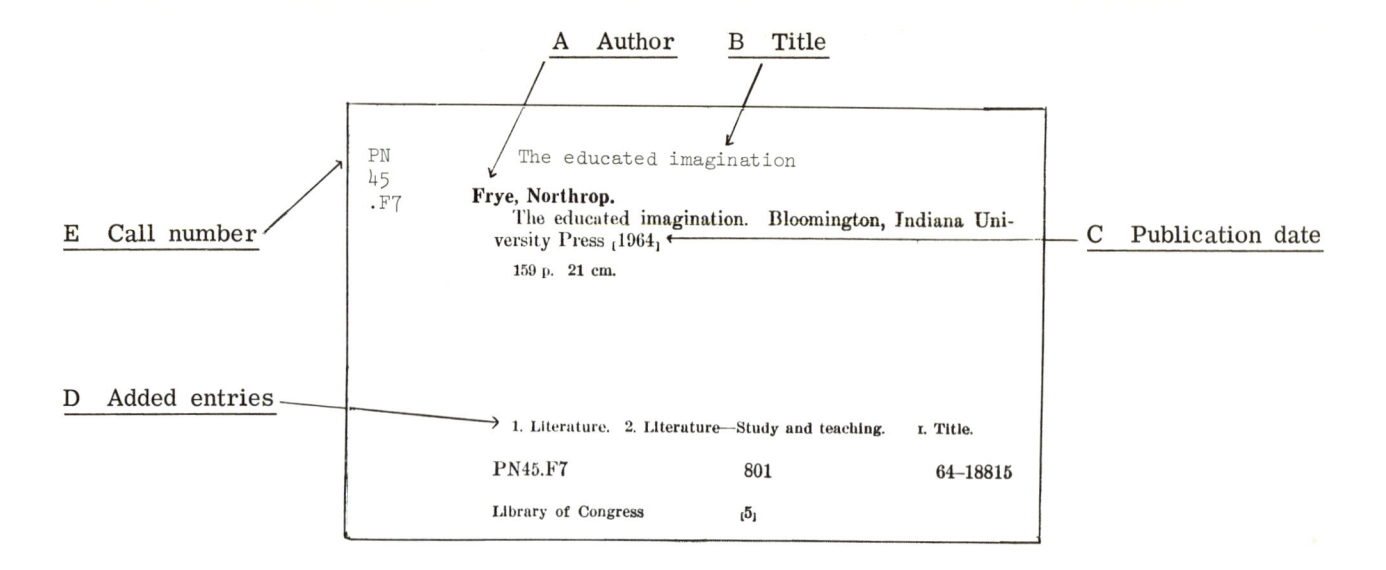

```
                    A Author     B Title

E Call number    PN       The educated imagination
                 45
                 .F7    Frye, Northrop.
                            The educated imagination.  Bloomington, Indiana Uni-     C Publication date
                        versity Press [1964]
                        159 p. 21 cm.


D Added entries         1. Literature. 2. Literature—Study and teaching.  I. Title.

                        PN45.F7                 801             64–18815
                        Library of Congress     [5]
```

You can tell that you have reached the title card because

   a) the title (B) comes under the author (A).
   b) the title (B) is typed above the author (A).
   c) the card looks exactly like the author card.
   d) the call number is the same.
   e) "I can't tell and that's the trouble."
   f) "I don't know what drawer to go to."

EXERCISE FRAME A 2.1

These cards are filed "by title." What determines their order in the file? (The cards are set up as if you were thumbing the cards from front to back in a file drawer.)

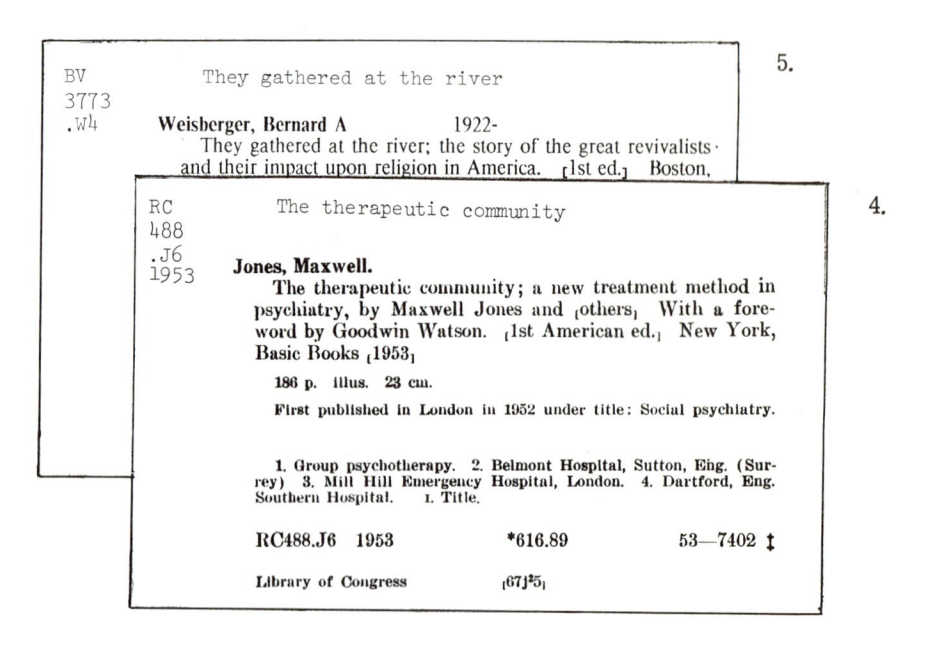

```
BV          They gathered at the river                          5.
3773
.W4       Weisberger, Bernard A      1922–
              They gathered at the river; the story of the great revivalists
          and their impact upon religion in America.  [1st ed.]  Boston,

    RC          The therapeutic community                       4.
    488
    .J6
    1953    Jones, Maxwell.
                The therapeutic community; a new treatment method in
            psychiatry, by Maxwell Jones and [others]  With a fore-
            word by Goodwin Watson.  [1st American ed.]  New York,
            Basic Books [1953]
                186 p. illus. 23 cm.

                First published in London in 1952 under title: Social psychiatry.

                1. Group psychotherapy.  2. Belmont Hospital, Sutton, Eng. (Sur-
            rey)  3. Mill Hill Emergency Hospital, London.  4. Dartford, Eng.
            Southern Hospital.   I. Title.

            RC488.J6 1953          *616.89          53–7402
            Library of Congress    [67]†5
```

Reading a Catalog Card   4

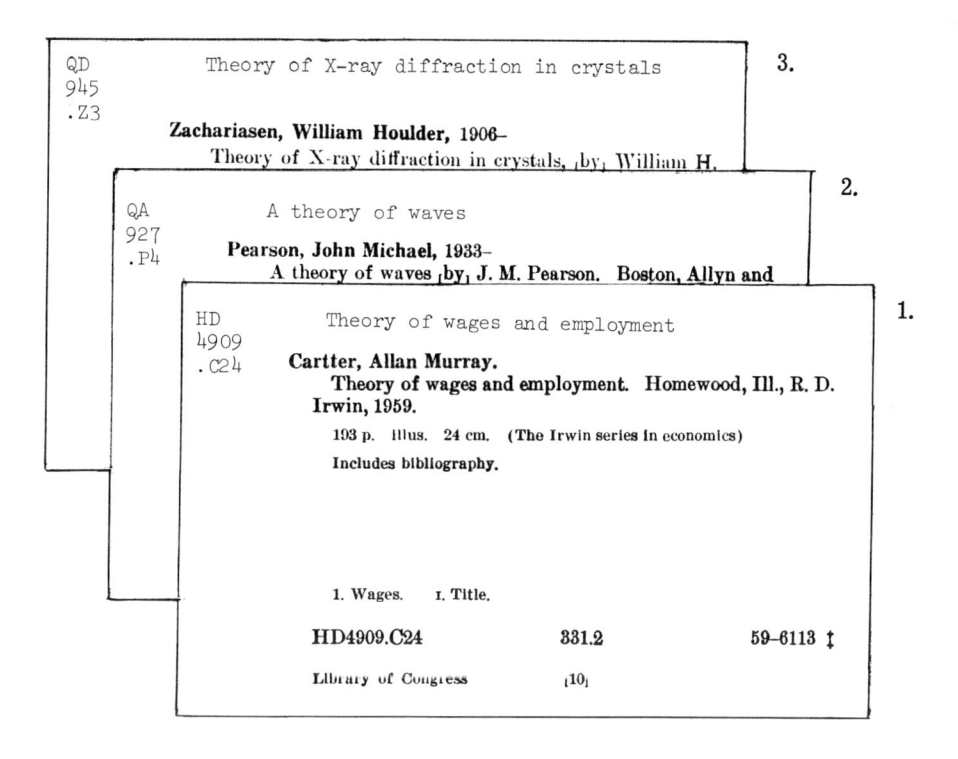

```
QD          Theory of X-ray diffraction in crystals            3.
945
.Z3   Zachariasen, William Houlder, 1906-
        Theory of X-ray diffraction in crystals, by William H.
```

```
QA          A theory of waves                                  2.
927
.P4   Pearson, John Michael, 1933-
        A theory of waves by J. M. Pearson.  Boston, Allyn and
```

```
HD          Theory of wages and employment                     1.
4909
.C24  Cartter, Allan Murray.
         Theory of wages and employment.  Homewood, Ill., R. D.
      Irwin, 1959.
         193 p.  illus.  24 cm.  (The Irwin series in economics)
         Includes bibliography.



         1. Wages.    I. Title.

      HD4909.C24            331.2            59-6113 ‡
      Library of Congress     [10]
```

EXERCISE FRAME A 2.2

Titles are arranged by "the first important word." All right, but which words are <u>not</u> important?

In the following arrangement by title the words <u>un</u>important to the filing are _____.

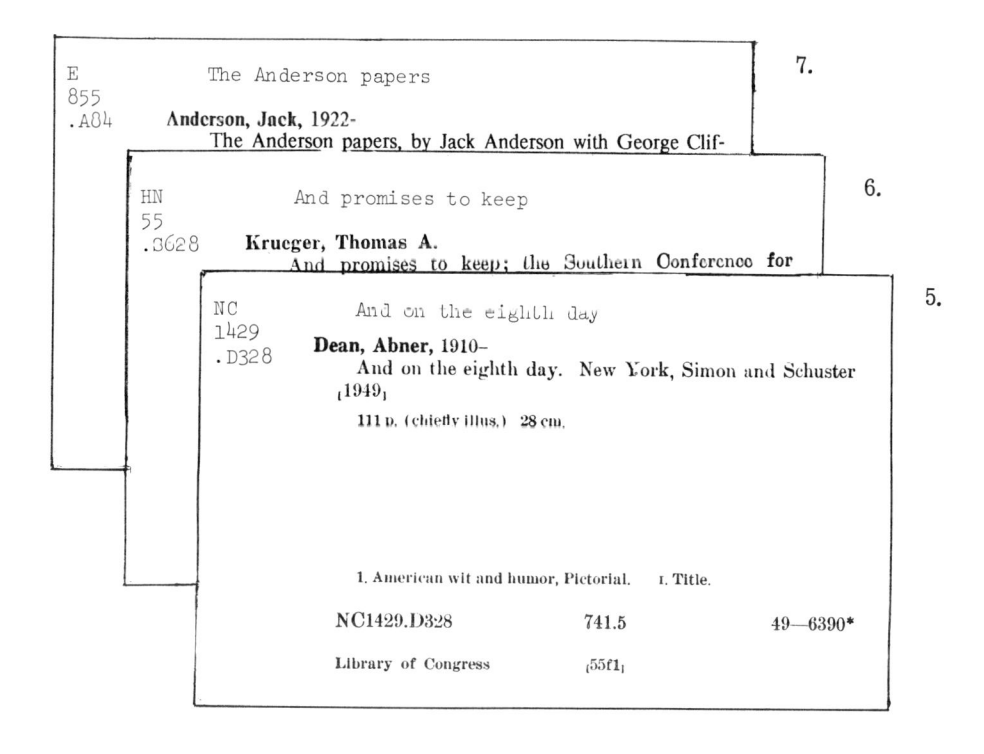

```
E           The Anderson papers                                7.
855
.A84  Anderson, Jack, 1922-
        The Anderson papers, by Jack Anderson with George Clif-
```

```
HN          And promises to keep                               6.
55
.3628 Krueger, Thomas A.
        And promises to keep; the Southern Conference for
```

```
NC          And on the eighth day                              5.
1429
.D328 Dean, Abner, 1910-
        And on the eighth day.  New York, Simon and Schuster
      [1949]
         111 p. (chiefly illus.)  28 cm.



         1. American wit and humor, Pictorial.   I. Title.

      NC1429.D328           741.5            49—6390*
      Library of Congress     [55f1]
```

Frame A 2.2

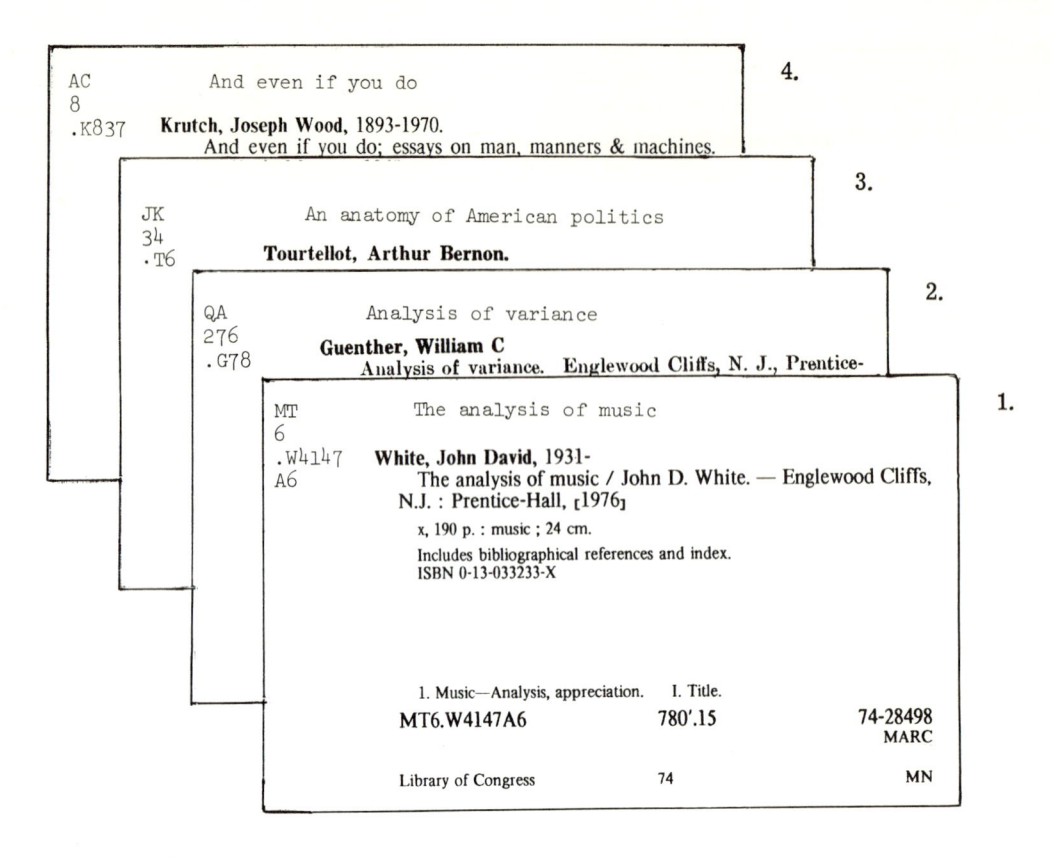

```
AC          And even if you do                            4.
 8
.K837   Krutch, Joseph Wood, 1893-1970.
            And even if you do; essays on man, manners & machines.
```

```
JK          An anatomy of American politics               3.
 34
.T6     Tourtellot, Arthur Bernon.
```

```
QA          Analysis of variance                          2.
276
.G78    Guenther, William C
            Analysis of variance.  Englewood Cliffs, N. J., Prentice-
```

```
MT          The analysis of music                         1.
 6
.W4147  White, John David, 1931-
A6          The analysis of music / John D. White. — Englewood Cliffs,
        N.J. : Prentice-Hall, [1976]
            x, 190 p. : music ; 24 cm.
            Includes bibliographical references and index.
            ISBN 0-13-033233-X


            1. Music—Analysis, appreciation.    I. Title.
        MT6.W4147A6              780'.15               74-28498
                                                         MARC
        Library of Congress        74                     MN
```

EXERCISE FRAME A 2.3

Since you're concerned with the title now, try the first word of the title--excluding an article (<u>a</u>, <u>an</u>, <u>the</u>). For example:

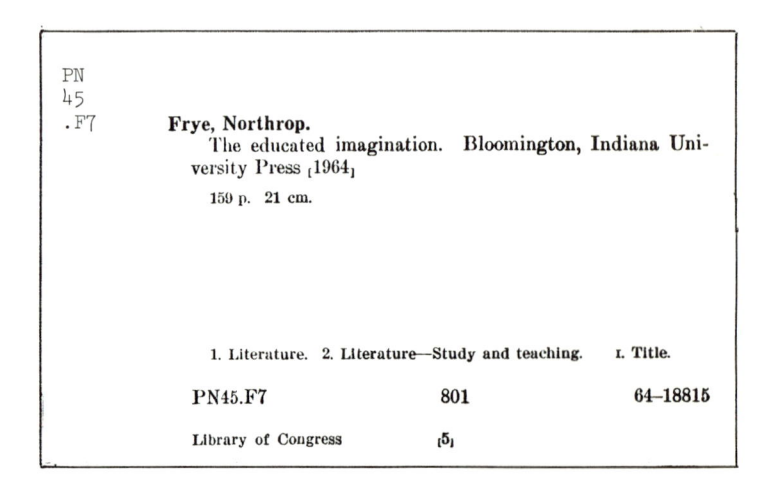

```
PN
45
.F7     Frye, Northrop.
            The educated imagination.  Bloomington, Indiana Uni-
        versity Press [1964]
            159 p.  21 cm.




            1. Literature.  2. Literature—Study and teaching.  I. Title.
        PN45.F7                  801                   64-18815
        Library of Congress      [5]
```

The title card that corresponds to that author card will be filed in the drawer labeled, for instance,

    a) EDU--EDUCATION, E.
    b) FRU--FUNC
    c) TERT--THEATER
    d) PLP--POETQ
    e) EDUCATIONAL P--EF

Reading a Catalog Card   6

EXERCISE FRAME A 2.4

To practice filing titles before you go on to locate your title card, arrange these title cards properly. (They are arranged here by author.)

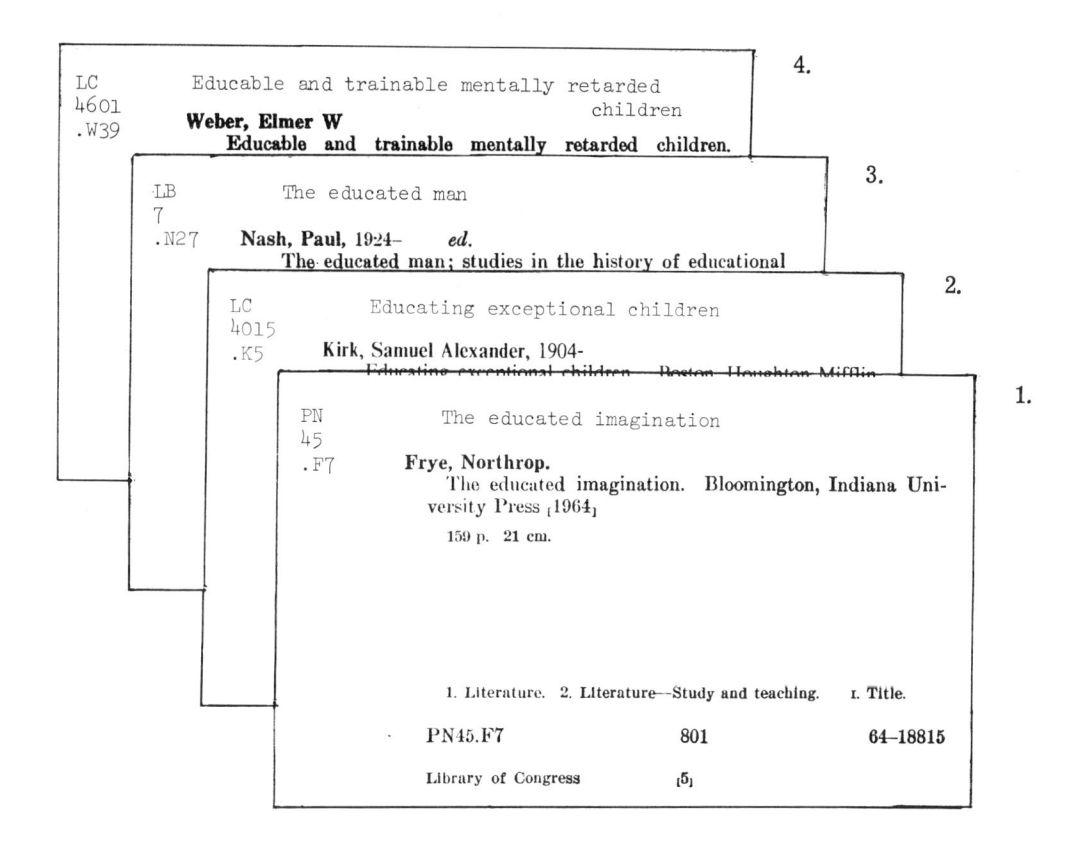

```
    LC       Educable and trainable mentally retarded      4.
    4601    Weber, Elmer W                    children
    .W39       Educable and trainable mentally retarded children.

         LB           The educated man                    3.
         7
         .N27    Nash, Paul, 1924-     ed.
                    The educated man; studies in the history of educational

              LC          Educating exceptional children         2.
              4015
              .K5     Kirk, Samuel Alexander, 1904-
                                                                    1.
                   PN          The educated imagination
                   45
                   .F7    Frye, Northrop.
                             The educated imagination. Bloomington, Indiana Uni-
                          versity Press [1964]
                             159 p.  21 cm.


                          1. Literature. 2. Literature—Study and teaching.  I. Title.
                             PN45.F7              801           64-18815
                             Library of Congress        [5]
```

The proper order, according to title, is _____.
                                         (List the numbers.)

EXERCISE FRAME A 2.5

Now that you know what word the title will be filed under, go to the proper drawer and find the title card that corresponds to your author card. Here again is the title card to match the author card in frame A 1:

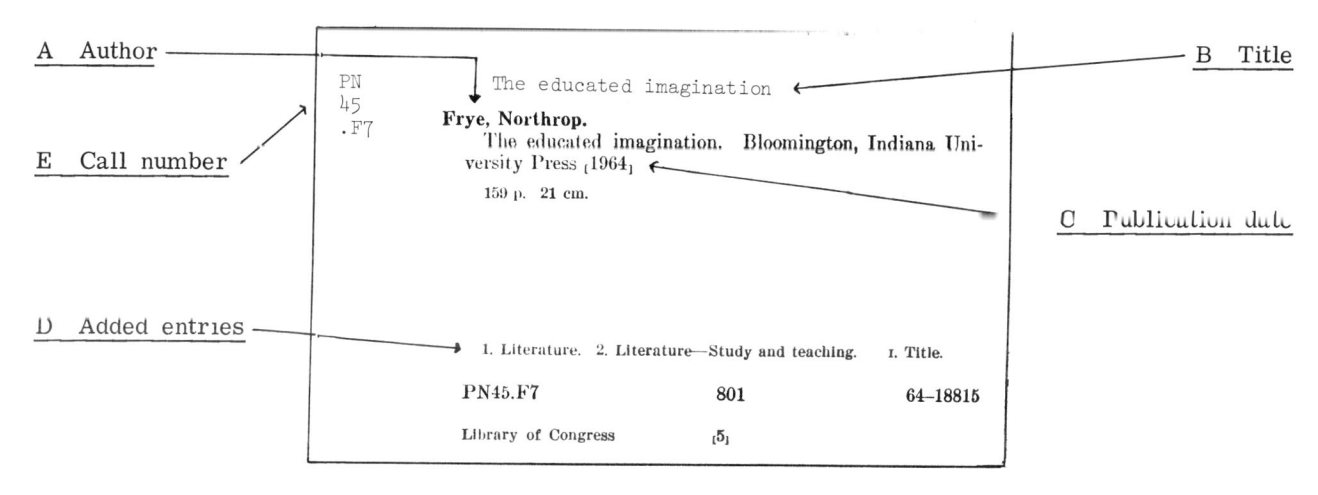

```
A  Author ──────┐                                            ┌───── B  Title
                │   PN      The educated imagination ◄───────┘
                │   45
                │   .F7   Frye, Northrop.
E  Call number ─┘           The educated imagination. Bloomington, Indiana Uni-
                          versity Press [1964] ◄─────────────┐
                             159 p.  21 cm.                  │
                                                             └───── C  Publication date


D  Added entries ────────►  1. Literature. 2. Literature—Study and teaching.  I. Title.
                               PN45.F7              801           64-18815
                               Library of Congress        [5]
```

You can tell that you have reached the title card because

    a) the title (B) comes under the author (A).
    b) the title (B) is typed in small letters above the author (A).
    c) "I can't tell and that's the trouble."

EXERCISE FRAME A 3

What we want now is a card with added entries--like (D) at the bottom of the example here:

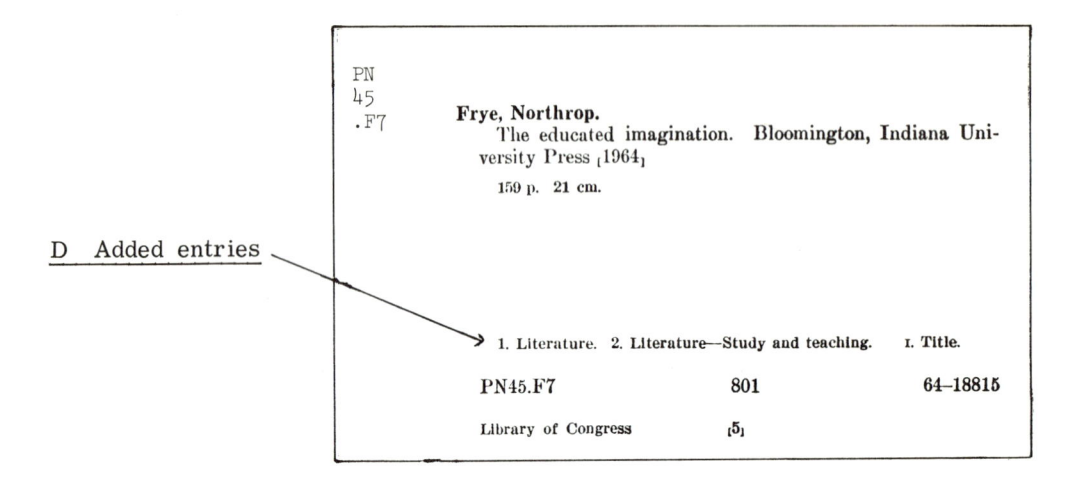

```
PN
45
.F7     Frye, Northrop.
            The educated imagination.  Bloomington, Indiana Uni-
        versity Press [1964]
            159 p.  21 cm.



            1. Literature.  2. Literature—Study and teaching.    I. Title.

        PN45.F7                    801                    64-18815

        Library of Congress        [5]
```

D Added entries → (points to the "1. Literature..." line)

We want at least one entry with an Arabic numeral (1), not a Roman numeral (I). If you are already working with such a card, stick with it. If not, flip to a main-entry author card with an Arabic-numeral added entry.

On that card the term or terms in the Arabic-numeral entry sound like

    a) another author--go to frame A 4.
    b) another title--go to frame A 5.
    c) a subject--go to frame A 6.

CHOOSE THE ONE (a, b, OR c) THAT FITS YOUR CARD & FOLLOW THE DIRECTION. IF MORE THAN ONE FITS YOUR CARD, TAKE YOUR PICK.

EXERCISE FRAME A 4

The Arabic-numeral added entry sounds like another author, perhaps like this:

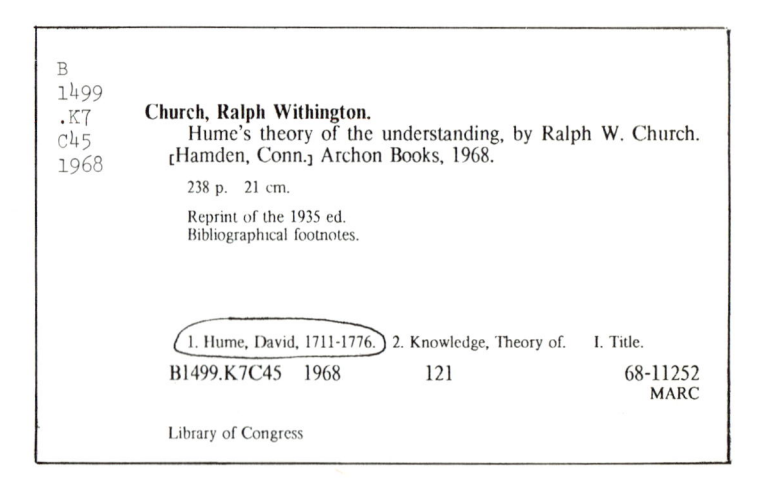

```
B
1499
.K7     Church, Ralph Withington.
C45         Hume's theory of the understanding, by Ralph W. Church.
1968    [Hamden, Conn.] Archon Books, 1968.
            238 p.  21 cm.

            Reprint of the 1935 ed.
            Bibliographical footnotes.


            (1. Hume, David, 1711-1776.)  2. Knowledge, Theory of.   I. Title.
        B1499.K7C45    1968               121                68-11252
                                                              MARC
        Library of Congress
```

Reading a Catalog Card   8

In that example, David Hume is

    a) the author of the book.
    b) one of the subjects of the book.
    c) the title of the book.

"Knowledge, Theory of" is

    d) the title of the book.
    e) the only subject of the book.
    f) one of the subjects of the book.

EXERCISE FRAME A 4.1

Arabic-numeral added entries are SUBJECTS. They help indicate what the book is ABOUT. When they are typed on a main-entry card (like the author card, for example), they are typed in CAPITALS.

B

```
PQ          CALDERON DE LA BARCA, PEDRO, 1600-1681
6315
.W3     Wardropper, Bruce W       ed.
          Critical essays on the theatre of Calderón. Edited by
        Bruce W. Wardropper. [New York] New York University
        Press, 1965.
            xvi, 239 p.  22 cm.
            Bibliography: p. 227-231. Bibliographical footnotes.


            1. Calderón de la Barca, Pedro, 1600-1681.   I. Title.

        PQ6315.W3           862.3              65-14336
        Library of Congress       [5]
```

A

```
NB           Calder, Alexander, 1898-
237
.C28    Arnason, H       Harvard.
A8         Calder, text by H. H. Arnason. Photos. by Pedro E.
        Guerrero. [Princeton, N. J.] Van Nostrand [1966]
            xi, 192 p.  illus. (part col.)  ports. (part col.)  29 cm.
            Bibliography: p. 184-185.




                  I. Calder, Alexander, 1898-
        NB237.C28A8          730.924           66-31776
                             rev
        Library of Congress  [r71d2]
```

    1. Card B shows that the book contains principally material (a) [by or about?] Calderón. You can tell that because "Calderón de la Barca, Pedro" is typed at the top in (b) [CAPITALS or Lower Case?] and the added entry at the bottom has (c) [an Arabic or a Roman?] numeral.

    2. Card A shows that the book contains principally material (d) [by or about?] Calder. You can tell that because "Calder, Alexander" is in (e) [CAPITALS or Lower Case?] and you notice that the added entry at the bottom has (f) [an Arabic or a Roman?] numeral.

Frame A 4.1

3. Card A has no Roman-numeral title entry ("II. Title"), because such an entry would merely generate a card beginning (g) ["Calder" or "CALDER"?], and that would not add usefully to the author entry ("Calder, Alexander, 1898- ").

If you want to practice with the distinction between titles and subjects, go to frame A 5. If that's enough, go to frame A 7.

EXERCISE FRAME A 5

Titles are often subjects, in a way; they tell what a book is about:
Moravcsik, J. H. E. <u>Aristotle.</u>
Lubac, Henri de. <u>The religion of Teilhard de Chardin.</u>
Cho, Soon Sung. <u>Korea in world politics.</u>
Weinstock, Herbert. <u>Rossini, a biography.</u>
Bazin, André. <u>What is cinema?</u>

Titles are also often misleading as subjects; they do not tell what a book is about so much as they betoken the book:
Henderson, Joseph L. <u>Thresholds of initiation.</u> (Fraternities? No, psychoanalysis.)
MacLeish, Archibald. <u>Continuing journey.</u> (Travels? No, essays on the arts and public affairs.)
Martin, Jay. <u>Harvests of change.</u> (Slot machines? No, American literature, 1865-1914.)
Wiesenthal, Simon. <u>The murderers among us.</u> (FBI reports? No, memoirs of the concentration camps.)

Because titles are unreliable as subjects, the catalog does not treat them as subjects; it treats them as it does authors. SUBJECT headings are identified by Arabic numerals and are typed at the top of the card in CAPITALS. Other entries (authors, titles, names of series...) are identified by Roman numerals and are typed at the top of the card in Lower Case.

A
```
F                LANDON, ALFRED MOSSMAN, 1887-
686
.L26      McCoy, Donald R
             Landon of Kansas [by] Donald R. McCoy.  Lincoln, Univer-
          sity of Nebraska Press [1966]
             x, 607 p.  illus., ports.  24 cm.
             Includes bibliographical references.




                 1. Landon, Alfred Mossman, 1887-      I. Title.
             F686.L26              329.6'00924              65-16190
                                                             MARC

          Library of Congress
```

B
```
F                    Landon of Kansas
686
.L26      McCoy, Donald R
             Landon of Kansas [by] Donald R. McCoy.  Lincoln, Univer-
          sity of Nebraska Press [1966]
             x, 607 p.  illus., ports.  24 cm.
             Includes bibliographical references.




                 1. Landon, Alfred Mossman, 1887-      I. Title.
             F686.L26              329.6'00924              65-16190
                                                             MARC

          Library of Congress
```

Reading a Catalog Card   10

1. Card A shows a typical

   a) author entry.
   b) title entry.
   c) subject entry.

2. You can tell that because "Landon, Alfred Mossman" is typed in [Lower Case or CAPITALS?] and the added entry at the bottom, which generates this card, has [a Roman or an Arabic?] numeral.

3. Card B shows a typical

   d) author entry.
   e) title entry.
   f) subject entry.

4. You can tell that because "Landon of Kansas" is typed in [Lower Case or CAPITALS?] and the added entry at the bottom, which generates this card, has [a Roman or an Arabic?] numeral.

5. The author card will begin with

   g) McCoy, Donald R.
   h) Landon, Alfred Mossman.
   i) LANDON, ALFRED MOSSMAN.

Go to frame A 7.

EXERCISE FRAME A 6

The Arabic-numeral added entry sounds like a subject, perhaps like this one:

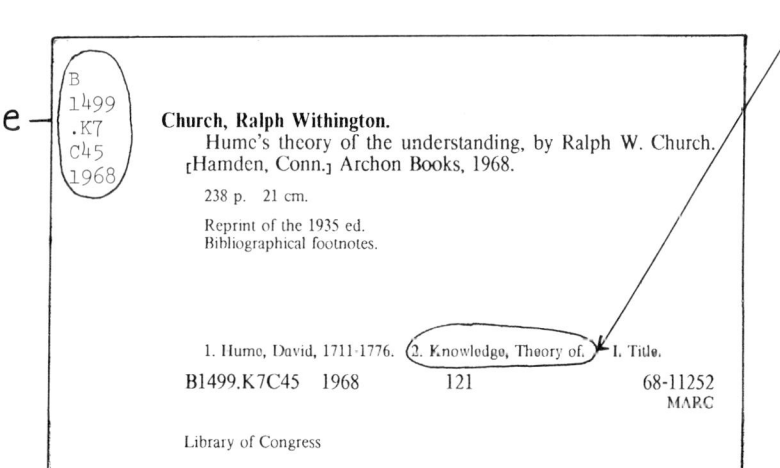

```
        ┌─────────────────────────────────────────────────────────┐
        │ ⌢                                                       │
        │(B    )                                                  │
        │ 1499                                                    │
  e ───▶│ .K7    Church, Ralph Withington.                        │
        │ C45       Hume's theory of the understanding, by Ralph W. Church.│
        │ 1968    [Hamden, Conn.] Archon Books, 1968.             │
        │ ⌣                                                       │
        │         238 p.  21 cm.                                  │
        │                                                         │
        │         Reprint of the 1935 ed.                         │
        │         Bibliographical footnotes.                      │
        │                                                         │
        │                                                         │
        │           1. Hume, David, 1711-1776. (2. Knowledge, Theory of.) I. Title. │
        │           B1499.K7C45   1968         121         68-11252│
        │                                                    MARC │
        │                                                         │
        │         Library of Congress                             │
        └─────────────────────────────────────────────────────────┘
```

On the example above, circle the following items and letter them with their respective letters (the call number is already done):

   a) the author
   b) the title
   c) a person used as a subject
   d) a topic used as a subject
   e) the call number

According to the example, subjects are identified by [Arabic or Roman?] numerals.

Any other added entry--a title or a co-author, for instance--will be identified by [an Arabic or a Roman?] numeral.

Go on to frame A 6.1.

EXERCISE FRAME A 6.1

Here is the set of cards for Church's book on Hume:

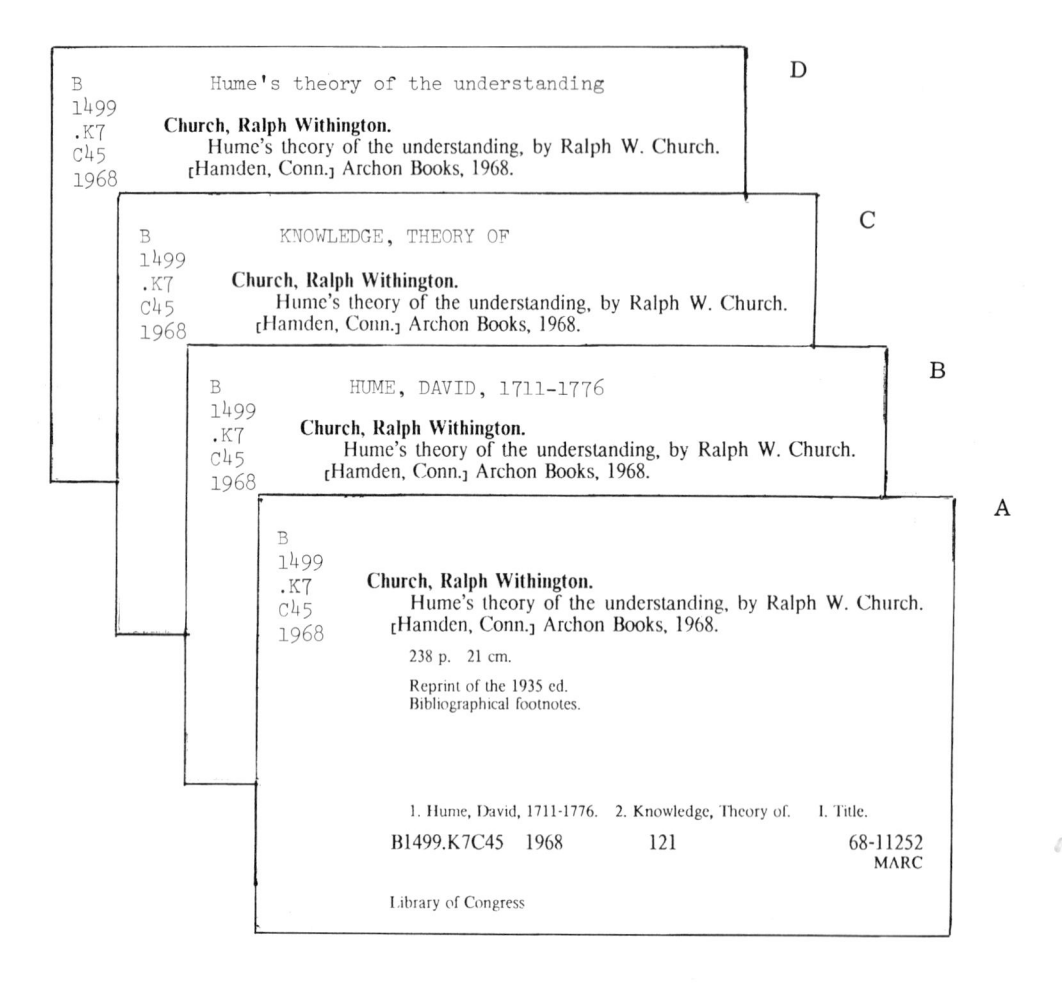

```
         D
    B                Hume's theory of the understanding
    1499
    .K7      Church, Ralph Withington.
    C45          Hume's theory of the understanding, by Ralph W. Church.
    1968         [Hamden, Conn.] Archon Books, 1968.
                                                                         C
         B                   KNOWLEDGE, THEORY OF
         1499
         .K7      Church, Ralph Withington.
         C45          Hume's theory of the understanding, by Ralph W. Church.
         1968         [Hamden, Conn.] Archon Books, 1968.
                                                                         B
              B                 HUME, DAVID, 1711-1776
              1499
              .K7      Church, Ralph Withington.
              C45          Hume's theory of the understanding, by Ralph W. Church.
              1968         [Hamden, Conn.] Archon Books, 1968.
                                                                         A
                   B
                   1499
                   .K7      Church, Ralph Withington.
                   C45          Hume's theory of the understanding, by Ralph W. Church.
                   1968         [Hamden, Conn.] Archon Books, 1968.

                              238 p.  21 cm.
                              Reprint of the 1935 ed.
                              Bibliographical footnotes.


                              1. Hume, David, 1711-1776.  2. Knowledge, Theory of.  I. Title.
                              B1499.K7C45   1968         121              68-11252
                                                                          MARC
                              Library of Congress
```

1. Card A, with nothing typed above the name of the author, is

    a) the main-entry card.
    b) the title card.
    c) a subject card.

2. Card B occurs--the catalog will contain a card like B--because the main entry has

    ? { d) the name "Hume" in the title.
        e) the Arabic-numeral subject entry: 1. Hume, David, 1711-1776.
        f) something to do with Hume.

3. Card B is

    g) an author card.
    h) a title card.
    i) a subject card.

Reading a Catalog Card

4. Card C occurs because the main entry has

    j) the word "understanding" in the title.
    k) "Hume, David, 1711-1776" as a subject entry, and because Hume wrote on knowledge.
    l) the Arabic-numeral subject entry: "Knowledge, Theory of"

5. Card C is

    m) an author card.
    n) a title card.
    o) a subject card.

6. Card D occurs because the main entry has

    p) the Roman-numeral indication: I. Title
    q) a title.

7. Card D is

    r) an author card.
    s) a title card.
    t) a subject card.

8. So it appears that [Arabic-numeral or Roman-numeral?] subject entries have the subject heading typed in [CAPITALS or Lower Case?]. Other cards have [Arabic-numeral or Roman-numeral?] author entries or title entries in [CAPITALS or Lower Case?].

If you want to practice with authors' names as subject entries, go to frame A 4. If you want to practice with the distinction between titles and subjects, go to frame A 5. If that's enough of that, go to frame A 7.

EXERCISE FRAME A 7

After that excursion, come back to your main-entry author card with the Arabic-numeral subject heading printed at the bottom of the card. Go to the proper drawer in the catalog and find the subject card that corresponds to your author card.

Which one is the "proper drawer"? That is to say, where will your subject card be filed? Try this example. Here is the first subject card to match the author card in frame A 1:

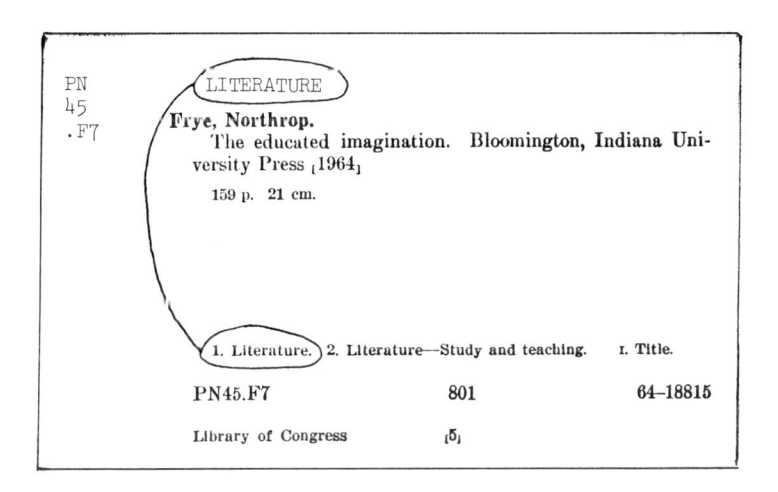

```
PN          LITERATURE
45      Frye, Northrop.
.F7         The educated imagination.  Bloomington, Indiana Uni-
         versity Press [1964]
            159 p.  21 cm.




                    1. Literature.  2. Literature—Study and teaching.   I. Title.

         PN45.F7                   801                    64-18815
              Library of Congress          [5]
```

You would find that subject card in the drawer labeled

    a) EDU--EDUCATION, L
    b) FRO--FT
    c) LINDS--LITERATURE, B

Now that you have a subject card, you are ready to practice a more difficult business: getting from one subject to another. For that process, go to Section B. You may want to take the pre-test of this section now as a post-test.

SUMMARY OF SECTION A

    A set of catalog cards for a given book includes the following:

An author card, or main entry; the name is in boldface type,* and nothing is typed above the author line.

As many cards as there are added entries at the bottom. (There may be none.) The added entries are numbered.

    Arabic numerals indicate subjects. On a subject card, the words of the added entry are typed above the main entry (the top line) in CAPITALS.

    Roman numerals indicate titles (or co-authors or titles of series). On a title card, the name of the book is typed above the main entry (the top line) in Lower Case. In filing a title card, one disregards an initial "The," "A," or "An"--including their equivalents in another language--and files by the next word after.

---

*If the card comes from the Library of Congress; if it does not, the typeface will probably be of one kind on the whole card.

SECTION B

WORDS AS POSSIBLE "SUBJECT HEADINGS"

INTRODUCTION

This section will teach you how to select from your topic some term to use as a possible subject heading with which to get into the card catalog. If your topic is already one word (like "Automation" or "Trees"), go to frame B 4. To find out whether you already know how to do what this section is about, do the short test below. You can do this section without using an actual card catalog in a library.

Answers to tests and exercises in Section B begin on page 68.

PRE-TEST

If you can do most of the following items, you already know the contents of Section B.

I. For each title, choose the most specific subject heading appropriate to the title.

    Campbell, P. N. The structure and function of animal cell components.
        a) Biology
        b) Biochemistry
        c) Man--Constitution

    Dance, J. B. Radioisotope experiments for schools and colleges.
        d) Radioactivity
        e) Radiobiology
        f) X-rays

    Palmer, F. R. A linguistic study of the English verb.
        g) English language
        h) English language--Verb
        i) Grammar, Comparative and general--Verb

    Moynihan, D. P. Maximum feasible misunderstanding; community action in the war on poverty.
        j) Community
        k) Community organization
        l) U. S. Office of Economic Opportunity. Community Action Program.

    Pilpel, H. F. When should abortion be legal?
        m) Abortion--U. S.--Popular works
        n) Conception--Prevention
        o) Obstetrics

II. In each topic, underline the most specific term (the single word or the phrase) to use as a possible subject heading.

    a. Politics of Medicare.

    b. William Bradford as a historian.

    c. Trade unionism in mid-19th-century England.

    d. Snake venoms.

e. Naturalism in 19th-century English fiction.

f. Birds and reptiles in the poetry of Emily Dickinson.

If you choose not to do the following exercises, you will find a summary of Section B on page 22.

EXERCISE FRAME B 1

(If your topic is already one word--like "Automation" or "Trees"--go to frame B 4.)

Topic: "The primary structure of proteins."

Problem: To find a term in the topic that will serve as a possible subject heading.

Reasoning: A "topic" is a "subject"--here the topic is given, so you have a subject. The trouble is you have a <u>subject</u> with several words in it, so the problem is really to find <u>one</u> of those words to use as a <u>subject heading</u>. Shall it be "primary" or "structure" or "proteins"?

The understanding about a subject heading in a card catalog is that it is <u>specific</u> (particular), not general. It names particularly the material which is on the same level of <u>specificity</u> as the heading.

Example: The subject heading BIOLOGY covers works that treat of the whole field of biology. A work in genetic theory in particular is more specific within the field of biology and falls under the more specific heading GENETICS.

Exercise: In each group below that you decide to work with, assign each book to a subject heading whose <u>scope</u> fits the scope of the book. (Do whatever fields you please until you feel that you have got the sense of "scope." Don't feel obliged to do all the items.)

<u>HISTORY, MODERN</u>   <u>HISTORY, MODERN--20TH CENTURY</u>   <u>EUROPE--HISTORY--1789-1900</u>

1. Taylor, Alan J. P. <u>From Napoleon to Lenin.</u> Harper & Row, 1966.

2. <u>Larousse encyclopedia of modern history, from 1500 to the present day.</u> Harper & Row, 1964.

3. Kohn, Hans. <u>Revolutions and dictatorships; essays in contemporary history.</u> Harvard University Press, 1941.

4. Fontaine, André. <u>History of the Cold War.</u> Pantheon, 1968-69.

5. Higby, Chester P. <u>History of modern Europe; a survey of the evolution of European society from the national risings against Napoleon to the present day.</u> The Century Co., 1932.

<u>LITERATURE</u>   <u>FICTION--HISTORY & CRITICISM</u>   <u>NEGRO LITERATURE (AMERICAN)</u>

6. Pritchett, V. S. <u>The living novel & later appreciations.</u> Random House, 1964.

7. Steiner, George. <u>Literature and silence; essays on language, literature, and the inhuman.</u> Atheneum, 1967.

8. Hill, Herbert. <u>Anger, and beyond: the Negro writer in the United States.</u> Harper & Row, 1966.

9. <u>Literary theory and structure; essays in honor of William K. Wimsatt....</u> Yale University Press, 1973.

10. Hardy, Barbara N. <u>Tellers and listeners: the narrative imagination.</u> Athlone Press, 1975.

Possible "Subject Headings"

PSYCHOLOGY   PSYCHOLOGY, COMPARATIVE   PSYCHOLOGY, PHYSIOLOGICAL

11. Kryter, Karl D. The effects of noise on man. Academic Press, 1970.

12. Miller, George A. Psychology, the science of mental life. Harper & Row, 1962.

13. Young, Paul T. Motivation and emotions; a survey of the determinants of human and animal activity. Wiley, 1961.

14. Eiduson, Samuel. Biochemistry and behavior. Van Nostrand, 1964.

15. Evans, Richard I. Konrad Lorenz: the man and his ideas. Harcourt Brace Jovanovich, 1975.

MUSIC--ANALYSIS, INTERPRETATION   MUSIC--PHILOSOPHY & AESTHETICS
MUSIC--DISCOGRAPHY   MUSIC--DICTIONARIES

16. Haggin, Bernard H. The new listener's companion and record guide. 4th ed., Horizon, 1974.

17. Kamien, Roger, comp. The Norton scores; an anthology for listening. W. W. Norton, 1970.

18. Scholes, Percy A. The Oxford companion to music; self-indexed and with a pronouncing glossary.... 9th ed., Oxford University Press, 1955; 10th ed., 1970.

19. Meyer, Leonard B. Emotion and meaning in music. University of Chicago Press, 1956.

20. Christ, William et al. Involvement with music. Harper's College Press, 1975.

CHEMISTRY   CHEMISTRY, ORGANIC   CHEMISTRY--BIBLIOGRAPHY   CHEMISTRY--DICTIONARIES

21. Mellon, Melvin G. Chemical publications, their nature and use. McGraw-Hill, 1965.

22. Hamlet, Peter. Introductory, organic, and biochemistry: a new view. Heath, 1975.

23. The encyclopedia of chemistry. Ed. by C. A. Hampel and G. G. Hawley, 3d ed., Van Nostrand Reinhold, 1973.

24. Vaczek, Louis C. The enjoyment of chemistry. Viking Press, 1964.

25. Silverstein, Robert M. et al. Spectrometric identification of organic compounds. Wiley, 1974.

BIBLIOGRAPHY--BIBLIOGRAPHY   REFERENCE BOOKS--BIBLIOGRAPHY
REFERENCE BOOKS--LITERATURE   REFERENCE BOOKS--PROBLEMS, EXERCISES, ETC.

26. Taylor, Margaret S. Basic reference sources; a self-study manual. Scarecrow Press, 1971.

27. Kehler, Dorothea. Problems in literary research: a guide to selected reference works. Scarecrow Press, 1975.

28. Murphey, Robert W. How and where to look it up; a guide to standard sources of information. McGraw-Hill, 1958.

29. Sheehy, Eugene P. Guide to reference books. 9th ed. [of C. M. Winchell]. American Library Association, 1976.

30. Downs, Robert B. American library resources; a bibliographical guide, 1951, supplement 1950-61, American Library Association, 1962.

EXERCISE FRAME B 2

Back to the problem.

Topic: "The primary structure of proteins."

Problem: To find a term in that topic which will serve as a possible subject heading.

Rule: The best bet is the most specific term.

Applying the rule to the topic, it seems that in the title below the most specific term is

["The primary structure of proteins"]

    a) <u>primary</u>, because it means "first in importance."
    b) <u>structure</u>, because like "skeleton" or "framework" it stands for the basic part.
    c) <u>structure</u>, because all proteins have a structure.
    d) <u>proteins</u>, because proteins are tiny.
    e) <u>proteins</u>, because it is what "primary structures" makes sense with.

For further exercise in finding specific terms, go to frame B 2.1. For a side-trip into another way to find a possible subject heading, go to frame B 3. For straight-line progression, go to frame B 4.

EXERCISE FRAME B 2.1

    More exercises in finding specific terms to use as possible subject headings. Work on topics in whatever subjects matter to you, until you feel you have the sense of "specific term."

    In the following topics, underline the term you think is most specific <u>within</u> that topic:

    1. Reviews of books of fiction.

    2. The social aspects of art.

    3. Courtship in 19th-century America.

    4. The microbiology of winemaking.

    5. Blood imagery in "Macbeth."

    6. International liquidity.

    7. A modern understanding of salvation.

    8. State support for treatment of the handicapped.

    9. Theory of sets.

For a side-trip into another way to find a possible subject heading, go to frame B 3. For straight-line progress, go to frame B 4.

EXERCISE FRAME B 3

    Another way to think about specificity is to think of "specific" as meaning "subordinate" or "on a lower branch."

    Fill in the boxes with terms from this topic: "Ancient lives of Vergil."

Possible "Subject Headings"   18

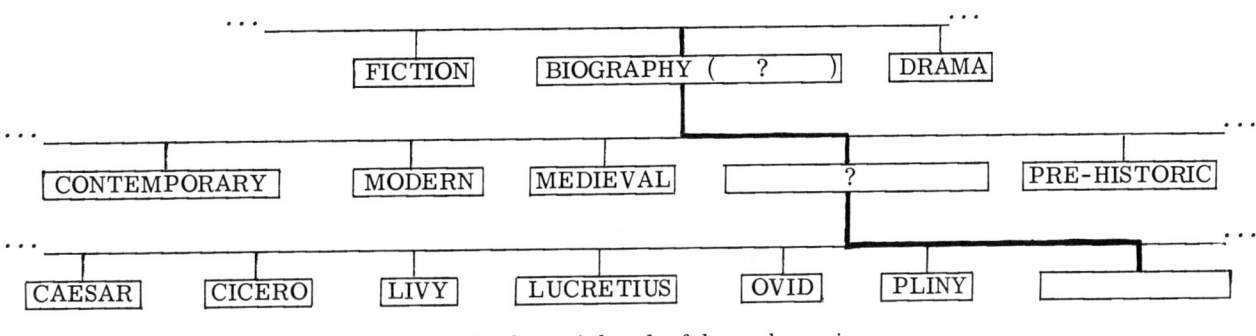

```
 ...┌─────────┬──────────────┬──────┬──────────┐...
    FICTION   BIOGRAPHY ( ? )         DRAMA
 ...┬──────────┬────────┬──────────┬────────────┬...
 CONTEMPORARY  MODERN  MEDIEVAL    ?         PRE-HISTORIC
 ...┬─────┬──────┬────────┬───────┬──────┬──────┐...
  CAESAR CICERO LIVY  LUCRETIUS  OVID  PLINY   □
```

The most specific term, the one on the lowest level of branches, is _____.

For a harder problem, go to frame B 3.1.   To return to the main line, go to frame B 4.

EXERCISE FRAME B 3.1

Now try a less obvious set-up. Arrange these terms in the boxes of the "tree" below:

    RURAL
    STAGNATION
    PATTERNS
    EXPLORATION
    IRREGULARITY
    MIGRATION
    RANDOMNESS
    URBAN
    NATIONAL
    EXCHANGE
    FOREIGN

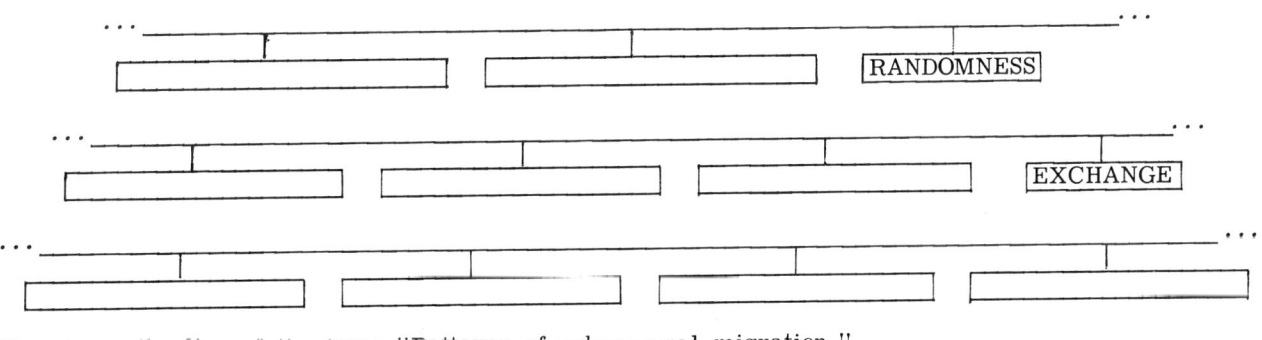

```
 ...┬────────────────┬──────────────┬────────────────...
    □                □                    RANDOMNESS
 ...┬────────┬────────────┬───────────────┬──────────...
    □        □            □                   EXCHANGE
 ...┬─────┬───────┬──────┬──────┬──────...
    □     □       □      □      □
```

Now trace the line of the topic "Patterns of urban-rural migration."

The most specific (lowest-level) term(s) in the topic is (are) _____.

   If you're a sucker for punishment and you want another exercise of the same kind, go to frame B 3.2.   That's enough? Go to frame B 4.

EXERCISE FRAME B 3.2

Arrange these terms on the tree:

    SETTING   ST. JOAN   LINCOLN
    LIBRETTO   NOVELLA   VIDEOSCRIPT
    SONNET   VOICE   ELIZABETH I
    FREUD   CHARACTER   GALILEO
    PLOT   PLAY   POINT OF VIEW

Now trace the line of the topic "St. Joan as a character in plays."

The most specific term, in the context of the topic, is _____.

No More? Go to frame B 4. What? More? Go to frame B 3.3.

EXERCISE FRAME B 3.3

Now, without the lines and blocks but with the same idea of levels, arrange these terms on four increasingly specific levels. You will not necessarily have an equal number of terms on each level.

    SIMPLE   IDENTITY
    ANONYMITY   CHAOTIC
    DISCOVERY   WORLD
    COMPLEX   UNIFORM
    REFUSAL   SEARCH

Now trace the line of the topic "The search for identity in a complex world."

The most specific term with which to enter the card catalog is _____.

Go to frame B 4.

EXERCISE FRAME B 4

So far, you have found in each topic <u>one specific</u> term that might serve as a subject heading:
    "Reviews of books of <u>fiction</u>"
    "The social aspects of <u>art</u>"
    "Ancient lives of <u>Vergil</u>"

But not every kind of information can be classified under one-word terms. Often it will take a phrase--such as an adjective plus a noun--to do the job with discrimination:

Possible "Subject Headings"

Topic: "The rise of the detective story"

As a possible subject heading, the phrase "detective story" is a better bet than the one word "story" because "detective story" is more

? { a) prominent.
   b) specific.
   c) inclusive.

As a possible subject heading, the phrase "detective story" is preferable to the one word "detective" because

? { d) "detective" will have to change to "detectives."
   e) "detective story" is more explicit.
   f) "detective story" is the name of the thing that the topic is about.

For an exercise in isolating adjective-plus-noun phrases as possible subject headings, go to frame B 4.1. For straight-line progress, go to frame B 5.

EXERCISE B 4.1

How can you tell how to handle a phrase of adjective + noun (like "perpetual calendars" or "Christian persecutions of pagans")? Will they be treated as one term, like "collective bargaining"? Or will they be treated as a basic term (the noun) with a specifying qualifier (the adjective), like "psychological normality"?

↑   ↑
SPECIFIER   BASE

It will matter to you when you start looking in the card catalog. For instance, shall you look in the B's for "BARGAINING, COLLECTIVE" or in the C's for "COLLECTIVE BARGAINING"? The guidelines are not very clear, and the reasons for treating certain terms in certain ways are complicated--and not always sensible. Here are some samples of actual Library of Congress subject headings:

Two-word "names":
   APPLE JUICE (not JUICE, APPLE)
   ARTIFICIAL SATELLITES (not SATELLITES, ARTIFICIAL)
   AUTOMATIC PILOT (not PILOTS, AUTOMATIC)
   BALD EAGLE (not EAGLES, BALD)
   BASKET MAKING (not MAKING OF BASKETS)

Inverted terms or terms transformed into phrases:

   LIGHTING, ARCHITECTURAL ... (not ARCHITECTURAL LIGHTING)
   ART, AFRICAN (not AFRICAN ART)
   COMMISSIONS OF INQUIRY, INTERNATIONAL (not INTERNATIONAL COMMISSIONS OF INQUIRY)

One way to approach the problem is to try thinking of the phrase as a name (like "Center Hall"). If it seems like one, treat the phrase as one term.

Here is an exercise in "seeming":

Topic: "The nature of the social encyclicals"

"Social encyclicals" seems like
? { a) a noun ("encyclicals") qualified for the present topic by the specifying term "social."
   b) a two-word term or name, like "Vatican Council."

Topic: "The efficiency of open market operations"

"Open market operations" seems like
? { c) a noun ("operations") qualified by the two-word term "open-market."
   d) a three-word term or name, like "Thirty Years War."

Frame B 4.1

Topic: "Regulation of chromosome functions"

"Chromosome functions" seems like

? { e) a noun ("function") qualified for the present by the more specific term "chromosome."
   f) a two-word term or name, like "slime molds."

Topic: "The commercial use of whale oil, 1840-1850"

"Whale oil" seems like

? { g) a noun ("term") qualified for the present by the specifying term "whale."
   h) a two-word term or name, like "beech tree."

Go on to frame B 4.2.

EXERCISE FRAME B 4.2

Having interpreted the words of the topics as you did in frame B 4.1, now underline the most specific term--one word or more than one word--within each topic ... the best bet as a possible subject heading:

1. "The nature of the social encyclicals"

2. "The efficiency of open market operations"

3. "Regulation of chromosome functions"

4. "The commercial use of whale oil, 1840-1850"

To practice locating the terms in the catalog, go to frame B 4.3. For straight-line progress, go to frame B 5.

EXERCISE FRAME B 4.3

If ENCYCLICALS (in "social encyclicals") is a subject heading, you may find it in the file drawer labeled, for example,

   a) SOCI--SOCIAL INTEL
   b) EMPL--END

If OPEN MARKET OPERATIONS is a subject heading, you may find it in the file drawer labeled

   c) OO--OQ for "OPEN"
   d) MARI--MARO
   e) OO--OQ for "OPERATIONS"

The heading CHROMOSOMES (in "chromosome function")? The drawer labeled

   f) CHRISTIANITY, E.--CHURCH
   g) FRU--FUNC

The heading WHALE OIL? The drawer labeled

   h) WESTA--WHA
   i) OF--OK

Go to frame B 5.

Possible "Subject Headings"

EXERCISE FRAME B 5

We said in frame B 4 that sometimes a term to use as a possible subject heading comes in a phrase of more than one word: "detective stories," "whale oil," "Middle English"...

Topic: "The arts in society"

As a possible subject heading, the most specific terminology that does justice to the topic is

? {
  a) The arts.
  b) Art.
  c) Society.
  d) The arts in society.
  e) Social art.
}

For a further exercise in deciding between a single term and a phrase, go to frame B 5.1. For straight-line progress, go to Section C.

EXERCISE FRAME B 5.1

This exercise presents more practice in choosing between a single term and a phrase as a likely subject heading.

Topic: "Separation of church and state"

As a possible subject heading, the most specific terminology is

? {
  a) Church.
  b) State.
  c) Church and state.
  d) Separation.
  e) Separation of church and state.
}

Topic: "Books written by lawyers"

As a possible subject heading, the most specific terminology is

? {
  f) Books.
  g) Lawyers.
  h) Lawyers as authors.
  i) Books about the law.
}

Topic: "Criteria for measuring distances"

As a possible subject heading, the most specific terminology is

? {
  j) Mensuration.
  k) Standards.
  l) Standards of length.
  m) Distances.
  n) Distances--Measurement.
}

You are now ready for Section C. You may want to take the Pre-Test of Section B now as a post-test. Below you will find a summary of this section.

SUMMARY OF SECTION B

If one's topic is expressed in one word (e.g., "Romanticism"), one has no problem with specificity: that word is the one to use in starting a search through the card catalog or a bibliography or an index.

If one's topic is expressed in more than one word (e.g., "Conceptions of physical causality," "Staging Wagner's Ring of the Nibelung"), one may need to choose one of the words as the specific term by which to enter the catalog or the bibliography or the index.

To decide which word is the most specific, one can arrange the words by their scope. Scope means how much of the world a word seems to cover. If one term seems to be included in another, then it is more specific than the other. For example, in "The Battle of Stalingrad," the term "Stalingrad" is more specific than the term "battle"; there are many instances of battles, there is only one Stalingrad.

Not all terms can be expressed by one word in English; sometimes it takes a phrase (often an adjective plus a noun): Gothic novel, school reorganization, council-manager government, quarter horses. Phrases present a problem when one tries to enter a card catalog, for instance. Shall one go in under the first word or under a subsequent word in the phrase? A rule of thumb is to try thinking of the phrase as the name of something; if it seems like a name, go into the catalog under the first word in the phrase. For "Gothic novel," go in under "Gothic" rather than under "novel."

SECTION C

HOW TO USE SUBJECT HEADINGS

INTRODUCTION

To find out whether you already know how to do what this section is about, do the short test below.

To do this section you will need to use an actual card catalog in a library, along with the following books:

United States. Library of Congress Subject Cataloguing Division. <u>Library of Congress subject headings</u>, 8th ed., Library of Congress, 2 vols., 1975.

[OR: Quattlebaum, Marguerite, ed., <u>Subject headings used in the dictionary catalogs of the Library of Congress</u>, 7th ed., 1966.]

<u>Readers' guide to periodical literature</u>.

<u>Roget's international thesaurus,</u> 3rd ed., Crowell, 1962, or a subsequent edition.

Answers to tests and exercises in Section C begin on page 73.

PRE-TEST

If you can do most of the following items, you already know the contents of Section C.

I. Using only the added subject entries on the catalog cards for the following two books (not their authors and not their titles), get from

```
JN
231
.B8     Butler, David E
            British political facts, 1900–1960, by David Butler and
        Jennie Freeman. London, Macmillan; New York, St Mar-
        tin's Press, 1963.
            xvi, 245 p.  tables.  26 cm.
            "Bibliographical note": p. 239–240. Bibliographical footnotes.


            1. Gt. Brit.—Pol. & govt.—20th cent.—Handbooks, manuals, etc.
        I. Freeman, Jennie, joint author.  II. Title.

        JN231.B8              354.42              62-20260
```

to

```
JN
401
.L6
```
Loewenstein, Karl, 1891-
British Cabinet government.   New York, Oxford University Press, 1967.
xv, 207 p.   21 cm.
Bibliography: p. 195-197.

1. Great Britain—Politics and government.   2. Cabinet system—Great Britain.   I. Title.
JN401.L6   320.9'42   67-25462
                                                          MARC
Library of Congress

List the chain of headings that you follow and the authors and titles of the books on whose cards you find the added subject entries.

II.   A.   Fill in the blanks in each entry according to the workings of the system of references (*sa*, *x*, *xx*, *see*) in LC Subject Headings.

Materialism   *(Metaphysics, BD331;*
  Philosophic systems: general, B825;
  by country, B851-4695)
  sa Dualism
      Idealism
      Lokāyata
  ⟶
      Monism
      Naturalism
      Realism
  xx Animism
      Dualism
      Idealism
  ⟶
      Monism
      Philosophy
      Positivism
      Realism

Mechanism (Philosophy)
  sa Materialism
      Naturalism
      Vitalism
  ⟶ *x*
      Philosophy, Mechanistic
  xx Biology—Philosophy
      Life (Biology)
  ⟶
      Naturalism
      Philosophy
      Science—Philosophy
      Vitalism
  Mechanisms, Interchangeable
      See Interchangeable mechanisms
  Mechanisms of defense
      See Defense mechanisms (Psychology)
  Mechanistic philosophy
      See Mechanism (Philosophy)

B.   According to the entries in II (A) above, the heading for La Mettrie, Julien Offray de, L'homme machine: a study in the origins of an idea, could be ["Philosophy, Mechanistic" or "Mechanism (Philosophy)"?].

III.   Using only subject entries in Readers' Guide to Periodical Literature, vol. 35 (not authors or titles), get from "Films" to "Two new films for super 8: a step forward?..." by L. Drukker in Popular Photography 76:68-9 Je '75.

IV.   Using LC Subject Headings, come as close as you can to a heading for the topic, "Infantry weapons in the Union Army during the Civil War." Start with "Weapons" and list the stages of your search.

Using Subject Headings

If you choose not to do the exercises on the following pages, you will find a summary of Section C on page 40.

EXERCISE FRAME C 1

Let's practice with a set topic first. Then you can try using your own after you complete this section of the program.

Topic: "Rights of defendants under American and British law"

Within the context of the topic, the most specific term on which to try to enter the catalog is
- a) Rights.
- b) Defendants [in legal proceedings].
- c) American (OR British).
- d) American law (OR British law).
- e) Law.

Go to frame C 1.1.

EXERCISE FRAME C 1.1

Now take that term to the catalog, use it as a subject heading, and try to get to publications that pertain to your topic: "Rights of defendants under American and British law."

What do you find? Is there ...
- f) a subject heading DEFENDANTS.
- ? g) a title that starts Defendants..., but not a subject heading.
- h) a subject heading DEFENDERS, but not DEFENDANTS.
- i) a title that starts Defenders..., but not even a subject heading.

EXERCISE FRAME C 2

If you flipped through several cards in the neighborhood of "Defend..." you were smart. Sometimes that way enables you to pick up hints to possible subject headings, or you realize that you've been making a mistake in the alphabet--or that the filing in the drawer is faulty. (Well, nobody's perfect.)

As a subject heading, "defendant" has taken us to a dead end. Where now?

One of three places:
1) another term in your topic,
2) a list of subject headings,
3) a synonym for "defendants" that you can think of right off the bat or that you can locate in a dictionary of synonyms or a thesaurus.

Topic: "Rights of defendants under American and British law"

If you want to try another term in your topic, go to frame C 3.

If you want to try a list of subject headings, go to frame C 4.

If you want to try a synonym, go to frame C 6.

EXERCISE FRAME C 3

Since "defendant" was no good, let's try the next most specific term in the topic: "Rights of defendants under American and British law." Let's by-pass "rights"; that term is perhaps less broad than the term "law" but it is conditional. It is conditioned by its context: the rights of man? the

rights of fishermen? the rights of whom doing what? Let's concentrate instead on "law" and on "American and British."

Here is a good place to notice the importance of geography in the catalog. Many a subject heading will get subdivided according to place, and many a place will get subdivided into its aspects. The question is, shall you head first for the place ("U.S." or "Great Britain") or for some other heading subdivided by place ("Law--U.S." or "Law--Gt. Brit.")?

The answer is not easy. It depends on what you have in your focus, what matters more to you. In the case of our topic, "law" seems to loom larger than "American and British." Let's try "law" as a subject heading. That is a subject important enough that your chances of finding it as a subject heading are good.

[If you came back to this frame from frame C 5, go on now to frame C 5.1. If you came back to this frame from frame C 6.4, go back now to its last paragraph.]

In the drawer in the card catalog that includes "LAW," the first card on which the spelling "l-a-w" occurs is
? a) a subject card.
   b) a title card.
   c) an author card.

Go on to frame C 3.1.

EXERCISE FRAME C 3.1

The cards headed LAW are for books that sound like very general treatises on the law. We need to get more specific. Let's do it by adding the geographical subdivision: LAW--U.S.

Try this card, for instance (for a book that your library may or may not have):

```
KF           LAW--UNITED STATES
8700
 .S5      Sigler, Jay A
              An introduction to the legal system [by] Jay A. Sigler.
           Homewood, Ill., Dorsey Press, 1968.
              viii, 248 p. 24 cm. (The Dorsey series in political science)
              Bibliographical footnotes.



              1. Justice, Administration of—United States.  2. Jurisprudence.  3. Law—
           United States.   I. Title.  II. Title: The legal system.
           KF8700.S5                  347.99'73              68-30857
                                                             MARC

           Library of Congress           [71]
```

Read the whole card with care; it has information that will help you get on (and some that will merely get in your way). For instance, you can move from this card to the actual book that it represents--you can go to the shelf where you know you will find "KF 8700.S5"--and perhaps get a lead on your topic. Why would you think it worthwhile to take that trouble? Because on the card you spot

   a) a mention that the book has a bibliography and an index.
   b) the classification "K..." for LAW.
   c) the subject entry, "1. Justice, Administration of--U.S."
   d) "What do all those things on the card stand for?"

Using Subject Headings

Go to frame C 3. 2.

EXERCISE FRAME C 3.2

So, shall you take the trouble to go to the shelf now? What is the alternative? You can go to the shelf on the strength of that one book or you can stay a while longer at the catalog searching for more clues. Save your feet. Stay at the catalog.

Now the problem is to move on from a card like the one for the Sigler book to something else. But in what direction? Among the rest of the cards headed LAW--U.S.? Try that.

From those titles it begins to look as if the subject heading LAW--U.S. labels books about

    a) defendants, specifically.
    b) fairly broad aspects of American law.
    c) federal law exclusively.

Go to frame C 3. 3.

EXERCISE FRAME C 3.3

"LAW--U.S. encompasses fairly broad aspects of American law." That sentence is worth noting until we can get to something better--which means something more specific and still pertinent to our topic. Maybe the other added entries on the subject card for the Sigler book will be what we are looking for.

```
KF           LAW--UNITED STATES
8700
.S5          Sigler, Jay A
                 An introduction to the legal system [by] Jay A. Sigler.
             Homewood, Ill., Dorsey Press, 1968.
                 viii, 248 p.  24 cm.  (The Dorsey series in political science)
                 Bibliographical footnotes.



                 1. Justice, Administration of--United States.  2. Jurisprudence.  3. Law--
             United States.   I. Title.  II. Title: The legal system.
             KF8700.S5                        347.99'13              68-30857
                                                                         MARC

             Library of Congress              [71]
```

The more specific--and pertinent--of numbers 1 and 2 is

    a) JUSTICE, ADMINISTRATION OF--U.S.
    b) JURISPRUDENCE.
    c) "Wait 'till I look up the word 'jurisprudence.'"

Go on to frame C 3. 4.

EXERCISE FRAME C 3.4

So go to the drawer for JUSTICE, ADMINISTRATION OF--U.S. and flip through the cards, watching the added entries for subjects--the Arabic-numeral headings.

Now the subject headings and the topic begin to come together. On the cards you have flipped through, you may have come on such added entries as these:

    COURTS--U. S.
    CRIMINAL PROCEDURE--U. S.
    CRIMINAL LAW--U. S.
    COURTS-MARTIAL AND COURTS OF INQUIRY--U. S.
    TRIAL PRACTICE--U. S.
    JUDGES--U. S.

The one most likely to bear directly on "defendants" in your topic--"Rights of defendants under American and British law"--is CRIMINAL PROCEDURE. To learn how one can know that fact, go to frame C 4, which works with lists of subject headings--the most useful tool at your command.

In flipping through cards to locate your heading, you may already have spotted subject headings with another geographical subdivision relevant to your topic: "--Gt. Brit." It is often a help to do that kind of scanning of the cards in front of and behind the one you are headed for; you may pick up clues to useful headings. The big disadvantage to the technique of search that you have just now practiced--using the added entries--is that your library may not have certain books whose cards bear added entries that would interest you if only you knew they existed. For instance, in your search through JUSTICE, ADMINISTRATION OF--U. S. you turned up useful subject headings but one that you may not have turned up (because no book bore it as an added entry) is CRIMINAL JUSTICE, ADMINISTRATION OF--U. S., which might have been fruitful. The search technique is a good one, still, but not as good as the use of the standard lists of subject headings (frames C 4 ff.).

EXERCISE FRAME C 4

You have got here either 1) because you came to a dead end in the catalog when you tried to get into it on the term "defendant" or 2) because you have acquired a list of subject headings relevant to your topic by scanning the added entries on some subject cards and now you want to know whether there are other useful entries that have not yet shown up, or 3) because you need to see whether a term you have is actually used as a subject heading.

With the cleverest mind in the world you can still hit a snag in this business of finding a useful subject heading for the simple reason that There Are Standards. Not only must you get into the catalog; you must get into it on its terms--you must use a term which is in fact used in the catalog.

In the United States many libraries follow one or the other of two standard lists of terms, either the one we will call LC Subject Headings (Library of Congress subject headings, 8th ed., Library of Congress, 1975) or the one called the Sears List (Barbara M. Westby. Sears list of subject headings, 11th edition, H. W. Wilson, 1977). The first is useful in many college libraries; the second is useful in public libraries that use the Dewey Decimal System of classification.

    [If you have the use of LC Subject Headings, continue working in this frame. If you do
    not, go to frame C 5.]

In LC Subject Headings your problem with "defendant" is going to be solved simply, as it happens, if you will let your eye wander a little. The list is alphabetical; if you look for "defendant," you come on the list on the following page.

From that list, the subject heading or headings useful to you will be (choose one or more):

    a) Defenders, Public.
    b) Defense (Civil procedure).
? c) Defense (Criminal procedure).
    d) Defense (Law).
    e) Defense (Military science).

Go on to frame C 4.1 unless you already know how an entry in LC Subject Headings works--what sa and xx and x do, for instance. In that case, go to C 4.5.1 for a review of those procedures or to C 4.5.3 for a note before you proceed.

Using Subject Headings

Defects in manufactures
    See Manufactures—Defects
Defence (Game) *(GV1469.D3)*
Defender of the bond
    See Defender of the marriage bond
Defender of the marriage bond
    sa Promoters of justice (Canon law)
     x Defender of the bond
   xx Divorce (Canon law)
      Marriage—Annulment (Canon law)
      Marriage (Canon law)
      Matrimonial actions (Canon law)
      Promoters of justice (Canon law)
Defenders, Public
    See Public defenders
Defense, Civil
    See Civil defense
Defense, Perceptual
    See Perceptual defense
Defense (Civil procedure) *(Direct)*
    x Defense (Law)
   xx Actions and defenses
      Civil procedure
      Trial practice
Defense (Courts-martial) *(Direct)*
    x Court martial defenses
   xx Defense (Criminal procedure)
Defense (Criminal procedure) *(Direct)*
    sa Alibi
      Defense (Courts-martial)
      Public defenders
      Right to counsel
    x Criminal defenses
      Defense (Law)
      Defenses, Criminal
   xx Actions and defenses
      Criminal procedure
      Due process of law
Defense (Law)
    See Actions and defenses
      Defense (Civil procedure)
      Defense (Criminal procedure)
Defense (Military science)
    See Attack and defense (Military science)

EXERCISE FRAME C 4.1

Let's look at the lay-out of headings in <u>LC Subject Headings</u> for a while before we narrow the range to a couple of headings that will clearly help you as you work on the topic.

Defense (Criminal procedure) *(Direct)*
    sa Alibi
      Defense (Courts-martial)
      Public defenders
      Right to counsel
    x Criminal defenses
      Defense (Law)
      Defenses, Criminal
   xx Actions and defenses
      Criminal procedure
      Due process of law
Defense (Law)
    See Actions and defenses
      Defense (Civil procedure)
      Defense (Criminal procedure)
Defense (Military science)
    See Attack and defense (Military science)

Actions and defenses *(Direct)*
    sa Actions on the case
      Bills of particulars
      Choses in action
      Citizen suits (Civil procedure)
      Civil procedure

Attack and defense (Military science)
    (UG443-9)
    Here are entered technical military works on siege warfare. Historical works on sieges are entered under the heading Sieges.
    sa Air defenses, Military
      Bombardment

Each element is significant: the typefaces, the indentations, the sa and x and xx and See marks. We will work on each element as we need to know its significance.

You will notice that "Defense (Law)" is marked "See Actions and defenses...," etc., and is in roman type (like this typeface that you are now reading). You also notice that when you follow up the "see" reference--when you actually "see" the headings "Actions and defenses" or "Defense (Civil procedure)" or "Defense (Criminal procedure)"--they are in boldface type. Then you notice that the same observations hold true for "Defense (Military science)"--roman type--and "Attack and defense (Military science)." Those observations lead you to think that the distinction in typeface in the main entries shows the difference between

    a) general ("Defense") and specific ("Attack and defense").
    b) headings used in the catalog (boldface) and headings not used in the catalog (roman).
    c) important and unimportant headings.

Finally, you notice that the distinction between boldface and roman applies to

    d) all words in an entry.
    e) entries "used" and entries "not used."
    f) main entries, at the margin, exclusively
    g) "What's an entry?"

EXERCISE FRAME C 4.2

    Main entries (at the left-hand margin of the column):
        boldface = used in the card catalog
        roman   = not used in the card catalog

Why bother to print main entries that are not going to be used as subject headings? Well, we have been thinking, for instance, that the word "defendants"--in the topic "Rights of defendants in American and British law"--was a legitimate term to try out as we entered the catalog ... and it might have turned out to be. (The only trouble was that it was too specific. If several specific terms--"criminal defenses," "defense (law)," "defenses, criminal"--can be summed up in a covering term that looks much like it--"Defense (Criminal procedure)"--the catalog will use the more general term for the sake of saving space.)

The "not used" main entries in roman type are put in the list of main entries in order to anticipate you, to second-guess you. They are terms that you are likely to think of as you work on a topic. But then, if the main entry in roman type is a not-used term, how can you know what related term is used? There will surely have to be a reference to a used term.

Let's look again at the lay-out of an entry:

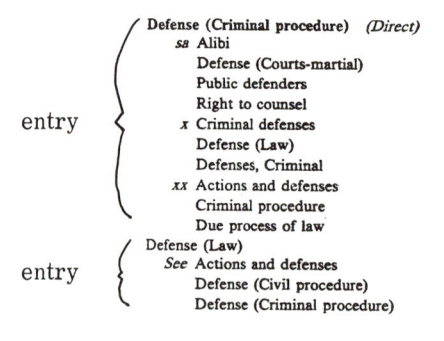

                          Defense (Criminal procedure)   *(Direct)*
                            sa Alibi
                                 Defense (Courts-martial)
                                 Public defenders
                                 Right to counsel
entry   *x* Criminal defenses
                                 Defense (Law)
                                 Defenses, Criminal
                          xx Actions and defenses
                                 Criminal procedure
                                 Due process of law
                        Defense (Law)
                          See Actions and defenses
entry   Defense (Civil procedure)
                               Defense (Criminal procedure)

Using Subject Headings   32

The italicized markers (*sa*, *x*, *xx*, *See*) are cross-reference markers. Each one of them signals a certain operation--a certain way to refer. To keep from cluttering up the entry, a marker is printed only beside the first term it controls; any other terms that are to be marked that same way are then simply listed. For instance, in the example above, s a marks "Public defenders." We understand that s a also applies to "_____."

Now ask yourself again the question, If the main entry in roman type is a not-used term, how can you know what related term is used? The answer is that you can follow the

    a) sa references.
    b) x references.
    c) xx references.
    d) See references.

If and when you refer to "Actions and defenses" as a main entry itself, it will be printed in

    e) boldface.
    f) roman.

Since "Defense (Law)" is a not-used term, the terms "Actions and defenses" and "Defense (Civil procedure)" and "Defense (Criminal procedure)"--the See references underneath it--

    g) are not used, either.
    h) are used.
    i) are not used but will lead you on.

EXERCISE FRAME C 4.3

So the used term is not DEFENDANTS but DEFENSE (CRIMINAL), for instance. Maybe you have looked for cards with that subject heading and the cupboard is bare! There are no books in your library with that heading, perhaps. Will LC Subject Headings serve you now?

    Defense (Criminal procedure)   *(Direct)*   Criminal defenses
       sa Alibi   *See* **Defense (Criminal procedure)**
          Defense (Courts-martial)
          Public defenders
          Right to counsel
      x Criminal defenses
          Defense (Law)   Defenses, Criminal
          Defenses, Criminal   *See* **Defense (Criminal procedure)**
     xx Actions and defenses
          Criminal procedure
          Due process of law
    Defense (Law)
      See Actions and defenses
         Defense (Civil procedure)
         Defense (Criminal procedure)

No sense using the x terms--"Criminal defenses" or "Defense (Law)" or "Defenses (Criminal)." They simply indicate, apparently,

    a) other used terms to which you are referred.
    b) not-used terms from which you are referred to a used term.
    c) not-used terms to which you are referred.

It probably makes sense to use the sa terms. Since they are in boldface as main entries, they represent

d) other _used_ terms related to the heading.
e) the on_ly used_ terms.
f) _not_-used _terms from_ which you are referred to the used term.

→ **Public defenders** *(Direct)* *(United States,*
    JK1548.P8)
  sa Legal aid
  xx Criminal procedure
    Defense (Criminal procedure)
    In forma pauperis
    Justice, Administration of
    Legal aid
    Legal assistance to the poor
    Right to counsel

→ **Right to counsel** *(Direct)*
  sa Public defenders
  x Right of counsel
  xx Civil rights
    Defense (Criminal procedure)
    Due process of law
    Lawyers

EXERCISE FRAME C 4.4

In LC Subject Headings try one of the _sa_ ("See also...") terms under "Defense (Criminal procedure)." If it _is_ a used heading, it will be in [a. boldface or roman?] at the place in the alphabetical list where it occurs as a main entry. (Turn to the place where one of the _sa_ references is listed as a main entry.) It [b. is or is not?] in boldface: it [c. is or is not?] a _used_ subject heading.

Go to frame C 4.5.

EXERCISE FRAME C 4.5

Stay at that _sa_ reference a moment. Consult it as you answer these questions to recapitulate what we have been _doing_.

What do you know so far?

1) Used subject headings are printed in _____.

2) Not-used subject headings, cited as examples of possible terms to second-guess you, are printed in _____.

3) _See_ references send you from a _____ term to a _____ term.

4) _X_ references ("_see_ from") cite the _____ terms from which you are referred to a _____ term.

5) _Sa_ ("_see also_") references send you from one _____ term to a _____ term.

That leaves us with _xx_ references to clarify. You came to the _sa_ reference where you are now working from the _used_ term, "Defense (Criminal procedure)." How is that term marked under the _sa_ reference where you are now?

So now you know that

6) _xx_ references ("_see also from_") cite the _____ terms from which you are referred to another _____.

To practice a little with the references, go to frame C 4.5.1. If you have their mechanism in your head, go to frame C 4.6.

Using Subject Headings

EXERCISE FRAME C 4.5.1

To get the mechanism of references in <u>LC Subject Headings</u> well in mind, work through the following questions.

1. In the excerpt below, the term "Great Northern War, 1700-1721" is [used or not used?] as a subject heading in the catalog.

>   **Great Northern War, 1700-1721**
>   *See* Northern War, 1700-1721
>   **Great Plains**
>   *x* Plains, The Great
>   *xx* Northwest, Canadian
>   The West
>   **Great powers**
>   *sa* Concert of Europe
>   Equality of states
>   States, Small
>   *xx* Balance of power
>   Equality of states
>   International law
>   International relations
>   States, Small
>   World politics

2. "Great Plains" and "Great powers" are [used or not used?].

3. You [will or will not?] find the <u>x</u> reference "Plains, The Great" in the book's alphabetical list of main entries. It is a [used or not used?] term in the card catalog.

4. You [will or will not?] find the <u>xx</u> reference "The West" in the book's list of main entries. It is a [used or not used?] term in the catalog.

5. The <u>sa</u> reference "Concert of Europe" is a [used or not used?] term. It will appear in [boldface or roman?] type.

6. The <u>xx</u> reference, "World politics," will be followed, at its place in the book's list of main entries, by "Great powers," which will be marked [<u>x</u>, <u>xx</u>, <u>sa</u> or <u>See</u>?].

7. At the proper alphabetical place for the <u>x</u> reference, "Plains, The Great," it will be followed by "Great Plains," which will be marked [<u>x</u>, <u>xx</u>, <u>sa</u> or <u>See</u>?].

Go to frame C 4.5.2 for another review exercise in using <u>LC Subject Headings</u> entries, or to C 4.5.3 for a quick note before you proceed.

World organization
  See International organization
World politics *(19th century, D363, D397; 20th century, D440-472; European War, D511, D523, D610-619)*
  Here are entered historical accounts of international intercourse. Theoretical works are entered under International relations. Works dealing with foreign relations from the point of view of an individual state are entered under the name of the state with subdivision Foreign relations, *e.g.* United States—Foreign relations; United States—Foreign relations—Japan.
  Afro-Asian politics
  Christianity and international affairs
  Eastern question
  Geography, Political
  Geopolitics
  Great powers
  International organization
  Peaceful change (International relations)
  Propaganda, International

EXERCISE FRAME C 4.5.2

Just for practice, try this exercise.

1. In the excerpt at the right, the term used as a subject heading in the catalog is ["Encephalitides" or "Encephalitis"?].

2. At its alphabetical place in the main listing (p. 221), the term "Brain--Inflammation" will be followed by _____.

3. At the alphabetical place in the main listing (p. 221) for "Brain--Diseases" the term "Encephalitis" will be marked [sa, x or xx?].

4. Add the proper markings to the entries under "Elementary education of adults" according to the excerpts below.

Reading (Adult education) (LC5225.R4)
   xx Adult education
      Elementary education of adults

Adult elementary education
   See Elementary education of adults

Elementary adult education
   See Elementary education of adults
Elementary education
   See Education, Elementary
Elementary education for adults
   See Elementary education of adults

Adult education (Direct) (LC5201-6660)
   sa Ability, Influence of age on
      Adult education and state
      Bachelor of liberal studies
      Catholic Church--Adult education
      Continuing education centers
      Education of the aged
      Elementary education of adults
      Folk high schools

Education, Elementary (Direct) (LB1555-1601)
   sa Eighth grade (Education)
      Elementary education of adults
      Elementary school teaching
      Elementary schools
      Fifth grade (Education)
      Global method of teaching
      Radio in elementary education
      School supervision, Elementary
      Seventh grade (Education)
      Sixth grade (Education)
      Television in elementary education
   x Elementary education
   xx Education of children

Illiteracy (Indirect) (LC149-160)
   sa Education and crime
      Elementary education of adults
      Libraries and new literates
      Mental tests for illiterates
      New literates, Writing for
      Right to Read program
   x Literacy
   xx Education
      Education and crime
   -- Juvenile literature

Encaustic painting (ND2480)
   x Wax-painting
   xx Mural painting and decoration
      Painting
      Painting, Ancient
Encephalitides
   See Encephalitis
Encephalitis
   sa Encephalomyelitis
   x Brain--Inflammation
      Encephalitides
   xx Brain--Diseases
Encephalitis, Epidemic
   sa Encephalitis, Tick-borne
      Equine encephalomyelitis
      Japanese encephalitis

Elema (Papuan people) (DU740)
   sa Toaripi (Papuan people)
   xx Papuans
   -- Religion
Elementary adult education
   See Elementary education of adults
Elementary education
   See Education, Elementary
Elementary education for adults
   See Elementary education of adults
Elementary education of adults
      Reading (Adult education)
      Adult elementary education
      Elementary adult education
      Elementary education for adults
      Adult education
      Education, Elementary
      Illiteracy
Elementary particles (Physics)
   See Particles (Nuclear physics)
Elementary school . . .

Using Subject Headings

EXERCISE FRAME C 4.5.3

For the sake of seeing how useful it can be to scan items in the neighborhood of the item you are looking for, try looking in LC Subject Headings for the term "Rights of defendants." Any luck? Let your eye wander up from "Rights, Civil, See Civil rights." You quickly come to "Right to speedy trial, See Speedy trial" and then to "Right to counsel," a used term with references-to (sa) and references-from (x, xx) that lead you immediately to "Defense (Criminal procedure)," for instance.

Quick scanning of the vicinity, like quick flipping through the cards around a sought-for card in the catalog, often pays off.

Go to frame C 5.

EXERCISE FRAME C 5

Now you have seen the network of LC Subject Headings and how to work its switches. But it is only 2,026 pages of terms! For what it omits, read p. viii, "Headings Omitted," then continue in this frame. You noticed there (on p. viii) that the entries "Lincoln," "Napoleon," "Shakespeare," "Richard Wagner," and "Washington" are used as types. You will work with an example from "Shakespeare" in Section E of this workbook.

Since LC Subject Headings is far from exhaustive and since its compilers will not have second-guessed you at every point, you may need to use your wits and other instruments when you reach a dead end in the catalog.

For "wits and other instruments," go to frame C 6. (If you have already practiced working with headings in the Readers' Guide, go to frame C 6.5.) We'll ask you to pretend for a while that you do not know that "Defense (Criminal procedure)" exists as a subject heading.

(If you came to section C 4 from section C 6--on using the thesaurus--return to frame C 6.7, "Try one of the terms....")

EXERCISE FRAME C 6

Helpful as the added entries on the catalog cards and helpful as the books like LC Subject Headings and the Sears List may be, you may still come to a halt. Then you must use either the dictionary-thesaurus-encyclopedia that you carry around with you in your head or else consult other arrangements of subjects.

What are you trying to do in this searching? You are trying to bridge a gap between (a) a term in your topic but not in the card catalog and (b) a heading used in the catalog. You can use two strategies: 1) find a term related to yours and on the same level of specificity (a synonym or an antonym or an analogous term) or 2) find a subject to which your subject is related and pick a term related to that subject.

Let's demonstrate the first strategy, using the Readers' Guide to Periodical Literature and a thesaurus.

Take "defendants" from your topic, "Rights of defendants under American and British law," to the Readers' Guide. Pick a volume from a period of years appropriate to your topic--if you can tell; if you can't, pick a recent volume at random. For the sake of this demonstration, pick volume 24--it's fairly recent. If "defendants" is to appear in it, it will come on p. 577,

    a) after the entries for "Defense."
    b) between "Defenders of American liberties" and "Defense, Civil."
    c) between "Defelice, J. and others" and "Defenders, Public."
    d) "Where's the Readers' Guide"?

EXERCISE FRAME C 6.1

No "Defendants." Glance ahead of "Defelice, J. ..." to see if you can pick up a clue.

No clue. Will "Defense" help? From the run of entries here, "Defense" seems to apply predominantly to

    a) military aspects.
    b) legal aspects.
    c) sports.

One term may help:

    d) "Defenders, Public. See Public defenders."
    e) "Defense, Civil. See Civil defense."
    f) "Defense, Self. See Self defense."

EXERCISE FRAME C 6.2

"Public defenders" comes

    a) after "Public debts. See Debts, public."
    b) after "Puberty" and before "Public address systems..."
    c) after "Public officers."

There are no see also references, only a list of titles of articles. Perhaps a word in a title will help. Maybe the word

?   d) "defenders" in "Dearth of defenders."
    e) "justice" in "Justice for the poor; the banner of Gideon."
    f) "defense" in "Rising to the defense."

EXERCISE FRAME C 6.3

The first entry spelled j-u-s-t-i-c-e is

    a) the legal term.
    b) a name.

At the legal term there are no see also references and the titles of articles sound

?   c) too specific for your topic.
    d) useful.
    e) too general for your topic.

    Scan the headings in the neighborhood--scanning is often useful for picking up clues. Here come "Justice, Administration of" and some see also references worth jotting down as possible subject headings: "Criminal law," "Criminal procedure," "Due process of law." Indeed, at the entry "Due process of law" you'll find a see also reference to "Right to counsel," which is specifically related to your topic.

Go on to frame C 6.4.

EXERCISE FRAME C 6.4

    That was a neat demonstration. But what if we choose a different volume of the Readers' Guide? We are interested in it just now not because we want references to magazine articles but because it will suggest subject headings for us to try out in the card catalog. And if none of the

Using Subject Headings

periodicals indexed in Readers' Guide have published an article on our topic or other topics related to it, there will be no call for the Readers' Guide to list the headings.

Try volume 27, for instance, to see if we can make it work like volume 24. Hunt for "Defendants."

No soap. So you go to another term in your topic. (Go back to frame C 3 if you haven't already been there. If you have, keep going here.)

The topic is still "Rights of defendants under British and American law." At your new term you will find several likely branches, especially if you will remember to check the geographical subdivisions. And so it goes in the Readers' Guide. You will still have to see whether the new possible subject headings are actually used in the card catalog. If you know how to do that, go on to frame C 6.5. If you're not sure, go to frame C 4 (Library of Congress Subject Headings).

EXERCISE FRAME C 6.5

When all else fails, try that other collection of nomenclature (list of "names" for things), the thesaurus--a "treasury" of terms. It may put you on the track of ideas (and consequently of terms) that are related to the one you started with.

For this demonstration we will use Roget's International Thesaurus, 3rd edition, Crowell, 1962.* It has two major sections, an arrangement by categories of ideas (numbered) and an alphabetical dictionary of words with references to the numbered categories. In the dictionary section turn to "defendant." It is on page _____. The reference number beside it is number _____.

Now scan the vicinity. You may pick up clues to other terms worth checking--such as "defense, defence, legal plea, 1002.6" in this case.

Go to frame C 6.6.

EXERCISE FRAME C 6.6

In the section of numbered categories turn to 1003.6. It is on page _____.

> 6. accused, defendant, respondent, correspondent, libelee, suspect, prisoner.

Not much help. But subject headings in a card catalog are often names of abstractions. It will be worth checking a little further. You notice that category 1003 is divided into 15 sections and that those 15 are grouped in three bigger sections labeled _____, _____, and _____.

Names of abstractions are nouns. Scan the other terms under NOUNS.

Boldface type signifies that the term is listed in the dictionary section of the thesaurus. Many of the boldface terms have a legal aspect; they seem

? a) more general than "defendant" or "rights of defendants."
   b) more specific than "defendant" or "rights of defendants."
   c) of no particular significance to "defendants."

---
*Ref.
PE
1591
.M37
1962

Frame C 6.7

Go on to frame C 6.7.

EXERCISE FRAME C 6.7

But will terms like <u>accusation</u>, <u>charge</u>, <u>arraignment</u>, <u>indictment</u>, <u>incrimination</u> serve you? You'll have to check. Where? Well, the catalog itself if you want to waste time, or one of the lists of subject headings if you want to save time.

If you know how to use the lists, stay in this frame. If you do not, go to frame C 4 for <u>LC Subject Headings</u>.

Try one of the terms above (in the first line) to see whether you can eventually get to the heading "Defense (Criminal procedure)." Or run our maze here, starting from the word <u>accusation</u>:

> Accusation
> *See* Charges and specifications
>   (Courts-martial)
>   Indictments
>   Informations
>   ?

Go to frame C 6.7.1

EXERCISE FRAME C 6.7.1

"Police charges" will be located like which arrangement here?

      A?   OR   B?

A?	B?
Police	Police
→ Police charges	Police, Air Line
Police Clubs	→ Police, State
Police, Air line	Police charges
Police, State	Police Clubs

Complete the following:

> **Police charges** *(Direct)*
>   *x* Accusation
>   Charges, Police
>   *xx* Criminal investigation
>   ?

The <u>xx</u> signifies that the terms so marked will be [used or not-used?] and that a reference is being made

    a) <u>from</u> them <u>to</u> "Police charges"--a path which you retrace.
    b) <u>to</u> them <u>from</u> "Police charges"--a path which you trace.

Go to frame C 6.7.2.

Using Subject Headings							40

EXERCISE FRAME C 6.7.2

"Criminal procedure (Direct)" will be located like which arrangement here?

A?　　　　　　　　　　　OR　　　　　　　　　　　B?

    Criminal omission　　　　　　　　　　　　　　　 Criminal omission
      See Omission, Criminal　　　　　　　　　　　 See Omission, Criminal
→ Criminal procedure (Direct)　　　　　　　　　　 Criminal procedure (Canon law)
    Criminal procedure (Canon law)　　　　　　　→ Criminal procedure (Direct)

Fill in the blank between "Default" and "Double jeopardy":

    Criminal procedure *(Direct)*
      sa Acquittals
        Alternative convictions
        Amparo (Writ)
        Appellate procedure
        Arrest
        Bail
        Complaints (Criminal procedure)
        Confession (Law)
        Contumacy
        Correctional law
        Courts-martial and courts of inquiry
        Criminal courts
        Criminal jurisdiction
        Criminal law
        Criminal registers
        Default (Law)

        Double jeopardy
        Evidence, Circumstantial
        Evidence, Criminal
        Executions and executioners
        Extradition
        Flagrans crimen
        Fugitives from justice
        Grand jury
        Habeas corpus
        Indeterminate sentence
        Indictments

For some exercises on specificity of heading, go to Section D.

SUMMARY OF SECTION C

    When you have chosen the most specific term in your topic and try to enter the card catalog or an index like Readers' Guide, you need to know whether the term is actually used as a subject heading and, if it is, whether there are related terms that will lead you to helpful books.

    The standard subject headings used by the Library of Congress and consequently by many a research library are listed in Library of Congress Subject Headings (8th edition, 1975). That book also lists many terms that a layman might think to use but that are not "standard" subject headings. It adds a system of cross-references, to make the book into a network rather than a mere alphabetical list:

A "used" ("standard") subject heading is printed in boldface in the main alphabetical list. Under a boldface heading the following symbols may appear:

  sa ("see also") precedes a list of other used terms that are directly related to the boldface term. (At their alphabetical places they, too, will be in boldface.)

  xx ("see also from...") precedes a list of other used terms under which, at their alphabetical places, there will be an sa reference back to the present boldface term.

   x ("see from...") precedes a list of terms not used as subject headings; terms which--at their alphabetical places--will refer to the present boldface term: "See ____." Such terms will be printed in ordinary type.

A term not in boldface is not a used subject heading. One is referred from it to a term that is used, by means of the phrase, "see ____." (For the reverse direction--from the used heading to the not-used, the sign is x.)

One may, of course, find a subject heading in LC Subject Headings but not find a book in the library under that heading. In that case one needs related terms that may let him into the catalog. LC Subject Headings may supply them through its system of cross-references; so may a similar guide like Readers' Guide or Humanities Index or Social Sciences Index, or a thesaurus like Roget's.

SECTION D

SPECIFICITY

INTRODUCTION

What do you do when you come to a dead end with a term that is too specific for your library's card catalog? To find out whether you already know how to do what this section is about, do the short test below. To do this section you will need a copy of <u>LC Subject Headings</u> and at one or two points you may want to go to an actual card catalog in a library.

Answers to tests and exercises in Section D begin on page 80. WORD OF WARNING: In this section all the choices will be marked ? {, and you will be tracing out the consequences of whatever choices you make. You may find yourself running around from frame to frame; be patient with yourself, there's a pay-off at the end.

PRE-TEST

If you can do the following item, you already know the contents of Section D.

Using <u>LC Subject Headings</u>, the card catalog, and a dictionary, move from the topic, "The popularity of penny dreadfuls" to this quotation about them in a certain book and identify the book:

> At the bottom of the scale remained the hardy penny leaflets, usually running to thirty-two pages and inclosed in a garish wrapper. Some of these leaflets were penny bloods, pure and simple; but in response to a renewed clamor in the press against cheap thrillers, some firms made a brave show of promoting more wholesome literature for the masses....

_____, page _____.
AUTHOR & TITLE

If you choose not to do the following exercise, you will find that pages 45 and 46 summarize Section D.

EXERCISE FRAME D 1

Starting as early as frame B 1, and here and there in later frames, we have worked with the notion of specificity. The rule has been to start with the most specific term in the topic. But there are physical limits to how specific the subject headings in a card catalog can be. The catalog has only so many drawers; the library has only so many books. There is also a conceptual limit. The library has decided to buy only so much information on only so many topics.

As you use a certain library, you come to know its characteristics--what to expect and what not to expect. A project for which a small college library may have three or four cards may occupy a whole drawer at the Library of Congress.

When you come to a dead end, either in the catalog or in one of the lists of subject headings because the term that you are trying is too specific, one trick is to put that term in a category larger than itself and then try using the name of the category as a lead-in to the lists of headings. (Another trick is to check for titles beginning with your term, in the hope that the added entries on the title card will put you on the track. But beware of ambiguous titles.)

For example, "Confrontation," in its political sense, is not a used heading in the catalog, so think of politics and try "Political action" or "Political"-something-or-other and scan the headings to

see if you can get a clue. Perhaps "Political behavior, See Political psychology" or "Political psychology, xx Political science" or "Political science, sa Pressure groups."

For an exercise in threading your way from the too-specific to a particular work, try this problem: To get from the term "ambiguity" to a particular book on ambiguity in literature whose author and title you do not yet know.

"Ambiguity" is not a used term in the catalog. A thinkable category to leap to might be

? { a) Literary problems.
    b) Literature.
    c) Meaning.

EXERCISE FRAME D 2

"Literary problems" [from frame D 1]

When I scan LC Subject Headings in the neighborhood of "Literary...," I gather that "Literary problems" must be too general a heading. The closest term I can find is "Literary style, See Style, Literary" and even that is not quite it. But if I keep scanning, I come to "Literature." The "scope note" under it--"Here are entered..."--makes it sound too broad, but the wealth of sa references looks promising.

"Literature" [from frame D 1
or D 2.2.2]

When I scan the sa references and the also phrases--"Agnosticism in literature" and similar phrases--and the xx ("see also" from) references--like "Language and languages"--that heading of "Style, Literary" doesn't sound bad, after all. In any case, I am most likely to pick out one of these sa or xx references:

? { a) "Creation (Literary, artistic, etc.)."
    b) "Style, Literary."
    c) "Language and languages."

EXERCISE FRAME D 2.1

You've come here from frame D 2 because you think the sa references under "Style, Literary" may lead you closer to a book about ambiguity in literature--or from frame D 2.3 in order to get out of a closed circle. Of the sa references under "Style, Literary" one of the most promising (in your judgment) is

? { a) "Diction."
    b) "Literature--Aesthetics."
    c) "Rhetoric."

EXERCISE FRAME D 2.1.1

You came here from D 2.1 or D 2.4 because "Diction" may get you close to a book about ambiguity in literature. Under "Diction" the most promising sa or xx reference (in your judgment) is

? { a) "Vocabulary."
    b) "Rhetoric."

EXERCISE FRAME D 2.1.2

You came here from frame D 2.1.1 because "Vocabulary" may get you close to "ambiguity in

Specificity

literature." Under "Vocabulary" the sa and the xx references make you think that you're on a track toward

?(a) technical aspects of vocabulary that relate to "ambiguity."
 (b) technical aspects of vocabulary that move off to who knows where.

Go back to any junction you please and follow a different path (using the frame numbers).

EXERCISE FRAME D 2.2

You've come here from frame D 2 because you think the sa references under "Language and languages" may lead you closer to a book about ambiguity in literature. On page 1007 the "scope note" under the heading--"Here are entered..."--and the sa references make you want to check first

?(a) the list of sa references.
 (b) under "Languages--Philosophy" and "Languages--Psychology."

EXERCISE FRAME D 2.2.1

Of the sa references under "Language and languages," the most useful for your topic--"ambiguity in literature"--is probably

 (a) "Communication."
?(b) "Rhetoric."
 (c) "Semantics."

EXERCISE FRAME D 2.2.2

Well, "Semantics" is tempting but not satisfying. It is only half the point, the "meaning" half but not the "literature" part. What we want is a term that will blend "ambiguity of meaning" with "literature," and we're not getting it.

The point is that we're trying on the one hand to be too specific for the catalog--there's no heading "Ambiguity" or "Ambiguity in literature"--and on the other hand we can't find a term to substitute for "ambiguity in literature." We'll have to be less specific and rise to a higher level of generalization. It might make sense to rise as high as

 (a) "Art."
?(b) "Literature."
 (c) "Poetry."

EXERCISE FRAME D 2.3

You have come here from frame D 2.1 because "Literature--Aesthetics" may get you closer to a book about "ambiguity in literature." Check the sa references under the heading. We're in a closed loop:

$$\begin{pmatrix} \nearrow \text{"Style, Literary"} \\ \text{"Literature--Aesthetics"} \swarrow \end{pmatrix}$$

The reasonable thing to do, then, is

 (a) try the heading in the catalog.
?(b) go to PN45 on the shelf and check the books.
 (c) back-track to frame D 2.1 and try another choice.

EXERCISE FRAME D 2.4

You came here from frame D 2.1.1 or D 2.2.1 because "Rhetoric" may get you closer to "ambiguity in literature." The sa references make me think that my understanding of "ambiguity" needs to be less ambiguous. Is it, for instance, a figure of speech? Perhaps you should check a large dictionary first; try Webster's Third New International Dictionary..., for instance.

A likely path to follow, then, is

? (a) the sa reference, "Diction."
   (b) the one back to frame D 1, choice (c), "Meaning."
   (c) the one back to "Literature" where there was an sa reference to "Poetry."
   (d) the author cited, William Empson.

EXERCISE FRAME D 2.5

On the strength of that clue in the Webster's Third definition of "ambiguity" and the fact that under "Literature" in LC Subject Headings there is an sa reference to "Poetry," turn to "Poetry" in LC Subject Headings.

The "scope note"--"Here are entered..."--makes you think that

? (a) it's worth trying the catalog under POETRY... and maybe POETICS.
   (b) you're not much closer to "ambiguity" than before.

If you want to keep tracing the network, go back to any junction and follow a different path from the one you took just now. If that's enough of that, go to frame D 4.

EXERCISE FRAME D 3

With "Meaning" the first problem is to decide whether to work with "Meaning (Psychology)" or "Meaning (Philosophy)." They have a common term: "Semantics (Philosophy)," if that's any help. But there are more sa references under "Meaning (Psychology)," so maybe it's a more fruitful choice.

The sa references under "Meaning (Psychology)" make you decide to follow the reference to

   (a) "Language and languages." Go to frame D 2.2.
? (b) "Semantics." Go to frame D 2.2.2.
   (c) "Semantics (Philosophy)." Go to frame D 3.1.

EXERCISE FRAME D 3.1

"Semantics (Philosophy)" seems a likely lead? Turn to it in LC Subject Headings (p. 1632) and compare the entry with the entry above it for "Semantics."

The entry for "Semantics (Philosophy)" sounds like technical philosophy more than technical literature. It's leading us astray. Try to head back for literature by choosing.

? (a) the heading "Semantics." Go to frame D 2.2.2.
   (b) the xx reference from "Language and languages." Go to frame D 2.2.

EXERCISE FRAME D 4 AND
SUMMARY

You have come here from a variety of frames, either expecting to come closer to answering the question, "How close can I come to 'ambiguity in literature'?" or wondering whether any of the paths you have followed will lead you very close.

Specificity 46

Remember that our main concern in this excursion has been to see how some terms are too specific for the catalog. Now that we are at the end, let me spring a sudden revelation on you. Not only do you have to be aware of specificity, of the size of the library and the nature of its collections, but also you have to rely on the good sense of the cataloguer. Will he have put the book in categories that will do justice to the contents of the book and also put a reader onto the track of the book?

Concerning "ambiguity in literature" there is a book by William Empson, Seven types of ambiguity, that will fill the bill--and that you may have come upon. But look at its added entries:

```
PN
1031
.E45      Empson, William, 1906-
              Seven types of ambiguity. [2d ed., rev. and re-set. New
          York] New Directions [1947]
              xv, 258 p. 21 cm.




              1. Poetry.  2. English poetry—Hist. & crit.   I. Title.
                                              808.1           A 48—78*
              Yale Univ. Library
              for Library of Congress   [a64h½]
```

I will not quibble with those three entries--as far as they go. But just one more would have made the book accessible to us quickly: "II. Title: Ambiguity, Seven types of." That inversion would have let us find the book filed by the title-word, "Ambiguity."

Moral: If the compilers of the lists of subject headings must second-guess you in supplying possible, not-used headings, you will sometimes have to second-guess the cataloguers by thinking of categories--usually relatively general ones--to which they might have assigned a book on a subject you seek.

Strategy: When you come to a halt on one level of specificity, try moving up one or two levels of generality to an embracing heading, to see if you can then come down at some other point.

Headings that are relatively general are often made relatively specific by the addition of a subdivision: e.g., the one on the card for the Empson book, "POETRY--HISTORY & CRITICISM." For exercises in their use, go to section F of this program.

SECTION E

SUBDIVISIONS

INTRODUCTION

This section will show you what subdivisions to expect under a general catalog heading. To find out whether you already know how to do this, complete the short test below. To do this section you will need to use an actual card catalog in a library.

Answers to tests and exercises in Section E begin on page 83.

PRE-TEST

If you can do the following items, you already know the contents of Section E.

I. Use <u>LC Subject Headings</u> and the card catalog in your library. Complete the subject heading for each topic by adding a likely subdivision. The book title is a suggestion of what you might find on the shelf according to the subject heading.

Topic: "Britain and the Common Market."

a) EUROPEAN ECONOMIC COMMUNITY--_____

e.g., Gelber, Lionel A. <u>The alliance of necessity: Britain's crisis, the new Europe and American interests.</u>

Topic: "The development of a racial-group image in the U.S. among Blacks."

b) NEGROES--_____

e.g., Pettigrew, Thomas F. <u>A profile of the Negro American.</u>

Topic: "Protestantism and the coming of the American Revolution."

c) UNITED STATES--_____--REVOLUTION

e.g., Jameson, John F. <u>The American revolution considered as a social movement.</u>

Topic: "Economic uses of green algae."

d) ALGAE--_____

e.g., NATO Advanced Study Institute, Louisville, Ky., 1962. <u>Algae and man.</u>

Topic: "The garden image in Shakespeare's history plays."

e) SHAKESPEARE, WILLIAM--_____

e.g., Charney, Maurice. <u>Shakespeare's Roman plays; the function of imagery in the drama.</u>

Topic: "Chaucer's use of Statius."

f) CHAUCER, GEOFFREY--_____

Subdivisions   48

    e. g., Plimpton, George A. <u>The education of Chaucer illustrated from the schoolbooks in use in his time.</u>

II. Under what subdivision will you find additional works on the subject of Masataka Banno, <u>China and the West, 1858-1861: the origins of the Tsungli yamen</u> or Jack Beeching, <u>The Chinese Opium Wars</u>?

    CHINA--HISTORY--_____

III. What period subdivision precedes that one (in item II)?

    CHINA--HISTORY--_____

    If you choose not to do the following exercises, you will find a Summary of Section E on page 54.

EXERCISE FRAME E 1

    A heading that is relatively general (like "Space science") can keep its usefulness--it can be left as the "filing word" that you look under in the catalog--but can also be made relatively specific by the addition of a subdivision: "SPACE SCIENCES--<u>INTERNATIONAL COOPERATION</u>." You notice that the subdivision is separated from the primary heading by a dash.

    Subdivisions are of four main kinds:

    1) Topic: "ELECTRONS--<u>EMISSION</u>"
    2) Form, or kind of organization: "SPACE SCIENCES--<u>BIBLIOGRAPHY</u>"
    3) Period: "FRANCE--HISTORY--<u>MEDIEVAL PERIOD TO 1515</u>"
    4) Locale: "LAW--<u>UNITED STATES</u>"

Here are "subdivisions of general application" (from <u>LC Subject Headings</u>, 7th ed.) that can be applied to any subject as appropriate:

Abstracts	Film catalogs
Addresses, essays, lectures	Handbooks, manuals, etc.
Bibliography	History [or History and criticism]
Bio-bibliography	Indexes
Case studies	Outlines, syllabi, etc.
Collected works	Periodicals
Collections	Societies, etc.
Congresses	Statistics
Dictionaries	Study and teaching
Directories	Yearbooks
Exhibitions	

And here also is the list of abbreviations made in subdivisions:

Antiquities--Antiq.	Economic conditions--Econ. condit.
Bibliography--Bibl.	Emigration and immigration--
Bio-bibliography--Bio-bibl.	Emig. & immig.
Biography--Biog.	Foreign relations--For. rel.
Boundaries--Bound.	Genealogy--Geneal.
Commerce--Comm.	History--Hist.
Description--Descr.	History and criticism--Hist. & crit.
Description and travel--	Industries--Indus.
Descr. & trav.	Manufactures--Manuf.
Dictionaries and encyclopedias--	Periodicals--Period.
Dict. & encyc.	Politics and government--Pol. & govt.
Directories--Direct.	Social conditions--Soc. condit.
Discovery and exploration--	Social life and customs--Soc. life & cust.
Disc. & explor.	Statistics--Stat.

Now act like a cataloguer and assign subdivisions from that list to the subject entry for each title below as it is described in Eugene P. Sheehy's Guide to reference works (9th edition):

Inter-Territorial Language (Swahili) Committee to the East African Dependencies. A standard English-Swahili [Swahili-English] dictionary (founded on Madan's English-Swahili dictionary), [prep.] under the direction of the late Frederick Johnson. London, Oxford Univ. Pr., H. Milford, 1939. 2v.   AD662

    Various reprintings. The two parts are also published separately.

?

Yearbook of comparative and general literature. Bloomington, Indiana Univ., 1952- . v. 1- . Annual.   BD20

    Published in collaboration with the Comparative Literature Committee of the National Council of Teachers of English; the American Comparative Literature Association; and the Comparative Literature Section of the Modern Language Association.
    Includes articles, news items, biographical sketches, and, in v. 1-19, an Annual bibliography designed to serve as a supplement to Baldensperger, Bibliography of comparative literature (BD1). The bibliography was discontinued after v. 19 (covering publications of 1969); thereafter, only a list of English translations from other languages appears annually as a bibliographic feature.   PN851.Y4

?

White, Carl M. and associates. Sources of information in the social sciences; a guide to the literature. 2d ed. Chicago, Amer. Lib. Assoc., 1973. 702p.   CA10

    1st ed. 1964

    A new and greatly enlarged edition of this now standard guide to the literature of the social sciences. Although originally designed primarily for graduate library school students, the work is widely useful to research workers as well. Nine principal chapters treat, respectively: social science in general; history; geography; economics and business administration; sociology; anthropology; psychology; education; and political science. Each consists of two main sections: (1) a bibliographic essay written by a specialist to explain the history and methodology of the discipline, and to cite, as applicable, a substantial number of pertinent, significant monographs; (2) annotated lists of reference sources, grouped by form, type, or specialized aspect, e.g., guides to the literature, abstracts, bibliographies, encyclopedias, handbooks, etc. Periodicals are listed in each category. Detailed table of contents and index of authors, titles and subjects.
    Sources of information in the social sciences should be consulted for many specialized sources not included in this Guide.   Z7161.W49

?

Subdivisions 50

> U. S. Bureau of the Census. Statistical abstract of the
> United States, 1878- . Wash., Govt. Prt. Off., 1879- .
> v. 1- . Annual.   CG69
>
>   v. 1-25, 1878-1902, prep. by the Bureau of Statistics (Treasury Dept.); v. 26-34, 1903-11, by the Bureau of Statistics (Dept. of Commerce and Labor); 1912-37, by the Bureau of Foreign and Domestic Commerce.
>   A single-volume work presenting quantitative summary statistics on the political, social, and economic organization of the United States. Indispensable in any library; it serves not only as a first source for statistics of national importance but also as a guide to further information, as references are given to the sources of all tables.
>   Statistics given in the tables cover a period of several years, usually about 15 or 20; some tables run back to 1789 or 1800.   HA202

_____?_____

   Finally, scan the paragraph on p. viii (in the 8th edition) about terms that <u>LC Subject Headings</u> does not list. Now go to frame E 2.

EXERCISE FRAME E 2

   Keep concentrating on subdivisions by <u>form</u> and keep acting like a cataloguer. Subdivide the heading for each book title. Use the subdivisions of general application which you have just rehearsed and the entries in <u>LC Subject Headings</u>.

Spitz, Armand N. <u>Dictionary of astronomy and astronautics.</u>

   (1) ASTRONAUTICS--_____

Schwartz, Leonard E. <u>International organizations and space cooperation.</u>

   (2) ASTRONAUTICS--_____

Wise, John. <u>Through the air: a narrative of forty years' experience as an aëronaut. Comprising a history of the various attempts in the art of flying by artificial means from the earliest period down to the present time. With an account of the author's most important air-voyages and his many thrilling adventures and hairbreadth escapes.</u> 1873.

   (3) AERONAUTICS--_____

International Symposium on Submarine and Space Medicine. <u>1st</u>, New London, Conn., 1958. <u>Environmental effects on consciousness; proceedings.</u>

   (4) SPACE MEDICINE--_____

Go to frame E 3.

EXERCISE FRAME E 3

   Now try completing some <u>form</u> subdivisions for an author. LC Subject Headings uses Shakespeare (p. <u>1647</u>) as a type. How would you subdivide the headings for the following books (judging by the titles)?

   Friedman, William Frederick and Elizabeth S. <u>The Shakespeare ciphers examined; an analysis</u>

of cryptographic systems used as evidence that some author other than William Shakespeare wrote the plays commonly attributed to him.

   (1) SHAKESPEARE, WILLIAM--_____

Furnivall, Frederick James. <u>Shakespeare: life and work.</u>

   (2) SHAKESPEARE, WILLIAM, 1564-1616--_____

Harbage, Alfred. <u>Conceptions of Shakespeare.</u>

   (3) SHAKESPEARE, WILLIAM--_____

Shattuck, Charles H. <u>The Shakespeare promptbooks; a descriptive catalog.</u>

   (4) SHAKESPEARE, WILLIAM--_____

Dickey, Franklin M. <u>Not wisely but too well; Shakespeare's love tragedies.</u>

   (5) SHAKESPEARE, WILLIAM--_____

For an exercise in applying the Shakespeare entries to another author, go to frame E 3.1. For straight-line progress, go to frame E 4.

EXERCISE FRAME E 3.1

Using the subdivisions under "Shakespeare, William" in <u>LC Subject Headings</u> as a sample, try subdividing the headings for these titles:

International Goethe Bicentennial Convocation and Music Festival, <u>Aspen, Colo.</u>, 1949. <u>Goethe and the modern age....</u> Regnery, 1950.

   (1) GOETHE, JOHANN WOLFGANG VON--_____

Kaulbach, Wilhelm von. <u>Goethe's female characters....</u> Stroefer & Kirchner, 1867.

   (2) GOETHE, JOHANN WOLFGANG VON--_____--_____

Hatfield, Henry C. <u>Goethe, a critical introduction.</u> Harvard, 1964.

   (3) GOETHE, JOHANN WOLFGANG VON--_____

Gray, Ronald D. <u>Goethe, the alchemist; a study of alchemical symbolism in Goethe's literary and scientific works.</u> Cambridge, 1952.

   (4) GOETHE, JOHANN WOLFGANG VON--_____--_____

Go to frame E 4.

EXERCISE FRAME E 4

You often find yourself working on a topic that includes a geographical term of some sort, and in the card catalog you will find many entries by <u>locale</u>, both as subdivisions ("Law--<u>United States</u>") and as primary entries ("<u>United States</u>--Politics and government"). Locale presents us with three concerns:

   1) What name has been adopted as standard in cases where there are variations in use ("Vienna" or "Wien"?),

   2) Whether the name of the locale will occur by itself as the first subdivision or will be

Subdivisions 52

preceded by the name of some larger geographical unit ("Antiquities--London" or "Antiquities--Great Britain--London"?),

    3) Whether it makes more sense to look under the name of the place, subdivided by subject ("Indiana--Election laws") or under the name of the subject, subdivided by the place ("Election laws--Indiana").

1. Cataloguers try to use--and stick to--the version of the name that occurs most commonly in English, regardless of "official" lists ("Vienna," not "Wien"). In case of conflict, you can expect to find a see reference from the term you have sought to the version of the name used in the catalog ("Formosa, See Taiwan").

2. LC Subject Headings distinguishes "direct" and "indirect" order.

"Education (Indirect)": the name of a bigger pertinent governmental unit must come after "Education" and before the name of a lesser locale--it will be "Education--France--Pau," not "Education--Pau." The Library of Congress now tends away from the indirect form and has persistently avoided it where the "bigger pertinent governmental units" are so large that many cards would accumulate at that point in the filing (i.e., "U.S."). You may want to read about local subdivision in LC Subject Headings, pp. xii, xiii, for procedures and exceptions.

"Land tenure (Direct)": the name of the locale can come next regardless of any larger governmental unit--it will be "Land tenure--Uttar Pradesh, India" and not "Land tenure--India--Uttar Pradesh."

3. As always, it makes sense to look first under the more specific of two terms, and if they seem equally specific, to look under both of them. Pick one of the following topics and follow it through the catalog to a certain title which will be vouchsafed to you in a later frame.

    a) "The mechanics of modern British elections."
    b) "Trappers and Indians in the American fur trade."
    c) "Slavery and anti-slavery in the border territory of Kansas."

EXERCISE FRAME E 5

In your search concerning the topic, "The mechanics of modern British elections," you have discovered that

TRUE   FALSE

_____   _____   a) "Elections--Great Britain" is a used heading.

_____   _____   b) "Great Britain--Elections" is a used heading.

_____   _____   c) "Great Britain. Parliament--Elections" is a used heading.

_____   _____   d) "Election law--Great Britain" would be a possibility.

Go on to frame E 8.

EXERCISE FRAME E 6

In your search concerning "Trappers and Indians in the American fur trade" you have discovered that

TRUE   FALSE

_____   _____   a) "Trappers" is a used heading.

___	___	b)	there is a useful <u>sa</u> reference at "Trapping."
___	___	c)	"Indians" is a used heading.
___	___	d)	"Indians" is clear enough as a heading for your purposes.
___	___	e)	"Indians of North America" in your library is too big a section in the card catalog to make it a good place to start.
___	___	f)	"Fur trade" can be subdivided by place.
___	___	g)	"America" is a used heading but apparently not a used subdivision.
___	___	h)	"Fur trade--North America" is an efficient heading for the topic.

If you have found these: Ross, Alexander. <u>The fur hunters of the far West.</u> <u>John Long's voyages and travels in the years 1768-1788</u> and Greenbie, Sydney. <u>Frontiers and the fur trade,</u> you're not there yet.

Go on to frame E 8.

EXERCISE FRAME E 7

In your search concerning "Slavery and anti-slavery in the border territory of Kansas" you have discovered that

TRUE	FALSE		
___	___	a)	"Slavery" pertains only to the United States.
___	___	b)	if you start with "Kansas" you will need to know what historical period to deal with.
___	___	c)	"Slavery in the U.S." cannot be subdivided.
___	___	d)	"Anti-slavery" is a used heading.
___	___	e)	"Slavery in the U.S.--Kansas" is an efficient heading.

Go to frame E 8.

EXERCISE FRAME E 8

Now concentrate on subdivision by <u>period of time</u>--often a prime consideration when you are working on a history topic. <u>LC Subject Headings</u> lists period subdivisions under the name of the geographical entity:

        U. S.
        Europe
        Spanish America } --History-- ...
        New York (City)
        ...

Much the same list, place by place, can be used after other subdivisions ("Politics & government," "Social conditions," "History & criticism") and after other headings where a division by time is appropriate ("Social groups--20th century," "Chemistry--Early works to 1800").

The time periods used are either "generally recognized epochs" or generally used names that are appropriate to a given heading. If the name does not include a number, a number is usually

Subdivisions   54

added, because the cards will be arranged by chronology, not by the alphabet, with inclusive dates coming before the included*:

 China--History--1766 B.C.-220 A.D. inclusive of
 China--History--Shang dynasty, 1766-1122 B.D. included in
 China--History--Northern Wei dynasty, 386-636 inclusive of
 China--History--Sui dynasty, 581-618 included in

Try the following exercise. Between what two entries would you insert "1898-" [which means "from 1898 on"]?

 1. U.S.--History--1865-
 2. U.S.--History--1865-1898
 3. U.S.--History--War of 1898
 4. U.S.--History--20th century
 5. U.S.--History--1901-1953
 6. U.S.--History--1913-1921

... "13th century"?

 7. Great Britain--History--Norman period, 1066-1154
 8. Great Britain--History--Plantagenets, 1154-1399
 9. Great Britain--History--Angevin period, 1154-1216
 10. Great Britain--History--Richard I, 1189-1199
 11. Great Britain--History--Henry III, 1216-1272
 12. Great Britain--History--Edward I-III, 1272-1377

Go to frame E 9.

EXERCISE FRAME E 9

 Applying your wits and LC Subject Headings to the following topic, see if you can reach a certain book that I have in mind. This time I won't guide you with true-false statements. Go it on your own.

   TOPIC: "The panic of 1819 and the rise of Jacksonian democracy."

Incidentally, Murray N. Rothbard's The panic of 1819; reactions and policies (Columbia University Press, 1962) is not it. Sorry.

For a few exercises in filing, go to Section F.

SUMMARY OF SECTION E

 A subject heading can be made more specific by the addition of a subdivision (after a dash). Subdivisions are of four kinds:

 by topic--"SYMPHONIES--ANALYSIS, INTERPRETATION"
 by form--"SYMPHONIES--SCORES"
 by time period--"INSTRUMENTAL MUSIC--TO 1800"
 by locale--"MUSIC--LOUISIANA--NEW ORLEANS"

 The common, standard subdivisions used by the Library of Congress are listed in LC Subject Headings, 8th ed., starting at page xviii. The categories of those usually omitted are listed on p. viii. And the headings "serving as patterns for sets of subdivisions--Shakespeare for literary authors,

---

*NOTE: LC Subject Headings (8th ed.) does precisely the reverse: included dates come before the inclusive (for the convenience of the computer, not that of an undergraduate searcher). Check the catalog in your library to see which practice your librarians now follow.

Lincoln for U. S. Presidents, etc."--are listed on p. xiv. On page 48 of this book are the subdivisions of general application and the standard abbreviations used in added entries on LC catalog cards.

Subdivisions by time period are labeled sometimes with "generally recognized epochs" and always by date: "Irish language--To 1100; --Middle Irish, 1100-1550."

The order of the entries, in <u>LC Subject Headings</u>, 8th ed., is "includ<u>ed</u>" dates before "inclu<u>sive</u>" dates, an order that makes sense for a researcher:

>"Ireland--History--1649-1660
>   --1649-1775
>   --17th century"

The order in the catalog of a smallish library is likely to be "inclusive" dates before "included" dates, an order that makes sense for someone scanning the catalog:

>"Ireland--History--17th century
>   --1649-1775
>   --1649-1660"

The order of the entries is by number, not alphabetical.

Subdivisions by locale present three concerns:

--the standard form of the name, where there are variations (it will be "Taiwan" now, not "Formosa," as it used to be); the form is likely to be the one most common in English ("Moscow," not "Moskova");

--whether a given locale will occur by itself--the so-called "Direct" way ("Art--Indianapolis--Exhibits," not "Art--Indiana--Indianapolis--Exhibits")--or as a subdivision after another locale ("Music--Austria--Vienna," not "Music--Vienna"), the so-called "Indirect" way; the trend is toward the "direct," but with several exceptions (p. xii);

--whether it makes sense to look under a place-name subdivided by subject ("India--Politics and government"), or under a subject subdivided by place ("Liberty of the press--India"); one should favor the more specific term, as usual.

SECTION F

FILING

INTRODUCTION

This section will alert you to what "alphabetical" means in the card catalog. To find out whether you already know how to do what this section is about, do the short test below. To do this section you do not need to go to a card catalog in a library.

Answers to tests and exercises in Section F begin on page 88.

PRE-TEST

If you can do the following items, you already know the content of Section F.

I. In LC Subject Headings, between "Indians of North America" and "Indians of South America," what will you expect the order of these headings to be?

    a) Indians of North America, Civilization of
    b) Indians of North America--Picture-writing
    c) Indians of North America--Wars--1775-1783
    d) Indians of North America--Wars--1750-1815
    e) Indians of North America as soldiers
    f) Indians of North America--Indian Territory

II. What would be the order of entries (a) through (f) above in a single-alphabet file, such as the card catalog in many small libraries?

III. In a single-alphabet file, single catalog--not divided into author-title and subject catalogs--what would be the order of these items?

    a)   The child's conception of physical causality
        Piaget, Jean, 1896-
           The child's conception of physical causality...

    b)   CHILDS, RICHARD SPENCER, 1882-
        East, John Porter.
           Council-manager government: the political thought of its founder, Richard S. Childs...

    c)   Childs, Richard Spencer, 1882-
           Short-ballot principles...

    d)   China after Mao
        Barnett, A. Doak
           China after Mao...

    e)   CHINA
        China yearbook. 1937-43...

    f)   CHINA
        China. Ministry of information.
           China after five years of war...

   g)   CHINA
          China. Ministry of information.
             China handbook, 1937-1945...

   h)   CHINA (PEOPLE'S REPUBLIC OF CHINA, 1949-)--STATISTICS
          Chen, Nai-ruenn, 1926-
             Chinese economic statistics

   i)   CHINA--ANTIQUITIES
          Li, Chi.
             The beginnings of Chinese civilization...

   j)   CHINA--FOREIGN RELATIONS--TO 1912
          Yen, Sophia Su-fei, 1935-
             Taiwan in China's foreign relations, 1836-1874...

   k)   CHINA--FOREIGN RELATIONS--UNITED STATES
          Chen, Lung-Chu, 1935-
             Formosa, China, and the United Nations...

   l)   CHINA--POLITICS & GOVERNMENT
          Mao, Tsê-tung, 1893-
             Selected works...

If you choose not to do the following exercises, you will find a summary of Section F on page 64.

EXERCISE FRAME F 1

There are a good many ways to file a run of headings in a card catalog, and a justification (of sorts) for every practice. In your library you will have to discover for yourself what the practice is--or ask a librarian about it.

However, there are two main "authorities" for filing, and you can exercise yourself a little on them both: the Library of Congress "dictionary" rules and the ALA (American Library Association) "dictionary" rules. I put "dictionary" in quotation marks because neither practice is actually like that of a dictionary, and yet in both practices--as in the dictionary--the alphabet is the source of the basic order:

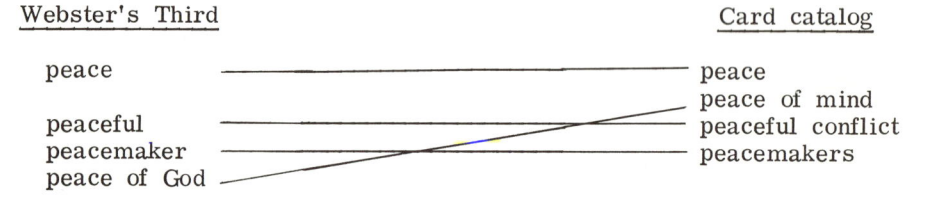

Webster's Third	Card catalog
peace	peace
	peace of mind
peaceful	peaceful conflict
peacemaker	peacemakers
peace of God	

Judging by those examples, true dictionary order is [letter-by-letter or word-by-word?].

Card catalog "dictionary" order is [letter-by-letter or word-by-word?].

Go to frame F 2.

EXERCISE FRAME F 2

With letter-by-letter order, no problems. You disregard spaces and punctuation marks and arrange the letters alphabetically:

Filing

can_
cana_
canaan
canaba
canace
canada

With word-by-word order, there can be problems. For one thing, the library has to decide whether to observe or to disregard punctuation.

"Observe punctuation" = use alphabetical order in more than one series of words, or do sub-arrangements under a head word.

"Disregard punctuation" = use only one alphabet, with no subarrangements.

Here is a word-by-word order that <u>observes</u> punctuation:

```
         MUSHROOMS, POISONOUS
    I    MUSIC
         MUSIC--ACOUSTICS AND PHYSICS        ⎫  subarranged
         MUSIC--ANALYSIS, APPRECIATION       ⎬  alphabetically
   I A   MUSIC--INSTRUCTION AND STUDY        ⎭  under MUSIC
         MUSIC--INTERPRETATION (PHRASING, DYNAMICS, ETC.)
         MUSIC--U. S.
         MUSIC, BAROQUE                      ⎫
   I B   MUSIC, INCIDENTAL                   ⎬  subarranged alphabetically under MUSIC
         MUSIC, POPULAR (SONGS, ETC.)        ⎭
    II   MUSIC AND COLOR
   III   MUSIC IN THE HOME
   IV    MUSIC LIBRARIES
         MUSICAL ABILITY
```

Here are the same entries arranged in a single alphabet, still word-by-word, but <u>disregarding</u> punctuation:

```
         MUSHROOMS, POISONOUS
         MUSIC
         MUSIC--ACOUSTICS AND PHYSICS
         MUSIC--ANALYSIS, APPRECIATION
         MUSIC AND COLOR
         MUSIC, BAROQUE
         MUSIC IN THE HOME
         MUSIC, INCIDENTAL
         MUSIC--INSTRUCTION AND STUDY
         MUSIC--INTERPRETATION (PHRASING, DYNAMICS, ETC.)
         MUSIC LIBRARIES
         MUSIC, POPULAR (SONGS, ETC.)
         MUSIC--U. S.
         MUSICAL ABILITY
```

Now try your hand at converting an arrangement-with-subarrangements that observes punctuation into a single-alphabet arrangement that disregards punctuation. Still word-by-word.

<u>Observes punctuation</u>   <u>Disregards punctuation</u>
0. ARSON
1. ART
2. ART--ADDRESSES
3. ART--AFRICA
4. ART, ABSTRACT
5. ART, AFRICAN
6. ART, APPLIED
7. ART AND LITERATURE

Observes punctuation	Disregards punctuation

8. ART OBJECTS
9. ARTERIES

Now let's see whether we can discriminate the kinds of meaning that the dash and the comma signal. We already know from Section E of this book that the dash signals a subdivision and that subdivisions in LC Subject Headings are of four chief kinds: topic, form, period (of time), and locale [see frame E 1]. What might the comma signal, then? To take an example, what is the difference between ART--AFRICA and ART, AFRICAN? We take it that in ART--AFRICA the main idea is ART and that the subdivision AFRICA has to do with the presence or significance of any kind of art in Africa; the art may be Chinese or European or what-have-you. ART--AFRICA is a likely heading for this book:

Fleming, D. J. Each with his own brush; contemporary Christian art in Asia and Africa, Friendship Press, 1968.

Then the inverted phrase ART, AFRICAN (= AFRICAN ART) probably signals

? a) the presence of art forms in Africa, regardless of their origin.
   b) the elements of art forms created by Africans.
   c) African-like art forms.

It would be a good heading for such a book as this:

Robbins, W. M. African art in American collections, Praeger, 1966.

[Incidentally, the point to the inversion is probably that under AFRICAN there would be many cards to file--"African" applies to a host of things--whereas ART is more restricted. But one could quibble easily with that interpretation of the scope of the two terms. Anyhow, the point to an inversion is usually to get a prominent word up front as the "filing word."]

Go on to frame F 3.

EXERCISE FRAME F 3

LC Subject Headings observes punctuation. Subdivisions (after dashes) precede inverted qualifications (after commas). You will discover in frame F 5 that there is a further refinement--a further set of distinctions to make.

Between what two headings in LC Subject Headings will you find "Mathematics--Tables, etc." then?

1. Mathematics
2. Mathematics--Programmed instruction
3. Mathematics--Study and teaching (Secondary)
4. Mathematics, Arabic
5. Mathematics, Maya
6. Mathematics as a profession
7. Mathematics teachers

Go to frame F 4.

EXERCISE FRAME F 4

In LC Subject Headings, subdivisions (after dashes) precede inverted qualifications (after commas) and qualifications precede extensions (words after the first word) that are free of punctuation.

Between what two entries, then, will you find "English language in foreign countries"?

Filing 60

1. English language
2. English language--Middle English, 1100-1500
3. English language--Early modern, 1500-1700
4. English language--18th century
5. English language--Dictionaries
6. English language--Etymology
7. English language--Grammar
8. English language--Rhetoric
9. English language--Study and teaching--Foreign students
10. English language--Text-books for foreigners
11. English language in India
12. English letters

Go to frame F 5.

EXERCISE FRAME F 5

In <u>LC Subject Headings</u> subdivisions precede inverted qualifications and qualifications precede extensions. The set of subdivisions following dashes may itself have sub-sets of arrangements: chronological subheads are grouped together first, then come form and topic subdivisions, and finally come the geographical subdivisions.

For the following series, list the numbers of the entries whose subdivisions belong to the sets named:

      MAIN HEAD   SUBDIVISIONS

1. English literature--To 1100. <u>See</u> Anglo-Saxon Literature
2. English literature--Early modern, to 1700
3. English literature--History & criticism
4. English literature--Indic authors
5. English literature--Jewish authors
6. English literature--Outlines, syllabi, etc.
7. English literature--Translations from French
8. English literature--Canada. <u>See</u> Canadian literature

SUB-SETS

Form: _____
Periodic (chronological): _____
Locale (geographical): _____

Between what two entries will you find "English literature--Middle English, 1100-1500"?

And between what two entries above will you find "English literature--Japanese authors"?

Go on to frame F 6.

EXERCISE FRAME F 6

The second "authority" for filing entries--one used by many libraries--is the ALA rules. They describe several procedures, which can be reduced to two main orders: (1) the grouped order that you saw in <u>LC Subject Headings</u> and that observes punctuation, and (2) an order that comes closer to using a single alphabet without subarrangements.

Some libraries observe the dashes and the commas in subject entries, as do <u>LC Subject Headings</u> and an index like <u>Readers' Guide</u>. In their card catalog they file subdivisions (after dashes) be-

fore qualifiers (after commas) and file both of them before extensions of the head word. (That is the practice suggested for large collections in A. L. A. rules for filing catalog cards, 1st edition, 1942.)

Here's one more exercise in that kind of order. According to that scheme, between what two entries in the card catalog will you find "Philosophy, Buddhist"?

1. Philosophy--Dictionaries ⎤
2. Philosophy--History   ⎬ Subdivisions
3. Philosophy--Terminology ⎦
4. Philosophy, American ⎤
5. Philosophy, Ancient   ⎪
6. Philosophy, Chinese   ⎬ Qualifiers
7. Philosophy, Medieval   ⎪
8. Philosophy, Modern   ⎦
9. Philosophy and religion ⎤ Extensions
10. Philosophy in literature ⎦

Go on to frame F 7.

EXERCISE FRAME F 7

Some libraries, especially smaller ones, come as close to a single alphabet as they can come. That is the practice recommended for small collections in the 1942 ALA rules and for all collections in the revision (2nd edition) of 1968. With any luck, your library will have shifted to the practice of a single alphabet. It has its drawbacks, but for the ordinary user of the card catalog the drawbacks are few.

According to that scheme, between what two entries will you find "Philosophy--History"?

1. Philosophy, Greek
2. Philosophy, Hindu
3. Philosophy in literature
4. Philosophy, Indic
5. Philosophy--Introductions
6. Philosophy, Islamic
7. Philosophy, Jewish
8. Philosophy, Medieval
9. Philosophy, Modern

Go on to frame F 8.

EXERCISE FRAME F 8

The ALA rules cover the many problems that arise in filing,* but you need to concern yourself with only one more: what order for several entries of the same word? Assume that the card catalog in your library has authors and subjects and titles interfiled in one catalog. (If they are actually divided, go to frame F 9.) You come to a run of cards where the same word functions as a person's name and as a subject heading and also as the first word of a title.

RULE: The cards are arranged in that order--person [often an author], subject heading [other than a person], title.

So, between what two entries will you find "Glass," a book by George Savage, Putnam, 1965?

---

*For example: Disregard apostrophes. Treat hyphenated words as one word. Disregard initial articles. File initial numbers by their spelling, not their rank. File forename entries before the same word as a surname. File abbreviations as if they were spelled out. File "Mc" as "Mac." File an initial before a word beginning with that letter. File umlauts (ä...) as simple letters (a...).

Filing 62

1. Glass, Bryan P.
    A key to the skulls of North American mammals...

2. GLASS, CARTER, 1858-
    Smith, Rixey, 1892-
    Carter Glass; a biography...

3. Glass, Hiram Bentley, 1906-
    Science and ethical values...

4. GLASS
    Logan, Harlan, ed.
    How much do you know about glass?...

5. Glass: a world history
    Kampfer, Fritz and Beyer, K. G.
    Glass: a world history...

6. The glass bees
    Jünger, Ernst, 1895-
    The glass bees...

Go to frame F 9.

EXERCISE FRAME F 9

What happens within an author or within a subject or within a title, where there are several cards in each category?

RULES: a) Arrange author (person) entries by the titles.
       b) Arrange subject entries by the authors.
       c) Arrange title entries by the authors (anonymous titles preceding the same title with an author).

a) Between what two entries will you find

    "Glass, Hiram Bentley, 1906-
        Science and ethical values..."?

1. Glass, Hiram Bentley, 1906-   ed.
    Forerunners of Darwin: 1745-1859...

2. Glass, Hiram Bentley, 1906-   ed.
    Symposium on Phosphorus Metabolism, Johns Hopkins University, 1951.
    Phosphorus metabolism, a symposium on the role of phosphorus...

3. Glass, Hiram Bentley, 1906-
    Science and liberal education...

b) Between what two entries will you find

    "GLASS PAINTING AND STAINING--FRANCE
        Aubert, Marcel, 1884-
        Stained glass of the XIIth..."?

4. GLASS PAINTING AND STAINING--FRANCE
    Arnold, Hugh.
    Stained glass of the middle ages in England and France...

5. GLASS PAINTING AND STAINING--FRANCE
  Aubert, Marcel, 1884-
   French cathedral windows of the twelfth and thirteenth centuries...

6. GLASS PAINTING AND STAINING--FRANCE
  Verrier, Jean.
   Vitraux de France aux douzième et treizième siècles...

c) Between what two entries will you find

    "A glossary of literary terms
     Abrams, Meyer Howard.
      A glossary of literary terms...."?

7. Glossary of linguistic terminology
  Pei, Mario Andrew, 1901-
   Glossary of linguistic terminology...

8. A glossary of literary terms
  Norton, Daniel Silas, 1908-
   A glossary of literary terms...

9. A glossary of mycology
  Snell, Walter Henry, 1889-
   A glossary of mycology...

Go on to frame F 10.

EXERCISE FRAME F 10

Finally, entries <u>about</u> a person (upper case) are filed just after entries <u>by</u> that person (lower case) and before any <u>other</u> entries that begin with that same name.

Between what two entries will you find

    "PROUST, MARCEL, 1871-1922
     Maurois, André, 1885-
      A la recherche de Marcel Proust..."?

1. Proust, Marcel, 1871-1922
  Atget, Eugène, 1856-1927
   A vision of Paris. The photographs of Eugène Atget; the words of Marcel Proust...

2. PROUST, MARCEL, 1871-1922
  Brée, Germaine.
   The world of Marcel Proust...

3. Proust recaptured
  Johnson, Pamela Hansford, 1912-
   Proust recaptured; six radio sketches...

Go on to frame F 11.

EXERCISE FRAME F 11

In a library that divides its author-and-title catalog from its subject catalog, the filing problems which you have just encountered do not occur--but neither does one have the richness of suggestion and association that a single catalog provides.

Filing

We have not touched on many niceties of filing, but you will be able at least to get into the right neighborhood of an entry that you seek.

Do you remember that in LC Subject Headings we emphasized scanning the vicinity of a heading in order to pick up clues? The same thing is true when you are searching a file drawer for a certain card. If you don't find the card where you expect it, take a few seconds to scan the cards around that place. Mistakes do happen.

SUMMARY OF SECTION F

The alphabetical entries in a dictionary are arranged letter-by-letter through the word or the phrase, disregarding the white spaces. The alphabetical entries in a card catalog and LC Subject Headings are made letter-by-letter within a word; a white space counts as "nothing" (zero) and interrupts the filing.

Rule of thumb: file "nothing" (zero) before "something."

Small libraries usually have a single catalog for authors, subjects, and titles, arranged by one alphabet--disregarding punctuation (dashes, commas, parentheses). Subdivisions by time period often come at the end of a group and are arranged chronologically, with an inclusive period preceding an included period.

Large libraries often have a catalog for authors and one for subjects and titles. They usually observe punctuation. The same is true of LC Subject Headings and of an index like Readers' Guide to Periodical Literature.

> Subdivisions (after a dash) precede inverted qualifications (after a comma), which precede extensions (phrases free of punctuation).

> Within subdivisions, those by time period come first and are arranged chronologically. Time periods starting with the same date are arranged with an included period before an inclusive one. Subdivisions by topic and by form come next, interfiled. Subdivisions by locale come last.

Cards with identical authors are sub-arranged alphabetically by their titles.

Cards with identical subject headings are sub-arranged alphabetically by their main entries.

Cards with identical title entries are sub-arranged alphabetically by their authors.

In a run of cards where the filing word is a person's name (Israel, John), a subject heading (ISRAEL: Isaac Deutscher, The non-Jewish Jew), and also a title (Israel; a personal history, by David Ben-Gurion), the cards come in that order: author, subject, title--or, as in many small libraries, the titles and the subjects may be interfiled, sub-arranged by their main entries.

Entries about a person (upper case; the person is a subject heading) are filed just after entries by that person (lower case: the person as author) and before any other entries (such as a title) that begin with that same name.

ANSWERS TO EXERCISES

SECTION A: PRE-TEST

a; h; j; q; 4, 3, 2, 1

A 1

a) The call number and the author are sometimes related, sometimes not. Concentrate on "<u>author</u> card"--the name of an author. Try the problem again.

b) The date is not the author, and you are looking for an <u>author</u> card. Try the problem again.

c) Not bad. But you will discover that names are typewritten at the top of a card for various reasons. For now, concentrate on matching the card illustrated in this problem. Try again.

d) All right. You've turned up a main-entry author card. Now go to frame A 2.

e) It had better not. That makes it what we call a "title card." Try again.

f) Ask yourself some questions to get yourself organized. What are you being asked to look for? What does the example have on it that will help you? Try any one of the choices and sneak a look at the answer. (Who knows? maybe trial-and-error is the smart way in.)

A 2

a) Yes, but then why should the card be filed in a different place? Try another explanation, one that will account for the filing.

b) Right, and consequently the card is filed where you found it. Now go to frame A 3--unless you feel that you kind of happened on your title card. If you're not sure about how titles are filed (does a word "the" count?), go to frame A 2.1.

c) If it does, you're not there. There will be at least one difference, as the example shows: the title appears twice. Try another explanation, one that will let the title appear twice.

d) Yes, it should be, it's the same book. But that says nothing about the title. Try another explanation.

e) Try comparing the example card in this frame with the example card in frame A 1. Find a difference and then see if one of the multiple-choices describes that difference.

f) Well, the catalog is arranged alphabetically word by word--with a few major exceptions--but the question is, which word on your card controls where the card will be filed? For a direct answer to that question, go to frame A 2.3. For an exercise in figuring out the answer, go to frame A 2.1.

A 2.1

If you answered some such phrase as "the first important word in the title," go to frame A 2.2.

Answers

If you answered some such phrase as "the first word in the title except an article," and want practice in filing titles, go to frame A 2.4. If you are ready to hunt for your title card, go to frame A 2.5.

If you answered anything except some such phrase as "the first important word in the title," go to frame A 2.3.

A 2.2

[Some such phrase as] words like a, an, the--the articles. (But the words And, I, They, Who, Toward are "important"--as you will discover as you work in the catalog.)

To practice filing titles, go to frame A 2.4.

To proceed with finding your title card, go to frame A 2.5.

A 2.3

a) Exactly, since the "filing word"--educated--begins with "edu...."

If you want to practice some filing, go to frame A 2.4. If you are ready to hunt for your title card, go to frame A 2.5.

b) Because of "Frye, Northrop"? But that's the author's name, and the title card will be filed according to the title. Try again.

c) Because of the "The"? Read the opening sentence of this frame again and mind the exception it indicates.

d) For the call number, PN? Call numbers determine where the books sit on the shelves, not where their cards are filed in the catalog. Try again.

e) Cancel letters from the "filing word" in your title ("educated") and letters in the first term of the drawer label:

E̶d̶u̶c̶a̶ted

E̶d̶u̶c̶a̶tional P.

At that point you see that since "e" precedes "i" in the alphabet, your filing word will occur in a drawer preceding this one.

A 2.4

4, 1, 3, 2

A 2.5

a) Yes, but then why should the card be filed in a different place rather than under the author's name?

b) Right, and consequently the card is filed where you found it. Now go on to frame A 3.

c) Try comparing the example card in this frame with the example card in frame A 1. Find a difference and then see if one of the multiple-choices describes that difference.

A 4

a) If Hume were the author, he would take over from "Church, Ralph W." Try again.

b) Right. Added entries with Arabic numerals are SUBJECTS. They indicate what the book is ABOUT. Now do the other question in this frame.

c) The title begins "Hume's...," it's true, but "Hume's" is not "Hume, David." Try again.

d) Hardly, since the title ("Hume's theory of the understanding") comes just after the author (Church, Ralph Withington). Try again.

e) It's identified by an Arabic numeral, so it's a subject. But it's number 2, and there's a number 1 which is presumably also a subject. Go to frame A 4.1.

f) Right, like number 1 (Arabic), "Hume, David, 1711-1776." Go to frame A 4.1.

A 4.1

1. a) about b) CAPITALS c) an Arabic (numeral). Now do number 2.

2. d) by e) Lower Case f) a Roman (numeral). Now do number 3.

3. g) "Calder" (Lower Case).

A 5

Card A

    1. c (subject entry) 2. CAPITALS Arabic (numeral)

Card B

    3. e (title entry) 4. Lower Case Roman (numeral)
    5. g

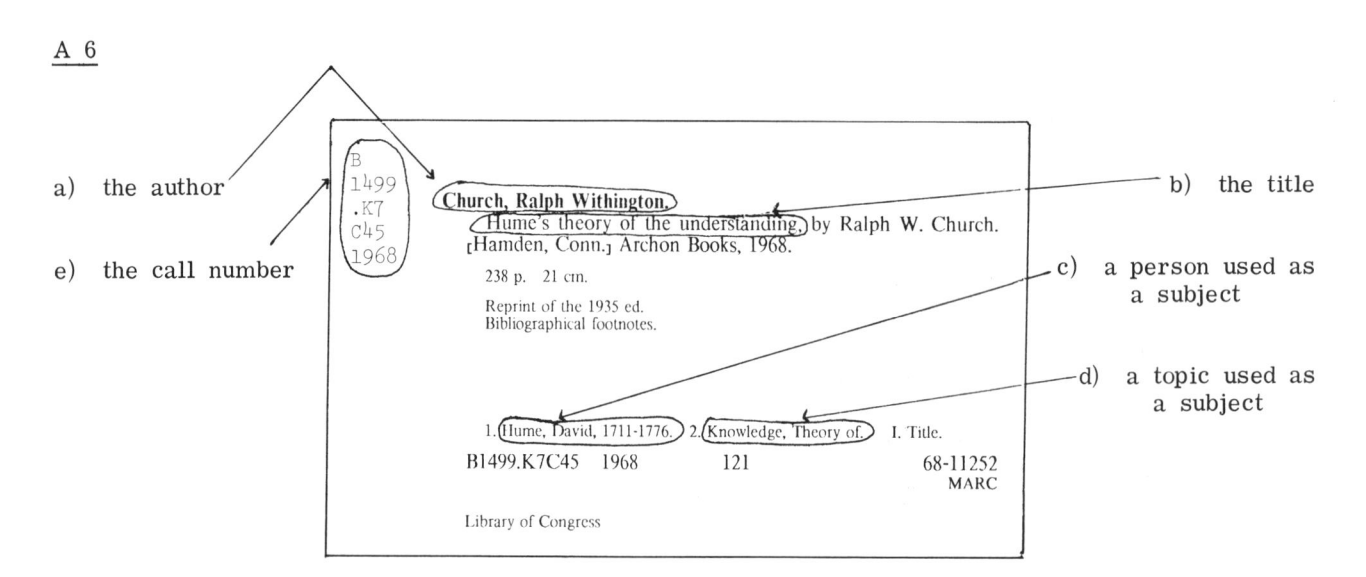

A 6

a) the author

e) the call number

b) the title

c) a person used as a subject

d) a topic used as a subject

[Catalog card: B1499.K7C45 1968. Church, Ralph Withington. Hume's theory of the understanding, by Ralph W. Church. [Hamden, Conn.] Archon Books, 1968. 238 p. 21 cm. Reprint of the 1935 ed. Bibliographical footnotes. 1. Hume, David, 1711-1776. 2. Knowledge, Theory of. I. Title. B1499.K7C45 1968 121 68-11252 MARC. Library of Congress]

Arabic (numerals for subjects)

a Roman (numeral for any other added entry)

Answers

A 6.1

1. a

2. e (f. Yes, the book has something to do with Hume--enough that the cataloguer saw fit to call for the subject heading.)

   (The trouble with "d" is that, according to the title, Hume may be an author rather than a subject. In that case the cataloguer would supply a Roman-numeral added entry.)

3. i

4. l (Choice "k" is a little muddy. The cataloguer saw fit to call for the two subject headings, "KNOWLEDGE, THEORY OF" and "HUME, DAVID, 1711-1776" because in this book the principal subject matter is precisely "knowledge" and "Hume.")

5. o

6. p (A cataloguer will not always "bring out" a title, especially not if it comes close to duplicating another card for the same book. See frame A 4.1, card A.)

7. s

8. Arabic-numeral (subject entries--1, 2, 3...); CAPITALS; Roman-numeral (other entries--authors, titles--I, II, III...); Lower Case

A 7

c (LINDS--LITERATURE, B.) since LITERATURE. falls between LINDS and LITERATURE, D.

(The filing principle is: File nothing before something. In this case the white space (nothing) after LITERATURE___ makes the word file in front of the B. (something) of LITERATURE, B.)

SECTION B: PRE-TEST

I. b; d; h; l; m;

II. a. Politics of <u>Medicare</u>.

   b. <u>William Bradford</u> as a historian.

   c. <u>Trade</u> unionism in mid-19th-century England.

   d. Snake <u>venoms</u>. OR <u>Snake venoms</u>.

   e. Naturalism in <u>19th-century English fiction</u>.

   f. Birds and reptiles in the poetry of <u>Emily Dickinson</u>

         OR PERHAPS

   Birds and reptiles in <u>the poetry of Emily Dickinson</u>.

B 1

HISTORY, MODERN	HISTORY, MODERN--20TH CENTURY	EUROPE--HISTORY--1789-1900
2	3, 4	1, 5*

*No, not under <u>HISTORY--MODERN</u>; it's only modern <u>Europe</u>.

B 1

LITERATURE	FICTION--HISTORY & CRITICISM	NEGRO LITERATURE (AMERICAN)
7, 9	6, 10	8

PSYCHOLOGY	PSYCHOLOGY, COMPARATIVE	PSYCHOLOGY, PHYSIOLOGICAL
12, 15	13	11, 14

MUSIC--ANALYSIS, INTERPRETATION	MUSIC--PHILOSOPHY & AESTHETICS
17, 20	19

MUSIC--DISCOGRAPHY	MUSIC--DICTIONARIES
16	18

CHEMISTRY	CHEMISTRY, ORGANIC	CHEMISTRY--BIBLIOGRAPHY	CHEMISTRY--DICTIONARIES
22, 24	25	21	23

BIBLIOGRAPHY--BIBLIOGRAPHY	REFERENCE BOOKS--BIBLIOGRAPHY
30	28, 29

REFERENCE BOOKS--LITERATURE	REFERENCE BOOKS--PROBLEMS, EXERCISES, ETC.
27	26

B 2

a) "Important" has nothing to do with "specific." Try again.

b) "Basic" has nothing to do with "specific." Try again.

c) To see if one term includes the other, try reversing the formula: "All structures have proteins." Clearly, "proteins" does not embrace "structures." Putting this topic in the context of all knowledge, "structure" is more general than "proteins," not more specific. Try again.

d) "Tiny" is not "specific." Mount Everest as a mountain is huge, but as a term it is more specific than "the Himalayas." Try again.

e) "Proteins" is the term that pins down the topic, so to speak. "Primary" and "structures" may apply to many things in the world, "proteins" to fewer. In this topic "proteins" is the most specific term.

B 2.1

1. Reviews of books of <u>fiction</u>.

    Reasoning: Fiction is a particular kind of book; it is a more specific category than "books." Reviews can apply to many kinds of works; as a category "reviews" overlaps with many others, is more general than "fiction."

2. The social aspects of <u>art</u>.

    Reasoning: "Social" and "aspect" can apply to many terms. "Art" can apply to fewer; it is more specific.

3. <u>Courtship</u> in 19th-century America.

    Reasoning: "19th-century" is an aspect of many subjects; "America" has many aspects. But "courtship" is contained in "America," according to the topic, and consequently is more specific.

4. The microbiology of <u>winemaking</u>.

    Reasoning: "Microbiology" embraces winemaking, among many other organic processes; it is more general.

Answers

5. Blood imagery in "Macbeth."

   Reasoning: "Imagery" occurs in many works. "Blood imagery"—to treat those two words as a single "term"—presumably can occur in more than one work. Macbeth is a single work, the most specific kind of term by virtue of being a name.

6. International liquidity.

   Reasoning: While "liquidity" may apply to more than economics, "international" applies even more broadly.

7. A modern understanding of salvation.

   Reasoning: "Modern" and "understanding" apply to many fields, "salvation" to fewer.

8. State support for treatment of the handicapped.

   Reasoning: The other terms apply in many fields, are more general.

9. Theory of sets.

   Reasoning: There are few phenomena without their theory; "sets" is of a much more limited application.

B 3

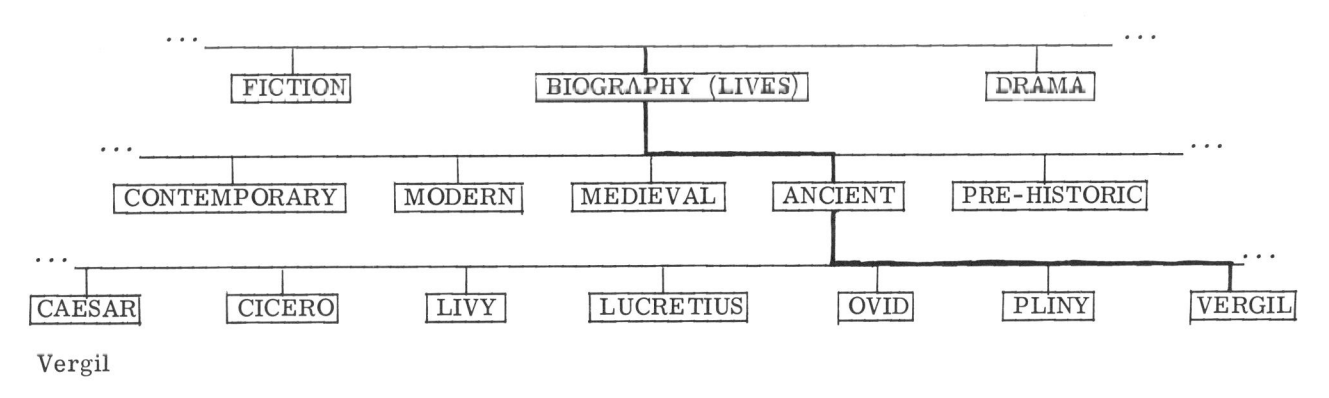

```
...─────────┬──────────────┬──────────────┬──────────...
         FICTION      BIOGRAPHY (LIVES)   DRAMA
...──┬──────────┬──────────┬──────────┬──────────┬──...
  CONTEMPORARY MODERN  MEDIEVAL  ANCIENT  PRE-HISTORIC
...┬────────┬────────┬──────────┬────────┬────────┬──────...
CAESAR  CICERO   LIVY    LUCRETIUS  OVID    PLINY   VERGIL
```

Vergil

B 3.1

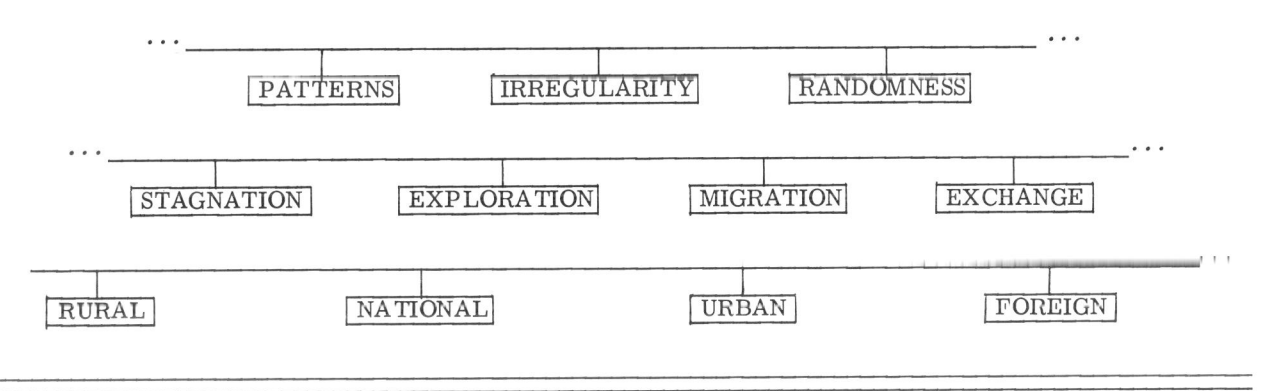

```
...──────────┬──────────────┬──────────────┬──────────...
         PATTERNS     IRREGULARITY    RANDOMNESS
...──┬──────────┬──────────────┬──────────────┬──────...
  STAGNATION  EXPLORATION    MIGRATION       EXCHANGE
─────┬──────────────┬──────────────┬──────────────┬──────
   RURAL        NATIONAL        URBAN          FOREIGN
```

B 3.1

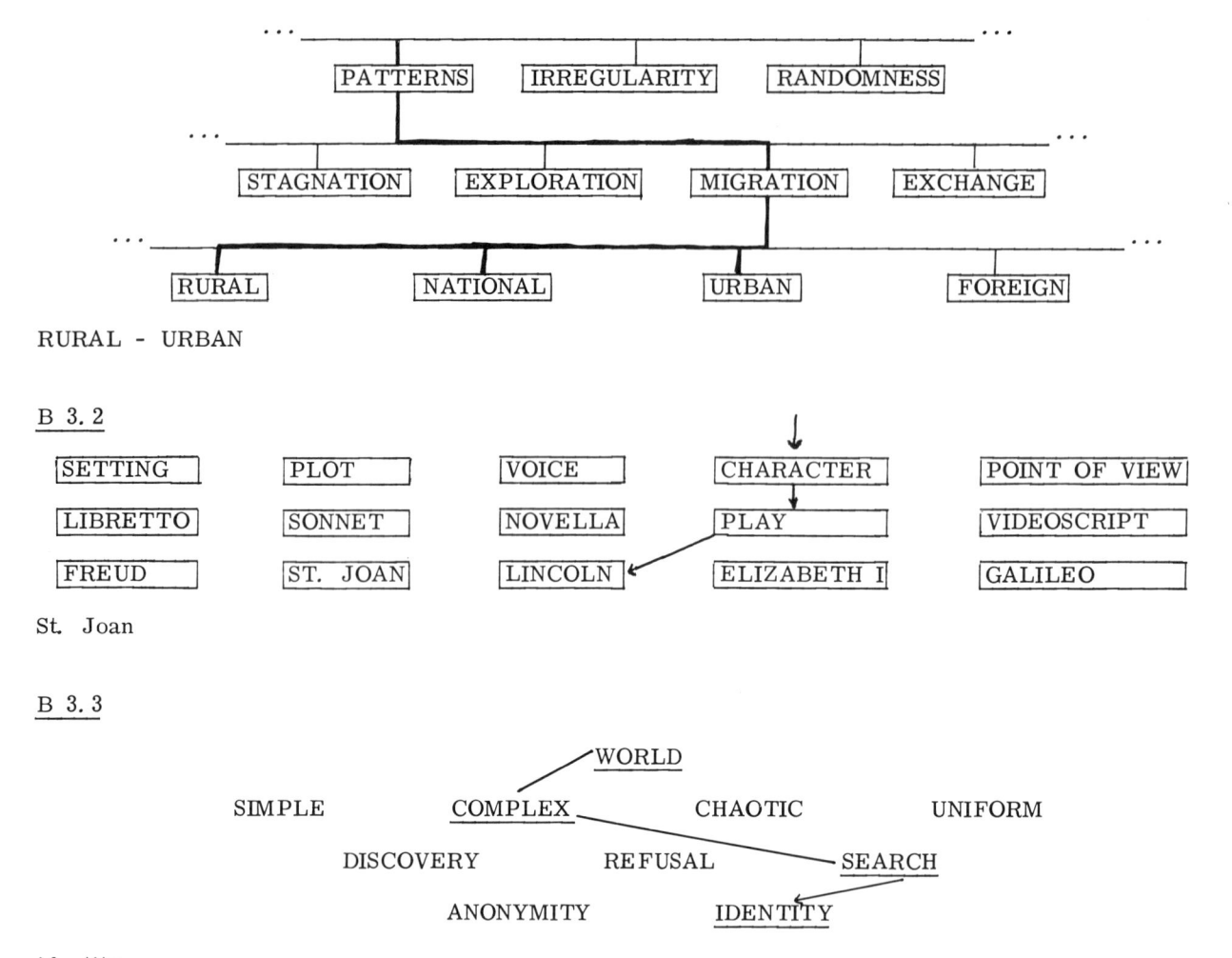

```
              PATTERNS    IRREGULARITY    RANDOMNESS
         STAGNATION   EXPLORATION   MIGRATION   EXCHANGE
         RURAL        NATIONAL      URBAN       FOREIGN
```

RURAL - URBAN

B 3.2

SETTING	PLOT	VOICE	CHARACTER	POINT OF VIEW
LIBRETTO	SONNET	NOVELLA	PLAY	VIDEOSCRIPT
FREUD	ST. JOAN	LINCOLN	ELIZABETH I	GALILEO

St. Joan

B 3.3

```
                    WORLD
   SIMPLE   COMPLEX      CHAOTIC      UNIFORM
       DISCOVERY   REFUSAL     SEARCH
             ANONYMITY   IDENTITY
```

identity

B 4

a) Because it comes earlier? or for some such reason? But prominence is one thing, specificity is another, and specificity is what matters in regard to subject headings. Try again.

b) Since "detective story" is a kind of story, yes, it is more specific--on a lower branch--than "story," and consequently a better bet than "story." Now do the second question in the frame.

c) Quite the reverse; there are many kinds of stories, including detective stories. Try again.

d) The heading would change to DETECTIVES but that would be a trivial difference since the words are spelled so much alike--not many cards would fall between DETECTIVE... and DETECTIVES. But the important thing is that even under DETECTIVES you would expect to find books about all manner of things that have to do with detectives. It would be a broad category--broader than DETECTIVE STORIES. Try again for a choice that has to do with specificity.

e) "Detective story" is more explicit about "stories," it is true, but as a general term (a term taken from the whole world of things that exist) it is not more explicit than "detective." Try again for a choice that has to do with specificity.

f) That's good. Names are the most specific terms we can deal with, and the rule we are operating with for the time being says that the best bet for a subject heading is the most specific term in the topic. Nor is there any handy one-word name in English for "detective story."

Answers

B 4.1

a) Like "presidential commission"? Yes.

c)
d) One or the other, probably more (d).

f) Like "protein synthesis"? Yes.

h)

B 4.2

1. "The nature of the social encyclicals."

    Reasoning: "Nature" and "social" apply to many things besides "encyclicals."

2. "The efficiency of open market operations."

    Reasoning: "Efficiency" applies to many processes besides open market operations. "Open market operations" is a name.

3. "Regulation of chromosome functions."

    Reasoning: "Regulation" and "functions" apply to many things besides chromosomes.

4. "The commercial use of whale oil, 1840-1850."

    Reasoning: "Use" has the broadest application, "commercial" can apply to many operations in many eras. The years "1840-1850" included whole worlds of events and things. "Whale oil" is a name.

B 4.3

b; c; f; h

B 5

a) The arts have many aspects--who performs them, where, how.... Not a very specific term, in the context of this topic. Try another choice.

b) Art embraces the who, how, where, when, why, and what kind of creativity. Not a very specific term, in the context of this topic. Try another choice.

c) Society, like Art, covers a broad range. Not a very specific term, in this context. Try another choice.

d) O.k. If "the arts" is one set and "society" is another, the place where they intersect will be a sub-set--a smaller area and more specific than either of the terms by itself.

e) Maybe the topic has to do with art as a reflection or token of society, maybe it has to do with art as one of the many ingredients of a society. "Social art" is specific, all right, but too specific to fit the topic. Try another choice.

B 5.1

a) The whole Church? Too broad.

b) Everything about government? Too broad.

c) Better than either of the single terms by itself, but still not the <u>most</u> specific terminology in the context of the topic. (Interestingly enough, though, this is the <u>subject</u> heading you will find in the catalog. Perhaps that is because there are more aspects to "Church and state" than their separation.) See the remark at choice (e).

d) Separation with regard to what? Of what from what? Too broad.

e) Yes, the most specific. Indeed, too specific, come to find out, when you start an actual search in the catalog; see the remark above, at choice (c).

f) All books? Books in their general aspect? Too broad.

g) All about lawyers? Too broad.

i) Including those written by laymen? More specific than either (f) or (g) but more general than (i).

h) The most specific; this is a subject heading used in the Library of Congress catalog.

l) or n)   The other terms are too broad for the topic.

SECTION C: PRE-TEST

I. Here's one way:

      Butler, David E.   <u>The electoral system in Britain, since 1918.</u>
ELECTIONS--GREAT BRITAIN
   ↓

      Pulzer, Peter G. J.   <u>Political representation and elections.</u>
POLITICAL PARTIES--GREAT BRITAIN
   ↓

      Jennings, Sir William Ivor.   <u>Party politics.</u>
GREAT BRITAIN--POLITICS & GOVERNMENT
   ↓

      Loewenstein, Karl.   <u>British Cabinet government.</u>

II. A.   <u>Materialism</u> (Metaphysics, BD331;
         Philosophic systems: general,
         B825; by country, B851-4695)
     <u>sa</u> Dualism
        Idealism
        Lokāyata
    → Mechanism (Philosophy)
        Monism
        Naturalism
        Realism
     <u>xx</u> Animism
        Dualism
        Idealism
        Immortality
    → Mechanism (Philosophy)
        Monism
        Philosophy
        Positivism
        Realism

<u>Mechanism</u> (Philosophy)
  <u>sa</u> Materialism
     Naturalism
     Vitalism
→ <u>x</u> Mechanistic philosophy
     Philosophy, Mechanistic
→ <u>xx</u> Materialism
     Naturalism
     Philosophy
     Science--Philosophy
     Vitalism
Mechanisms, Interchangeable
  See Interchangeable mechanisms
Mechanistic philosophy
  See Mechanism (Philosophy)

II. B.   "Mechanism (Philosophy)" [The other is not a heading used in the catalog.]

Answers

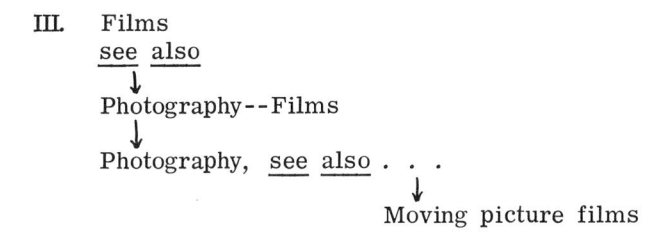

III. Films
    <u>see also</u>
    ↓
    Photography--Films
    ↓
    Photography, <u>see also</u> . . .
                    ↓
                  Moving picture films

IV. Here's one way:

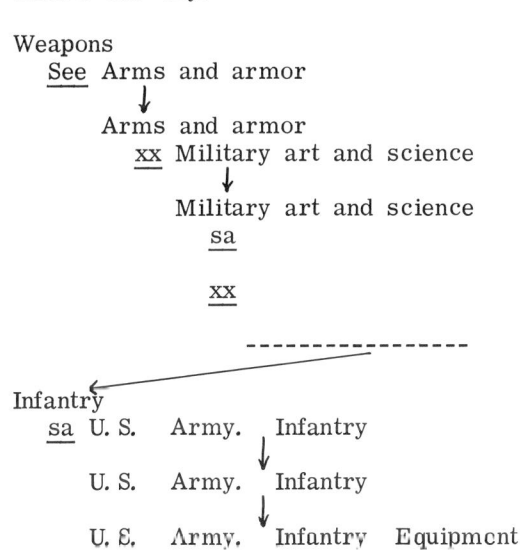

    Weapons
        <u>See</u> Arms and armor
                ↓
        Arms and armor
           <u>xx</u> Military art and science
                    ↓
            Military art and science
                <u>sa</u>

                <u>xx</u>

Infantry
    <u>sa</u> U. S. Army. Infantry
                      ↓
       U. S. Army. Infantry
                  ↓
       U. S. Army. Infantry Equipment
                      --History

[A search under "U. S.--History--Civil War" does not get you any closer.]

C 1

b) Defendants. I've saved you some trouble by not offering "Rights of defendants" as a choice. The phrase is not used in the catalogs as a subject heading.

C 1.1

f) You shouldn't have. If you did, tell the library cataloguer to mind his p's and q's, and look again.

g) The title itself may be just what you want, or it may be off the track. In either case, you can probably use some more leads. Go to frame B 3.3 to practice scanning the added entries for clues.

h)
i) Probably, and that's only indirectly helpful to the topic.

C 3

a) Perhaps, but not if the library has a book written by an author whose name is "Law." If so, his author card will precede any subject cards labeled "LAW," or title cards labelled "Law." [That assumes a single catalog. If your library has two separate catalogs--for instance, one for authors and one for subjects and titles--then a subject card may be the first one you come to.]

b) Perhaps, but not if the library has a book written by an author named "Law" (Law, John 1796-1873) or a book on the subject of the law. Authors precede subjects or titles of that name. Subjects and titles are interfiled with one another. [That assumes a single catalog for authors, subjects, and titles.]

c) Yes, if the library has a book written by an author named "Law." For a given word, an author by that name precedes that word as a subject or a title. [That assumes a single catalog for authors, subjects, and titles.]

C 3.1

a) Good, since a bibliography and an index are a little like a card catalog; they help reveal more information or they lead you along a path through the information that you are trying to locate.

b) Not much headway. Surely you already know that the book is about law; that's what the subject heading told you. Try another choice.

c) The added entry certainly interests you, but it does not much justify your leaving the catalog just yet in order to handle the book itself. Indeed, you would probably do better to stay at the catalog and look under JUSTICE, ADMINISTRATION OF--U.S. Try another choice.

d) Work through Section A of this program: "How to read a Library of Congress catalog card."

C 3.2

b) You remember that business of "scope" in frame B 1?

C 3.3

a) Right.

b) If you looked up a definition of "jurisprudence" and found something like "the science of law," you were--I hope--tempted to think that "jurisprudence" (theory of law) is more general than "administration of justice."

C 4

a) Somewhat useful, but the phrase "See Public defenders" underneath it sends you elsewhere right away.

b) Yes.

c) Yes.

d) Somewhat useful, but the "See..."-phrase underneath it sends you elsewhere right away.

e) Wrong area for your topic--but it is interesting to see how discriminating the catalog will have to be, given the fact that English words are likely to have multiple meanings.

C 4.1

a) The terms "general" and "specific" have meaning only within the context of a topic. Try another choice.

b) Exactly. The distinction is just that plain and drastic. Now do the next item in the frame.

Answers

"Headings used" = terms used as subject headings in the catalog.
"Headings not used" = terms not used as subject headings in the catalog.

c) Presumably all subject headings are "important" in some regard or other. Otherwise why bother to mention them? Try another choice.

d) In the entry for "Defense (Criminal procedure)" those words are in boldface and all others are in roman. But in the entry for "Defense (Law)" everything is in roman. So that's not the answer. Try another choice.

e) That's what you said above in choice (b), which doesn't advance us any further. Try again.

f) Right. Go on to frame C 4.2.

g) An entry is a unit that starts at the left margin. It may be that one line, or it may have several lines indented under it (as all our examples so far show). They are part of the entry. A new entry starts when the print returns to the left margin. Now try the item again.

entry
{
  Attar of roses
  x Oil of rose
  Oleum rosae
  Otto of roses
  Rose oil
  xx Roses
  Example under Essences and essential oils
}

entry
{
  Attempt, Criminal
  See Criminal attempt
}

entry
{
  Attendance, Church
  See Church attendance
}

entry
{
  Attendance, Football
  See Football attendance
}

C 4.2

"Right to counsel"

a)
b) Be careful. Those markers are being used under a boldface term. The question is about how to get from a roman entry (not-used) to a term that will be printed boldface where it oc-
c) curs as a main entry. Try again.

d) Right. That is the point to a See reference. Now do the next item in the frame.

e) Boldface, as a sign that it is a used term in the card catalog. Now do the last item in the frame.

g) Why mention them if they are not going to lead someplace where you want to go? Try another choice.

h) Right, and that, again, is the point to a See reference. Go on to frame C 4.3.

i) That's like leading you around Robin Hood's barn. Why bother to be indirect when it's possible to be direct? Try another choice.

C 4.3

a) Pardon me? We've seen that the roman-type "Defense (Law)" is a not-used term and here it is in the example, under "Defense (Criminal procedure)," as an x term. Try another choice.

b) Just as the roman-type "Defense (Law)," a not-used term, shows. Now do the last item in the frame.

c) Is it sensible to refer you to a dead end? Try another choice.

d) "Public defenders" and "Right to counsel" certainly sound like headings related to "Defense (Criminal procedure)" and they are clearly used terms, being in boldface type as main entries. Sa = see also. Go on to frame C 4.4.

e) "Only" is a tricky word. "The only ones used" where? Try another choice.

f) If they are not-used, why try to use them? Try another choice.

C 4.4

a) boldface

b) is (in boldface)

c) is (a used subject heading)

C 4.5

1) boldface (used)

2) roman (not used)

3) not-used ... used   (see references)
   roman   boldface

4) not-used ... used   (x references)

5) used ... used   (sa references)

xx

6) used ... used   (xx references)

C 4.5.1

1. not used

2. used

3. will (but not in boldface)   not-used

4. will   used

5. used   boldface

6. sa

7. See

C 4.5.2

1. (Encephalitis)
       sa Encephalomyelitis
        x Brain--Inflammation
          Encephalitides
       xx Brain--Diseases

Answers   78

2. Brain--Inflammation
        See Encephalitis

3. Brain--Diseases   (RC386-394)
        sa Acalculia
           Agraphia
           Alexia
           Amaurotic family idiocy
           Amnesia
           Aphasia
           Apoplexy
           Brain--Calcification
           Brain damage
           Brain--Radiography
           Cerebral arteriosclerosis
           Cerebral edema
           Cerebral palsy
           Cerebral sclerosis, Diffuse
           Cerebrovascular disease
           Cysticerosis, Cerebrospinal
           Encephalitis
           Fatigue, Mental
           Hepatolenticular degeneration

4. Elementary education of adults
        sa Reading (Adult education)
         x Adult elementary education
           Elementary adult education
           Elementary education for adults
        xx Adult education
           Education, Elementary
           Illiteracy

C 6

a)
b)   The list is alphabetical.   Try again.

c)   Go to frame C 6.1.

d)   Ask a librarian.

C 6.1

a)   Now do the last item in the frame.

d)   Because it sounds like a legal matter.   Turn to it in the Readers' Guide and go to frame C 6.2.

C 6.2

a)   Now do the last item in the frame.

d)   We just came from there; no point in going back.   Try another choice.

e)   Turn to that term in the Readers' Guide and go to frame C 6.3.

f)   That was mostly military aspects.   Try another choice.

C 6.3

b)   Now do the last item in the frame; e)

C 6.5

page 790; 1003.6

C 6.6

page 637

NOUNS   VERBS   ADJ[ECTIVE]S

b)   They name particular circumstances in which a defendant may find himself.

C 6.7

Accusation
   See   Charges and specifications
          (Courts-martial)
       Indictments
       Informations
→ Police charges

C 6.7.1

Arrangement B.   In LC Subject Headings the comma acts as a break in the filing.

Police charges (Direct)
    x Accusation
       Charges, Police
   xx Criminal investigation
 → Criminal procedure

used; a)

C 6.7.2

Arrangement A.   "(Direct)" is an indication of how to use the heading in subdivision; it is not part of the "official" heading.   We will work with it in Section E.

Criminal procedure (Direct)
   sa Acquittals
      Alternative convictions
      Amparo (Writ)
      Appellate procedure
      Arrest
      Bail
      Complaints (Criminal procedure)
      Confession (Law)
      Contumacy
      Correctional law
      Courts-martial and courts of inquiry
      Criminal courts
      Criminal jurisdiction
      Criminal law
      Criminal registers
      Default (Law)
→ Defense (Criminal procedure)   And you're in!
      Double jeopardy
      Evidence, Circumstantial
      Evidence, Criminal
      Executions and executioners
      Extradition
      Flagrans crimen
      Fugitives from justice

Answers

SECTION D: PRE-TEST

One way to do it:

    Dictionary definition of "penny dreadful"

  <u>LC Subject Headings</u>:
    Penny dreadfuls [too specific]

      Novels, <u>See</u> Fiction

                Fiction, [<u>also</u>] English fiction

                          English fiction--19th century

  Card catalog [that entry being not specific enough]

  <u>LC Subject Headings</u>:
    English <u>literature</u>--19th century

      OR

    Books

      OR

    Books and reading

      OR

    Booksellers and bookselling

      OR

    Publishers and publishing--Great Britain

  Card catalog: Richard D. Altick, <u>The English common reader; a social history of the mass reading public 1800-1900</u>, University of Chicago Press, 1957.

    index: Penny dreadfuls, 251, 292, <u>314</u>

D 1

a) Try "Literary problems" in <u>LC Subject Headings</u> and go to the beginning of frame D 2.

b) Perhaps the heading "Literature" is specific enough to put you on the track of a book about "ambiguity in literature." Since "Ambiguity" is not a used heading, the next best bet may well be the next most specific term in your topic--in this case the only other term. Try "Literature" in <u>LC Subject Headings</u> and go to frame D 2 at the flag, "Literature."

c) Try "Meaning" in <u>LC Subject Headings</u> and go to frame D 3.

D 2

a) I don't know ... I scan the <u>sa</u> and <u>xx</u> references under "Creation (Literary, artistic, etc.)" and I'm inclined to think I'm headed either away from my term "ambiguity" or up to too general a level. I'd try another choice, if I were you.

b) Have you looked at "Style, Literary" as a main entry, p. 1758? The <u>sa</u> references sound promising. Go to frame D 2.1.

c) There are lots of <u>sa</u> references. Go to frame D 2.2.

<u>D 2.1</u>

a) Look in <u>LC Subject Headings</u> under "Diction" and go to frame D 2.1.1.

b) Look in <u>LC Subject Headings</u> under "Literature--Aesthetics" and go to frame D 2.3.

c) Look in <u>LC Subject Headings</u> under "Rhetoric" and go to frame D 2.4.

<u>D 2.1.1</u>

a) Look under "Vocabulary" and go to frame D 2.1.2.

b) Look under "Rhetoric" and go to frame D 2.4.

<u>D 2.1.2</u>

a) In that case, follow up some of the references, see if you can get closer yet to "ambiguity in literature" and eventually find the book named in frame D 4.

b) That's my feeling. Might as well leave this track and retrace your steps. You've come by this route:

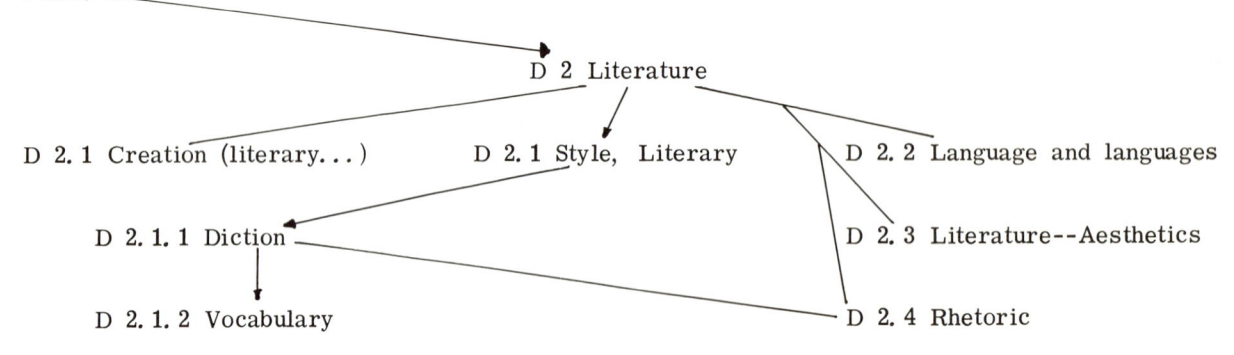

```
                              D 2 Literature
                                  /    \
   D 2.1 Creation (literary...)  D 2.1 Style, Literary    D 2.2 Language and languages
                                                          D 2.3 Literature--Aesthetics
        D 2.1.1 Diction
              |
        D 2.1.2 Vocabulary                                D 2.4 Rhetoric
```

<u>D 2.2</u>

a) Do that and go to frame D 2.2.1.

b) Can you find "Languages"?--page 1009, first column.

Under "Languages--Philosophy" one of the <u>sa</u> references sends you to "Languages--Psychology" and under that heading the interesting <u>sa</u> reference is to "Meaning (Psychology)." So now go to frame D 3.

<u>D 2.2.1</u>

a) Try " Communication." The "scope note" and the <u>sa</u> references show it to be a little technical for "ambiguity in literature." So try another choice.

b) "Very possibly, if I were sure of the definition of 'rhetoric.'" Read the definition in <u>Webster's Third</u>. If that still suits you, go to frame D 2.4. If not, try another choice.

Answers

c) Look at "Semantics" (bottom of p. 1631), then go to frame D 2.2.2.

D 2.2.2

a) That seems very general, when "Literature," for instance, is already available as a subject heading and is a concern of the topic. Try another choice.

b) Maybe so, since it is a subject heading and is a concern of the topic. Go to frame D 2 at the sign "Literature" and in LC Subject Headings turn to the main entry, "Literature," p. 1051.

c) Still so specific as that? It's not impossible, however. Go to frame D 2.5.

D 2.3

Any of the choices are reasonable.

a) All right, but if you come to a dead end there, either go back to frame D 2 or D 2.1 and follow a road not taken or go on to frame D 4 for an answer to the problem of specificity.

b) All right; PN45 in parentheses is the Library of Congress classification for works that deal principally with questions of esthetics in literature. You can look along the shelf there, check bibliographies and indexes and tables of contents in the books, and very likely get a lead. (If your library will let you consult its shelf list--catalog cards arranged according to the order of the books on the shelves--here is a chance to look at the added entries on all the cards labeled PN45.... That is probably a more fruitful technique at this point than going to the books themselves.) For an answer to the problem of specificity that we're dealing with, go to frame D 4.

c) All right; go back to frame D 2.1 and try either choice (a) or choice (c).

D 2.4

a) Go to frame D 2.1.1.

b) Go to frame D 1, choice (c), "Meaning."

c) Go to frame D 2.5.

d) Why not? It's the hottest lead yet. Hunt him up in the catalog, then go to frame D 4.

D 2.5

a) So try. Then go to frame D 4.

b) Now is a good time to remember how we got started on this search. We were talking about specificity in the card catalog, saying that it's possible to try to use a too-specific term. "Ambiguity" or "ambiguity in literature" is an example of the overly specific. The closest you are going to get is the heading POETRY or another heading which is equally general (relative to "ambiguity"). You have come here by this route [see next page]:

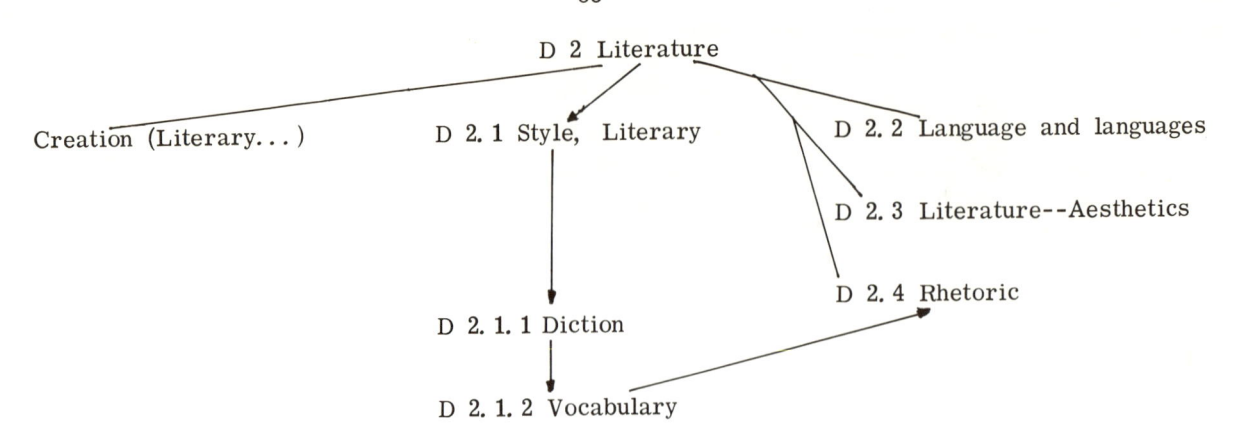

```
                              D 2 Literature
Creation (Literary...)    D 2.1 Style, Literary      D 2.2 Language and languages
                                                     D 2.3 Literature--Aesthetics
                           D 2.1.1 Diction           D 2.4 Rhetoric
                           D 2.1.2 Vocabulary
```

SECTION E: PRE-TEST

I. a) EUROPEAN ECONOMIC COMMUNITY--GREAT BRITAIN

    b) NEGROES--PSYCHOLOGY

    c) UNITED STATES--HISTORY--REVOLUTION

    d) ALGAE--ECONOMIC ASPECTS

    e) SHAKESPEARE, WILLIAM--HISTORIES

    f) CHAUCER, GEOFFREY--SOURCES

II. CHINA--HISTORY--FOREIGN INTERVENTION, 1857-1861

III. CHINA--HISTORY--WAR OF 1840-1842

E 1

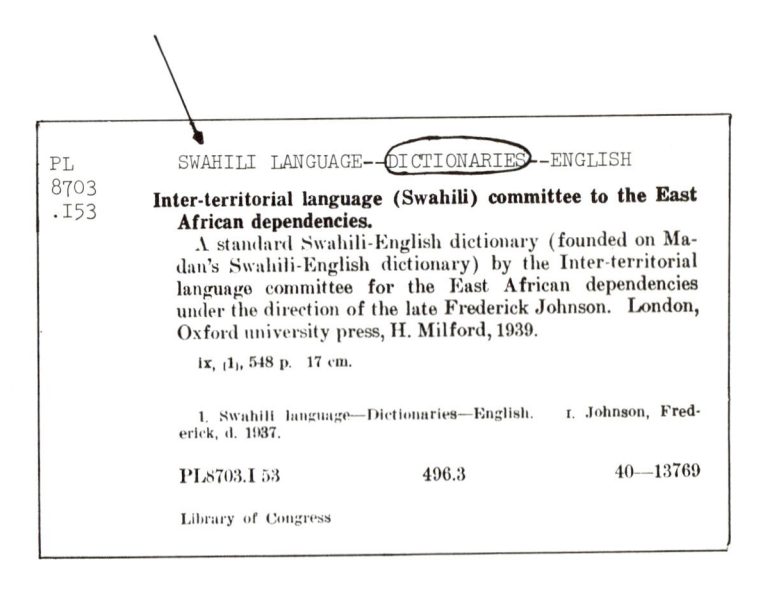

```
PL         SWAHILI LANGUAGE--(DICTIONARIES)--ENGLISH
8703
.I53       Inter-territorial language (Swahili) committee to the East
           African dependencies.
               A standard Swahili-English dictionary (founded on Ma-
           dan's Swahili-English dictionary) by the Inter-territorial
           language committee for the East African dependencies
           under the direction of the late Frederick Johnson. London,
           Oxford university press, H. Milford, 1939.
               ix, (1), 548 p. 17 cm.

               1. Swahili language—Dictionaries—English.    I. Johnson, Fred-
           erick, d. 1937.

                  PL8703.I53            496.3              40—13769
           Library of Congress
```

Answers 84

```
PN          LITERATURE, COMPARATIVE--YEARBOOKS
851
.Y4    Yearbook of comparative and general literature. 1-
        1952-
          [Bloomington] Indiana University.
              v.  ports.  26 cm.
           No. 1-9 issued as University of North Carolina studies in compara-
        tive literature.
           Vols. for 1952-60 published in Chapel Hill and sold by the Univer-
        sity of North Carolina Press.
           Published 1952-     in collaboration with the Comparative Lit-
        erature Committee of the National Council of Teachers of English
        and the Comparative Literature Section of the Modern Language As-
        sociation of America (1960-     with the American Comparative
        Literature Association)
           1. Literature, Comparative—Yearbooks.  (Series: North Caro-
        lina. University. Studies in comparative literature)

        PN851.Y4                                      53—62589

        Library of Congress         [69r630½]
```

```
Z           SOCIAL SCIENCES--BIBLIOGRAPHY
7161
.W49   White, Carl Milton, 1903-
1973       Sources of information in the social sciences, a guide to the
        literature [by] Carl M. White and associates: William W. Brick-
        man [and others]  2d ed.  Chicago, American Library Associa-
        tion, 1973.
              xviii, 702 p.  26 cm.




           1. Social sciences—Bibliography.   I. Title.
        Z7161.W49   1973           016.3                73-9825
        ISBN 0-8389-0134-4                                MARC

        Library of Congress            73
```

```
HA          UNITED STATES--STATISTICS
202
        United States. Bureau of the Census.
           Statistical abstract of the United States.  1st-    ed.;
        1878-
        Washington. U. S. Govt. Print. Off.
              v  24 cm  annual
           The 7th-8th editions combined in one issue; 66th ed., covers
        period 1944-45.
           Issued 1878-1902 by the Bureau of Statistics (Treasury Dept.);
        1903-11 by the Bureau of Statistics (Dept. of Commerce and Labor);
        1912-37 by the Bureau of Foreign and Domestic Commerce.
        ———— ———— Cities supplement: selected data for cities having
           25,000 or more inhabitants.  1940.  Washington.
              ii, 47 p.  27 cm.
           Superseded by its County and city data book, 1949.
                                       HA202  Cities suppl.
           1. United States—          Statistics.   I. Title.
        HA202                       -317.3                4—18089
        Library of Congress       [73r52q²⁴10]
```

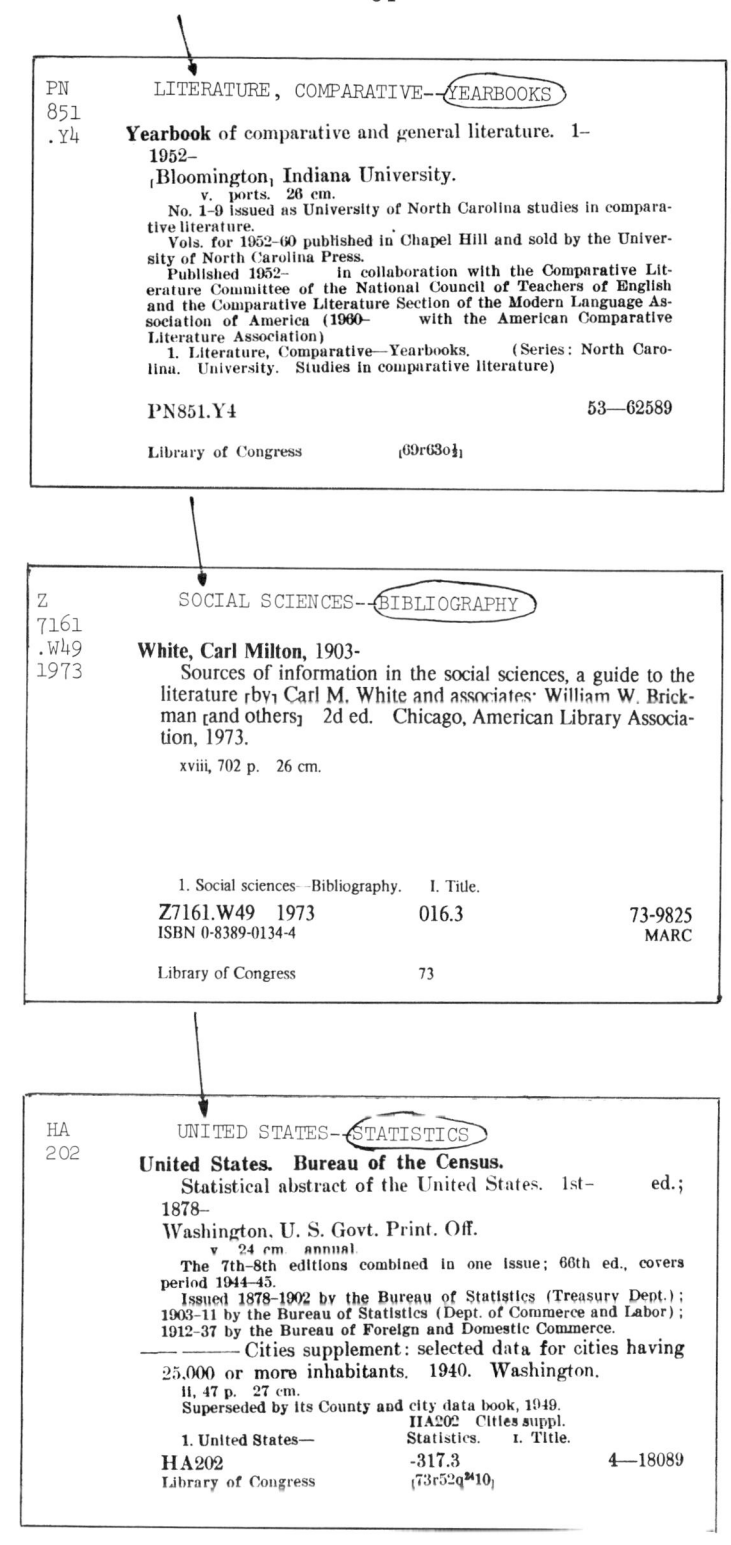

E 2

(1) ASTRONAUTICS--DICTIONARIES

(2) ASTRONAUTICS--INTERNATIONAL COOPERATION

(3) AERONAUTICS--HISTORY

(4) SPACE MEDICINE--CONGRESSES

E 3

(1) SHAKESPEARE, WILLIAM--AUTHORSHIP

(2) SHAKESPEARE, WILLIAM, 1564-1616--BIOGRAPHY

(3) SHAKESPEARE, WILLIAM--CRITICISM & INTERPRETATION

(4) SHAKESPEARE, WILLIAM--STAGE HISTORY

(5) SHAKESPEARE, WILLIAM--TRAGEDIES

E 3.1

(1) GOETHE, JOHANN WOLFGANG VON--ANNIVERSARIES, ETC. or APPRECIATION or CRITICISM & INTERPRETATION or INFLUENCE

(2) GOETHE, JOHANN WOLFGANG VON--CHARACTERS--WOMEN

(3) GOETHE, JOHANN WOLFGANG VON--CRITICISM & INTERPRETATION

(4) GOETHE, JOHANN WOLFGANG VON--KNOWLEDGE--ALCHEMY

E 4

a) How do you want to go?

   1) "Great Britain--_____" or
   2) "Elections--Great Britain"?

Is either (1) or (2) a used heading, according to LC Subject Headings?

What subdivision would be likely in (1)?*

Use your new wits and LC Subject Headings, hunt around in the card catalog, and when you think you have discovered the book that I have in mind, go to frame E 5.

b) Where do you want to start?

   1) "Trappers"?
   2) "Indians"?
   3) "Fur trade"?
   4) "America"?

Are they used headings, according to LC Subject Headings?

What subdivisions are likely to help?*

Use your wits--which means your strategies for searching--and LC Subject Headings, hunt around in the card catalog, and when you think you have discovered the book that I have in mind, go to frame E 6.

---

*In LC Subject Headings an entry preceded by a dash is a subdivision of the main entry.

Answers

c) How shall you start?

   1) "Slavery"?
   2) "Anti-slavery"?
   3) "Kansas--_____"?

Are those headings used in LC Subject Headings?

What subdivisions?*

Use the search techniques that you have practiced and LC Subject Headings, hunt around in the catalog, and when you think you have discovered the book that I have in mind, go to frame E 7.

E 5

TRUE	FALSE	
x		a)
	x	b)
x		c)
x		d)

Here's the book I had in mind, with a couple of its headings subdivided by place:

```
JN
955
.B82    Butler, David E
1963        The electoral system in Britain, since 1918.  2d ed.  Ox-
        ford, Clarendon Press, 1963.

            xiv, 232 p.  illus.  23 cm.

            "First published in 1953 under the title:  The electoral system in
        Britain, 1918-1951."
            "Bibliographical note": p. [221]-223.


            1.  Elections--Gt. Brit.   2.  Election law--Gt. Brit.   3.  Gt. Brit.
        Parliament--Elections.     I.  Title.

        JN955.B82       1963              342.42                    63-24311

        Library of Congress               [3]
```

E 6

TRUE	FALSE	
	x	a)
x		b) The one to "Fur trade."
x		c)
	x	d) or so it seems to me, when I see how many more subdivisions there are under "Indians of North America" and when I think about the implications of the terms of the topic.

---

*In LC Subject Headings an entry preceded by a dash is a subdivision of the main entry.

TRUE	FALSE		
(x)	(x)	e)	That depends, of course, upon your library's collection. Curiously enough, if the collection is large under "Indians of North America" it may be more efficient to start, rather, with "Fur trade--North America."
x	___	f)	
x	___	g)	
x	___	h)	or so it seems to me, since the topic touches on both Indians and trappers; "fur trade" is common to them and is the most specific term.

Here's the book I had in mind:

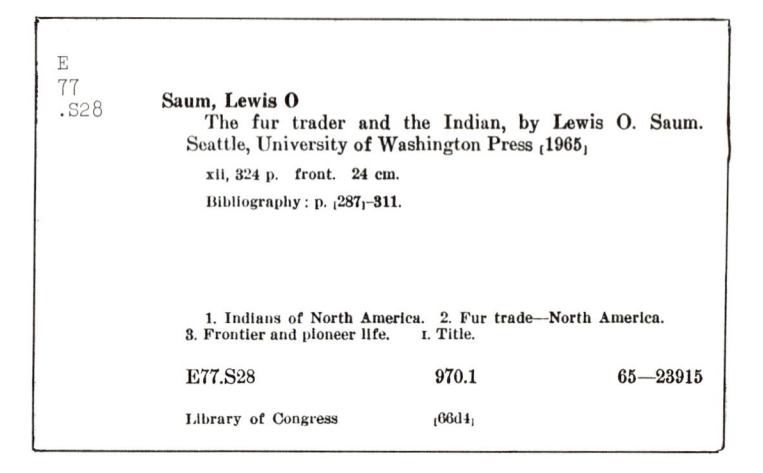

```
E
77      Saum, Lewis O
.S28        The fur trader and the Indian, by Lewis O. Saum.
        Seattle, University of Washington Press [1965]
            xii, 324 p.  front.  24 cm.
            Bibliography: p. [287]-311.


            1. Indians of North America.  2. Fur trade—North America.
         3. Frontier and pioneer life.   I. Title.
        E77.S28                 970.1            65—23915
        Library of Congress         [66d4]
```

E 7

TRUE	FALSE		
___	x	a)	"Slavery" pertains to the institution, not to a particular locale.
x	___	b)	in order to get to "Kansas--History--1854-1861."
___	x	c)	
___	x	d)	The closest heading is "Slavery--Anti-slavery movements."
x	___	e)	since it helps you get to where I want you to get!

The book I had in mind is this one:

```
F
685     Robinson, Charles, 1818-1894.
.R6         The Kansas conflict, by Charles Robinson ... New York,
        Harper & brothers, 1892.
            xxiii, 487 p.  21 cm.




         1. Kansas—Hist.—1854-1861.  2. Slavery in the U. S.—Kansas.
         I. Title.
                                                    Rc—89
        Library of Congress       F685.R6
                                  [4511]
```

Answers

E 8

"1898-" falls between (2) and (3) because it succeeds the period 1865-1898 and it includes the event of the War of 1898.

"13th century" falls between (10) and (11) because it succeeds 1199 and includes the dates of Henry VIII.

E 9

```
E
338
.D3
```

Dangerfield, George, 1904–
　　The awakening of American nationalism, 1815-1828. [1st ed.] New York, Harper & Row [ᶜ1965]
　　　　xiii, 331 p. illus., facsims., ports. 22 cm. (The New American Nation series)
　　　　"Bibliographical essay": p. 303-321. Bibliographical footnotes.

　　　　1. U. S.—Hist.—1815-1861.　2. Nationalism—U. S.　I. Title.

E338.D3　　　　973.5　　　　64—25112

Library of Congress　　[65n14]

SECTION F: PRE-TEST

I. b; c; d; f; a; e

II. e; a; f; b; d; c

III. c; b; a

　　f; g; e; d; i; k; j; h; l

F 1

True dictionary order: <u>letter-by-letter</u>

　　pea<u>c</u>e
　　pea<u>ce</u>ful
　　pea<u>ce</u>maker
　　pea<u>ce</u> of God

Card catalog "dictionary" order: <u>word-by-word</u>

　　pea<u>c</u>e
　　pea<u>c</u>e of mind
　　pea<u>c</u>eful
　　pea<u>c</u>emaker

F 2

Order that disregards punctuation:
- 0. ARSON
- 1. ART
- 4. ART--ABSTRACT
- 2. ART--ADDRESSES
- 3. ART--AFRICA
- 5. ART, AFRICAN
- 7. ART AND LITERATURE
- 6. ART, APPLIED
- 8. ART OBJECTS
- 9. ARTERIES

(b) for sure--and maybe (c), if I could figure out what it means, exactly.

F 3

Between No. 3 and No. 4 because it is a subdivision, to be subarranged within the set of subdivisions (Tables after Study...) and preceding any inverted qualifications.

    Mathematics--Study and teaching (Secondary)
→ Mathematics--Tables, etc.
    Mathematics, Arabic

F 4

Between No. 10 and No. 11 because extensions are subarranged ("in foreign..." before "in India") together and placed after any subdivisions or inverted qualifications.

    English language--Text-books for foreigners
→ English language in foreign countries
    English language in India

F 5

Form and topic: 4-7
Period (chronological): 1-2
Locale (geographical): 8

Between No. 1 and No. 2 because it is a chronological subdivision and is to be subarranged chronologically (1500 precedes 1700) with other chronological subdivisions.

    English literature--To 1100. See Anglo-Saxon literature
→ English literature--Middle English, 1100-1500
    English literature--Early modern, to 1700

Between No. 4 and No. 5 because it is a topical subdivision and is to be subarranged alphabetically (Indic, Japanese, Jewish) with other topical subdivisions.

    English literature--Indic authors
→ English literature--Japanese authors
    English literature--Jewish authors

F 6

Between No. 5 and No. 6 because it is an inverted qualification, to be subarranged alphabetically (Ancient, Buddhist, Chinese) with other inverted qualifications.

Answers

        Philosophy, Ancient
→   Philosophy, Buddhist
        Philosophy, Chinese

F 7

Between No. 2 and No. 3 because, alphabetically, Hindu precedes History, which precedes in literature.

        Philosophy, Hindu
→   Philosophy--History
        Philosophy in literature

F 8

Between No. 4 and No. 5. Incidentally, in some small libraries identical subjects and titles will be interfiled, sub-arranged by author.

        GLASS [subject heading]
→   Glass   [title]
        Glass: a world history [title]

F 9

a) Between No. 2 and No. 3 because you are arranging by title the works of one author.

        Glass, H. B.
           Forerunners...

        Glass, H. B.
           Phosphorus...

→   Glass, H. B.
           Science and ethical values...

        Glass, H. B.
           Science and liberal education...

b) Between No. 5 and No. 6: "Aubert, Marcel, 1884-" with "Aubert, Marcel, 1884-" and then within that author by title: "Stained..." after "French...."

c) Between No. 7 and No. 8: the title by Abrams before the same title by Norton.

F 10

Between No. 2 and No. 3.